Mama Africa

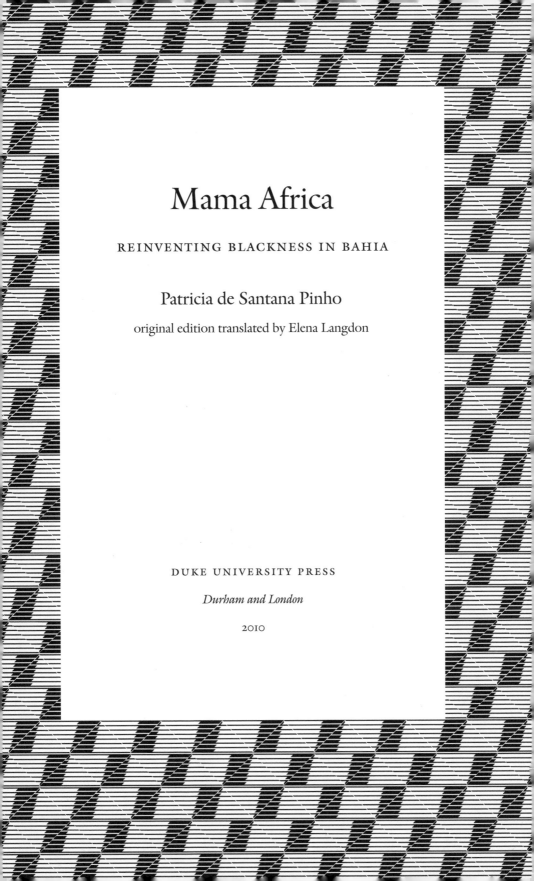

Mama Africa

REINVENTING BLACKNESS IN BAHIA

Patricia de Santana Pinho

original edition translated by Elena Langdon

DUKE UNIVERSITY PRESS

Durham and London

2010

First Portuguese edition published 2004

Expanded English edition
© 2010 Duke University Press

All rights reserved
Printed in the United States
of America on acid-free paper ∞
Designed by Amy Ruth Buchanan
Typeset in Carter + Cone Galliard
by Keystone Typesetting, Inc.
Library of Congress Cataloging-in-
Publication Data appear on the last
printed page of this book.

I dedicate this book to Gilson,
my best friend and the love of my life,
for sharing the certainty
that souls have no one color.

CONTENTS

ACKNOWLEDGMENTS

To thank is to think, to meditate about the special people who participate in our lives and help define who we are. Without them our own identities, our "narratives of the self," are not possible. Like ocean waves, the flows of life come and go, bringing and taking away people and feelings, but at the same time maintaining a certain constancy without which we have no reference. I hope that these few words are capable of expressing my deepest gratitude for those individuals that, in many different ways, have helped me throughout my life and academic career. I thank my parents, Fernando and Bernadette Pinho, for their everlasting generosity and for their example of love and tolerance, and my siblings, Marianna, Rodrigo, and Fernandinho, with whom I have learned the practice of coexisting in diversity. I am grateful to my grandmothers, Vovó Conceição, whose forward-thinking spirit is a source of inspiration to me, and Vó Isaura, who immersed us in beautiful hybrid traditions. Many thanks to Rosária, Elisa, Ciça, Emanuel, and Sonildes, as well as to my dear friend Creusa, for their constant love and support.

I am grateful for the wonderful learning experience offered to me by the Universidade Estadual de Campinas (UNICAMP), where I had great colleagues and professors, among whom are my advisor Teresa Sales and professors Fernando Lourenço, Célia Marinho de Azevedo, and Josué Pereira da Silva. Thanks to FAPESP (Fundação de Amparo à Pesquisa do Estado de São Paulo) for having supported my PhD studies at UNICAMP and my stay at Yale University as a visiting graduate student in 2001. Thanks to the Henry Hart Rice Foundation for supporting my postdoctoral fellowship in the African American Studies Department and the Council on Latin American and Iberian Studies at Yale in 2002–2003, and to the Mellon Foundation for supporting my postdoctoral fellowship in the Department of Black

Studies at Amherst College in 2003–2005. At Yale I was welcomed by Victoria Langland, Hazel Carby, Gil Joseph, Beatriz Riefkohl, Geneva Melvin, and Janet Giarratano. I express my deepest gratitude to Vron Ware and Paul Gilroy for their generosity toward my life and work.

Many thanks to my dear colleagues in the Department of Latin American, Caribbean, and U.S. Latino Studies at the University at Albany, where I have been teaching since 2005. It has been a blessing to be a part of such a convivial, intellectually engaging, and politically active environment. Special thanks to Glyne Griffith, Bert Nepaulsingh, and Edna Acosta-Belén for their selfless guidance.

My research on the *blocos afro* would not have been possible without the genuine commitment of my then–research assistant, sociologist Stela Soares, and all the folks who kindly allowed us to interview them. I am especially grateful to singer Graça Onasilê and composer Juracy Tavares da Silva for our constructive dialogues. Thanks also to Vera Lúcia Reis Serra for her competent transcription of the interviews. I am indebted to my translator Elena Langdon, who did a terrific job both in translating *Reinvenções da África na Bahia* into English and in editing my extensive rewriting of the chapters, as well as the new material. I am also very grateful to the two anonymous readers for their important suggestions and commendation of my book to Duke University Press.

The translation was generously supported by grants from the University at Albany's College of Arts and Sciences Faculty Research Award Program and Initiatives for Women. I thank the journals *Revista Brasileira de Ciências Sociais* and *Latin American Perspectives*, in the pages of which minor portions of this book's first chapter appeared. I would also like to thank Duke University Press and Sarah Nutall for allowing me to reprint parts of my essay "Afro-Aesthetics in Brazil," from the 2006 collection *Beautiful Ugly: African and Diaspora Aesthetics.*

Over the last few years I have been fortunate to meet several scholars who have, in different ways, contributed to my reflections on blackness, whiteness, *mestiçagem*, racism, and resistance to racism in Brazil and beyond, including Bob Stam, Sérgio Costa, John Burdick, Pat Mohammed, Shirley Tate, and Michelle Wright. My warmest thanks to Pedro Meira Monteiro, Malcolm McNee, Julio Corbea Calzado, and Rachel Jean-Baptiste for our friendship and stimulating conversations.

Lastly and most importantly I would like to express my deepest gratitude to my husband Gilson, *meu companheiro querido*, for his love, generosity, and support, and for offering me *a curva generosa da compreensão.*

ACKNOWLEDGMENTS

INTRODUCTION

"Mama Africa is a single mother who has to prepare baby bottles every day, besides wrapping gifts for a living at Casas Bahia [a Brazilian retail chain]." This famous verse by Brazilian singer and songwriter Chico César portrays Africa in a way that is quite different from its dominant representations in Brazilian popular culture. His words are not in tune with the prevalent festive discourses, and they call for contemplation rather than celebration. Chico's Mama Africa is an eloquent expression of this book's argument: reinventions of Africa have been tremendously important for black communities in the diaspora and have frequently spurred black resistance, but they have simultaneously helped corroborate preestablished notions of blackness. Although they have functioned as sources of inspiration, the myths of Africanness produced in the Americas have also served to wear out *Africa* by reducing it to a limited set of images. As Chico's song tells us, "Mama Africa has many other things to do besides taking care of the baby; she has blisters on her feet, she needs peace, and she doesn't want to play anymore."

Mama Africa's baby symbolizes the descendants of enslaved Africans who were dragged from their homeland, who have continuously imagined and reinvented Africa from afar. They have kept Africa alive in songs, legends, foods, dance forms, and, above all, myths. Unlike prevalent notions that associate myths with falsehood or deceiving narratives fabricated to mask reality, my use of the term *myth* is not in any way meant to diminish the power of the belief in a unity that exists among members of the diaspora, which I am calling the myth of Mama Africa. Rather, I opt for the term *myth* precisely because it contains the subtler and more powerful dimensions of the narratives that explain and interpret the world. By carrying values, messages, and ideals, myths are central to narratives and representations produced by dispersed peoples. The myth of Mama Africa establishes that black people around the world are connected to one another as much as they are to an imaginary entity from which the past, the traditions, the characteristics, and the "character" of all Afro-descendants purportedly emerge. Different versions of this myth have strongly permeated the imagination of numerous black groups in the African diaspora. While this book adopts a diaspora perspective and thus examines the local in connection to the global, it focuses on the versions of the myth of Mama Africa which have been invented in Bahia, generally believed to be the most African state in Brazil.

Throughout Brazilian history a wide array of black organizations have developed many forms of resistance. From the *quilombos* (communities formed by runaway slaves) of the 1600s to the present-day *blocos afro*, from the temples of Candomblé to the Frente Negra Brasileira of the 1930s, the Movimento Negro Unificado founded in the 1970s, and today's NGOs struggling to defend racial quotas, many organizations have sought a better quality of life for blacks in Brazil. Whether they define themselves as based on religion, culture, or politics, all modern black associations in Brazil have shared the need to deal with the meanings of Africa and Africanness, and to weave these meanings into their production of representations of blackness. These organizations are therefore simultaneously cultural and political.

In Bahia, among the major producers of discourses of blackness are the *blocos afro*, black cultural organizations that emerged in the capital city of Salvador during the 1970s, seeking to defeat racism within the sphere of Carnaval. Responding to racial discrimination, which excluded blacks from participating in Carnaval groups (*blocos*), a group of black activists founded their own *bloco*, Ilê Aiyê, which only accepted very dark-skinned blacks as members. *Blocos afro* have now extended past the boundaries of Carnaval and entertainment and produce new references of blackness that deeply influence the wider dynamics of cultural politics. Ilê Aiyê and Olodum are among Bahia's most important and well-known *blocos afro*. As the adjective *afro* indicates, the *blocos*' production is centered on reinventing the meanings of Africa and Africanness as a basis for constructing new cultural and aesthetic symbols. Arduously striving to create a distinct and specific black identity, *blocos afro* have put forward a version of the myth of

Mama Africa that is predominantly based on the black body, for which it establishes an ideal combination of "appearance," "essence," and "tendencies." Perceived as a flame that lightens up each and every black individual, Mama Africa functions as a source of the substance that fills the black body and the black soul, thus disseminating the notion that for a black appearance there is a corresponding black essence.

This book is an invitation to visit Bahia, or better yet, to revisit the state that is constantly labeled the most African part of Brazil. In addition to having the largest Afro-descendant population in the country, Bahia's vibrant black culture is a fundamental component of its public image, both nationally and internationally. Our journey will lead us into the spaces of black cultural production and down the paths of what has conventionally been called "blackness." Visualizing Bahia as part of the African diaspora, we will trace the routes of the black Atlantic, where we will discover the elements, local and global, used in the construction of race-based and Afro-referenced black identities. Our journey to Bahia will bring us to an encounter with Africa and its diaspora. Our continued travels will demand that we look beyond Bahia's enchantments and surface beauty in order to observe the complex relations between culture and politics. At the end of our journey, we will grapple with the notion of *baianidade*, or Bahianness, seeking to understand its intricate connections with blackness and Africanness and examining how these are constituted in relation to a broader ordering of power.

My discussion of blackness, black culture, and black identities in present-day Brazil engages with three major debates in cultural studies. The first concerns the significance of black cultures in the diaspora, and especially with the place that Brazil occupies within the black Atlantic. My analysis is informed by the assumption that the material and the symbolic cannot be analyzed in isolation, that discourses and practices are mutually constructed, and that culture and politics are interpenetrating. Culture, whether seen as a way of life or as objectified representations, exists in a hierarchical world in which some of its versions are hegemonic (Wade 1997). The intention here is to examine how culture participates in the operations of power, with the understanding that *culture is political*, because meanings are constitutive of the processes that seek to either transform or preserve the given hegemonic order.

I employ the term *black* as the generic designation of populations of African ancestry in the New World, keeping in mind that *black* and *white* are categories that exist because of each other. The meanings of these slippery categories vary according to the context and are constantly being redefined. The term *blackness* is used here to refer to black particularities and subjectivities, formed by black "structures of feeling" (Williams 1961) or, in other words, the characteristics related to the process of being, feeling, and becoming black. These characteristics are socially and culturally constructed. According to Stuart Hall (1992; 1996b), one of the major characteristics that make black diasporic cultures "black" is the strategic use of the body. As an important form of capital for slaves, their descendants, and the impoverished in general, the uses of the body have gone along with the centrality of music and style for diasporic black cultures. In tandem, Gilroy (1993a) defines diasporic black cultures as countercultures of modernity which share a common backdrop of experiences that includes a memory of slavery, a legacy of Africanisms, the effects of racism and racial discriminations, and dialogue and exchange with other diasporic black cultures. The various black cultures formed around the world have their own specificities, defined according to the local contexts in which they are produced. Nevertheless, some of their characteristics are shared, such as the belief in a common origin or past, the production of myths of Africanness, and the manipulation of the body as a locus for the construction of blackness.

Thus, black cultures are understood here as more than just automatic developments of the legacy brought to the Americas by enslaved Africans. A significant amount of academic work has put forward the notion that black cultures in the Americas are mostly constituted by "Africanisms," or the "retentions" of African cultural elements brought by the enslaved. Basing their claims on the African reminiscences that were transplanted to the New World, these perspectives insist on an ethnic homogeneity of the slave contingents who arrived in the Americas. In this vein, scholars seek to locate similar cultural elements and practices in Africa, in such realms as religion, music, and dance. However, instead of glorifying the persistence of Africanisms per se, as if they could possibly have a life of their own, this book analyzes how Afro-descendants have recreated, produced, manipulated, and employed culture for their own benefit. By focusing on how collectivities have chosen to reinvent Africa and Africanness as sources of empowerment, we can concentrate on the agency of black subjects in contexts marked by racism, inequality, and exclusion.

It is important to understand black cultures as formed within the interactions and dialogues of the black Atlantic, because it locates black cultures within a diaspora conceived of as dynamic and multicentered, countering the notion that there is only one center from which all forms of blackness emanate (Gilroy 1993a).[1] This brings us to the second debate I engage with in this book: the much-discussed essentialism of racial identities. The critique of essentialism—the belief that there are preexisting "African" molds that inform "black" characteristics—should not be carried out in the mere interest of theoretical rigor. Nor should it seek to negate the existence of a black particularity. I seek to transcend the binary opposition between the rigid perspectives of essentialism and antiessentialism by adopting an anti-antiessentialist position (Gilroy 1993a). In other words, I give value to black particularity and acknowledge it as constitutive of black subjectivities, but I nevertheless always regard it as being socially and historically constructed. The importance of analyzing black essentialism while there continues to be so much anti-black racism is to demonstrate the paradox of raciological antiracist struggles. In other words, it is necessary to lay bare the fact that racial essentialism ultimately preserves racist principles.

The third and probably most controversial debate I engage with focuses on the notion of "race." Contrary to those who argue that "race" should be used as a means of mobilization and unification of historically oppressed groups, I contend that the anti-racist struggle requires us to deconstruct the idea of "race," with the ultimate goal of superseding it. I deliberately write the word "race" in quotes even though I am well aware that the idea of "race" as a social construct has become commonplace among academics. Following such scholars as Paul Gilroy (1993a; 2000), Stuart Hall (1992; 1993; 1996a; 1996c), and Kwame Anthony Appiah (1992), I place "race" in quotes with the intention of preserving the term's discomfort. The quotes serve the purpose of interrupting the flow of the text, thus serving as a constant reminder of the artificiality and danger of raciological thought.

The more we understand the role of culture and politics in the construction of identities, the easier it becomes to recognize that blackness is not determined by characteristics fixed by "race" or nature. Feminist and anti-racist research has already shown how arguments based on nature are very rarely contested. In the past, their scientific authority bolstered discourses intended to subordinate women and blacks. Nonetheless, over the last decades, subordinated groups have also turned to notions of "nature" and "essence" to validate their claims and sustain the boundaries of their identities. This is the case with the *blocos afro* analyzed in this book, and especially so with Ilê Aiyê, which has relied heavily on a naturalized understanding of the black body as the main marker of difference.

This revised and expanded edition of my book *Reinvenções da África na Bahia* (2004) is more than a translation of the original. Although it preserves the central arguments and the earlier chapter arrangement, it has benefited from several factors. First, the concept of the myth of Mama Africa has been more fully developed and now occupies the central place it deserves. The myth of Mama Africa is presented in greater detail, acting as a guiding thread that permeates the entire text. This, consequently, allows for a greater dialogue among the chapters. Second, this book incorporates the recent literature on Brazilian racism and black identities that has blossomed over the past four years, as well as referencing earlier literature that had been overlooked in *Reinvenções*.

Third, this book benefited from the generous reviews of two anonymous readers. Their detailed comments, constructive criticism, and overall praise further convinced me that my main arguments were on the right track, while encouraging me to make some necessary changes. The most important of these revisions is a more nuanced approach to what has been termed in Brazil the "North American model of racial relations." I am less interested in the reality of U.S. racial politics than I am in how black activists in Brazil regard that reality and how their understanding of what happens in the United States is important in shaping their thoughts and attitudes toward their own racial identities. Therefore, when I argue that black activism in Brazil situates itself between an "African past" and a "North American future," I make it clear that both concepts refer to how Africa and the so-called U.S. model of racial relations have been imagined, conceived of, and thus reinvented within the sphere of black activism and black cultural production in Brazil.

Last but not least, the intricate process of translation has, in itself, enriched this book. More than transposing words from one language to another, translation also entails the discovery of new meanings. Because this book was written with an Anglophone readership in mind, terms and expressions that require no explanation for a Brazilian audience have received greater detail and contextualization here. Yet despite the many additions and the style changes, the final version reflects the same political positioning defended in *Reinvenções*; I continue to argue for the rescue of our shared human condition, regardless of the identities that appear, at times so profoundly, to fragment us.

The academic work that generated this book was based upon the alternating activities of literature review and field research, permeated by the constant analyses of culture. There were two primary periods of field research. The first consisted of research on the *blocos afro* Ilê Aiyê and Olodum in 1999 and 2000; I conducted interviews and participated, to the extent possible, in activities carried out by these two groups, including their rehearsals and festivals, Carnaval parades, as well as meetings, classes, and presentations. I have identified two groups within each *bloco afro* I worked with. The first group comprises the *blocos*' "producers of identity discourse," including directors, composers, musicians, and teachers. These are the internal leaders of the *blocos* who are responsible for research on Africa, defining the content of the classes, determining social action strategies, and establishing each *bloco*'s political stance. The second group comprises the *blocos*' "interlocutors of identity discourse," who are, above all, the young members of the *blocos* and those that benefit from their strategies for social action. This group receives, internalizes, and reelaborates the information about Africa, blackness, African essence, racism, and the forms of resistance to racism. Discourse producers are cited by name, since they are usually well-known public figures in Bahia, but I have not used the names of interlocutors in order to protect their individual identities.

The second period of field research consisted of interviews with African American tourists who visit Bahia—mainly its capital, Salvador, and the town of Cachoeira—in search of "African reminiscences" that might help them get closer to Africa. The first time I encountered one of these groups, I thought they were African tourists, since they were dressed in long, colorful tunics and sported either elaborate hairdos or large turbans. Only after the first conversations with those "Africans" did I discover that they were, in fact, African Americans. Their Africanness seemed so authentic and detailed that it permitted the (con)fusion with the original template, or at least with what is imagined of it. I had first noticed African American tourists in 1996, during the Festa da Boa Morte, the annual Celebration of Our Lady of the Good Death, but actual interviews began in August of 2000, when I had the opportunity to travel together with one of these groups from Salvador to Cachoeira.[2] I also interviewed tour guides who specialize in roots tourism, along with a few owners of travel agencies that cater specifically to African American tourists.

The analysis of Bahian black culture in general, and more specifically of the representations of the *blocos afro*, was also an important part of this research. Thus, my study included substantial examination of Bahian print and television media. This proved very valuable: it complemented my fieldwork impressions and allowed me to analyze the relationships between black culture and local politics by observing how images of blackness are associated with the official discourse of Bahianness.

Bahian black culture has simultaneously shaped and been shaped by references produced in other areas of the black diaspora, a topic I examine in chapter 1. I develop the concept of the myth of Mama Africa to explore how the belief in an idealized Africanness has spurred the construction of black identities. "Mama Africa" has become an increasingly ubiquitous expression in the songs, poems, and brochures produced by the *blocos afro*. Due to the frequent conflation of blackness with Bahianness, the term Mama Africa began to be used also in governmental advertising and hence became very present in everyday language. The mythification of Africa has been a common element in most, if not all, black communities of the diaspora. Black cultures are not the product of a frozen African heritage but have instead been constructed through dynamic processes within the black Atlantic system (Gilroy 1993a). The search for Africa in Bahia has made its capital, Salvador, even more "Africanized," thus amplifying its aura of blackness and attracting a growing number of African American tourists. Thus, both Bahia's own search for external black cultural references and the desire for Africanness projected on it from the outside have shaped its position within the black Atlantic network.

The black identities produced in the heart of the *blocos afro*, or whose central reference is the cultural production of the *blocos afro*, is analyzed in chapter 2. Inspired by the myth of Mama Africa, the *blocos afro* have been producing new representations of blackness, which have in turn affected the dynamics of Bahian cultural politics. I situate the production of Bahian black identities within the trajectory of black identities constructed in Brazil since the 1930s, and revisit the work of key scholars who contributed to a greater understanding of identities. While the *blocos afro* do not fit neatly into the definition of an ethnic group, their members are constantly attempting to produce an ethnic identity for which common lineage, ancestry, and pheno-type are deemed central. In order to enhance black distinctiveness, the body is transformed into a locus of affirmation of an Afro-referenced blackness.

I examine the centrality of the body in diasporic black cultures in chap-ter 3. There is a growing tendency among Brazilian blacks to define stan-dards of beauty according to an idealized African aesthetic as a means of confronting the negative images historically associated with blackness. The predominance of Eurocentric standards of beauty and the nefarious no-tions that historically degraded the black body in commonsense under-standings have contributed to the proliferation of stigmas and low self-esteem, primarily among black youth. The black body, weighted with an Africanness previously taken as negative, backwards, and associated with ugliness and filth, has been invested with an Africanness resignified to instill pride and beauty. In this way, Africa is *reinscribed* onto the body. The emergence of the *blocos afro* contributed to the adoption of black hairstyles and black styles of dress. Colorful fabrics from India and Bali, together with locally produced jewelry and clothes, are some of the elements used to invent an "Afro-aesthetics" in Brazil. Invoking the senses of sight, touch, and smell as connected to the black body, I examine the various ways in which Africanness — and consequently Africa itself — has been variously reinvented in order to produce beauty and restore dignity.

Africanness also entails an internal dimension, analyzed in chapter 4: the supposed essence of the black body. The myth of Mama Africa fosters the notion that for a black appearance there is a corresponding black essence, and that some traits naturally belong to black people, such as the gift for music and dance. Furthermore, these black tendencies are often believed to be transmitted through blood. I contend that the emphasis on nature — understood here as the combination of appearance and essence — puts culture at stake. Consequently, the powerful notion that it is necessary to "become black," so crucial to anti-racist groups, is threatened by the contradictory belief that one needs to reclaim tendencies already latent in the body or dormant in the soul. Grounded on the idea of "race," body-centric identities employ rigid subjectification techniques to guard the artificial boundaries built around cultures.

The narratives of blackness produced by black organizations have a significant amount of overlap with the concept of Bahianness employed by official discourse, which I examine in chapter 5. Certain Afro-Bahian cultural elements have been manipulated simultaneously by black groups in the construction of their identities and by the sectors of Bahia's elite that have invested in the concept of *baianidade*, namely local politicians and tourism-industry professionals. This process has promoted the notion that black bodies, endowed with a semi-mystical appearance and a quasi-magical essence, are responsible for disseminating Bahianness and providing it with authenticity. While at first this may give the impression that black organizations are in charge of the situation, a deeper look reveals that it is yet another circumstance in which blackness is held hostage of stereotypical representations. I argue that the myth of Mama Africa, in spite of its antiracist premises, intersects with, and to a great extent nourishes, the totalitarian notion of Bahianness. The expedient use of blackness by cultural groups (Yúdice 2003) and the exchange of favors carried out between key sectors of Bahian society have milked the myth of Mama Africa and allowed it to be used for purposes other than fighting racism and inequality.

An analysis of culture inevitably involves deconstructions and the revelation of contradictions. The process of deconstructing the essences operating at the core of identities can create divergences between the researcher and the researched. Postmodernism encouraged social scientists to challenge their foundations and question their position of authority with regard to the groups they research. The processes by which the researcher represents the researched has risen to the surface, as scholars self-critically observe how academic texts are constructed and how people are represented within them. I consider these interrogations extremely relevant, and I emphasize that my deconstructions of identities is not meant to reveal falsehoods, but rather to examine how truths have been produced. My goal is to reveal the incoherencies or contradictions that permeate the processes of constructing racial identities. My deconstructions are much less concerned with methodological or rational demands than with understanding the political meanings generated in the production of representations. We demystify beliefs not to diminish the beauty of myths, but to overcome the idea that identities must be fixed and that human beings are hostages of their culture or prisoners of their physical appearance.

The New Power of "Race"

During the three years I spent working on this book, an extremely important debate unfurled in Brazilian racial politics. Although the research for this book was carried out before this debate became so heated, I feel I should address, even if only briefly, this significant shift regarding anti-racist strategies. The concept of race has reemerged with tremendous force over the last few years following the proposal of two controversial new laws allegedly aimed at combating and repairing the country's record of racial inequality. The first is the Projeto de Lei de Cotas Raciais (Racial Quotas Bill, PL 73/99), which implements a quota system for blacks and indigenous students in Brazilian federal universities. Although the bill has not yet been voted on, several federal and state universities have already begun to implement the system in their entrance exams. Even more contentious is the Estatuto da Igualdade Racial (EIR), (Racial Equality Statute, PL 3,198/2000) which, if approved, will force all Brazilian citizens to specify their race and have it forever written on their ID cards and all types of official documents. The statute was approved by the senate in November

2005, but it has since faced serious opposition which has impeded congress from voting on it.

In this analysis of the debate surrounding the EIR and the quota system, I prefer not to opt for an easy partiality. Instead of grounding my commentary on an absolute position either for or against these racial laws, I have chosen the more difficult path of assessing the arguments that have informed both sides of the debate. The current, and very heated, discussion on the paradox of implementing race-based anti-racist laws has made it even more important to study the meanings of blackness, the myths of Africanness, and the significance of constructing separate black identities in Brazil today. The topics discussed in here will certainly contribute to a deeper understanding of why some black groups have found it necessary to establish a distinct black identity. The book also sheds light on the effects of this process on the subjectivities of those individuals who have "become black" by acquiring the identity formula provided by black cultural organizations.

Before I go any further, let me explain that this book is not about public policy. The reader will not find, beyond this introduction, a review of the Racial Equality Statute or an analysis of the recent implementation of racial quotas in Brazilian universities and public institutions. Yet because the study of black identities lies at its core, this book provides insight into how to respond to the undeniable reality of racism without further strengthening the notion of race. At the same time, I take very seriously the power of raciology — what Gilroy (2000) has defined as the race thinking and racial lore that inspires inhumanity — in Brazil; and while I invite readers to ultimately think beyond race, I also acknowledge and carefully analyze the effects of racism in shaping blackness, whiteness, and *mestiçagem* — racial and cultural mixture.[3]

One of the most strident reactions against the system of racial quotas was the cover of the 6 June 2007 edition of Brazilian newsweekly *Veja*, which claimed, in bright yellow capital letters, that "race does not exist." The magazine reported the attempt made by identical twin brothers to be classified as black for the University of Brasília's entrance exam so they could benefit from the recently implemented quotas for Afro-descendants. The caption that accompanied the picture of the two brown-skinned siblings had an alarming tone: the quota system had considered one twin black and the other white, therefore proving the unreality of race. To further enhance the shocking impact of *Veja*'s message, the cover portrayed one twin in a black T-shirt and the other wearing an otherwise identical white one, both standing against a half-black, half-white background.

Sensationalist and simplistic reactions have become ever more frequent in the debate surrounding racial inequalities in Brazil. Resorting to the biological notion that there are no human races, *Veja*'s commentary deliberately ignores the social effects of racism and its connections to the cultural interpretations of physical appearance. The same article joined the twins' story with the results of the DNA tests of a handful of black celebrities. The tests labeled the genes of dark-brown gymnast Daiane dos Santos as 40.8 percent European and only 39.7 percent African. Even more sensationalist was the revelation that the genetic make-up of jet-black samba composer Neguinho da Beija-Flor is 67.1 percent European. The discrepancy between genotype and phenotype was presented as evidence of the meaninglessness of racial categories.

Alongside the imprecision of the labels *African* and *European* is the problem of employing biology to discredit the social and cultural significance of race. Until as late as the 1940s, education and health systems in Brazil subscribed to theories of eugenics and social Darwinism to "correct" what was then understood as the nation's natural racial deficiencies. Among the most extreme consequences of such theories of scientific racism was the importation of European immigrants in order to "whiten" and therefore improve the country. In the early twenty-first century, biology is once again invoked, but this time to deny the existence of races and dismiss the effects of whitening ideologies. The increasingly heated debate on quotas and the EIR has generated, and in some instances revitalized, a series of key arguments against the revival of race. While some of the arguments are complex and others quite generic, they all need to be seriously examined if we are to understand this new moment of Brazilian history.

Possibly the most sweeping idea to figure prominently in the recent debate is that Brazil is not an essentially racist nation. This belief has been greatly disseminated in academic discussions, newspaper articles, and recently published books, including *Não somos racistas: Uma reação aos que querem nos transformar numa nação bicolor* [We Are Not Racists: A Reaction to Those Who Want to Transform Us into a Bicolor Nation] (2006), written by Ali Kamel, Globo Network's director of journalism. As the title of his bestseller indicates, Kamel argues that Brazilian society is not "constitutively racist." Instead, inequalities between blacks and whites are due solely to poverty and have no relation to racism. Kamel dedicates an entire chapter of his book to proving that there are no racial barriers that promote inequality between blacks and whites in the labor market. "If today the majority of the poor are blacks, this is not due to skin color. In Brazil this does not exist: 'if one is black, let him be poor.' Over the last 100 years, our model has concentrated income: those who are poor have great chances of staying poor. For about a decade now the country has tried to face this challenge, although it has done so timidly. With economic growth and better income distribution, the condition of blacks will improve significantly. Because here [in Brazil], color discrimination is not structural" (74).[4] Kamel not only denies that racism affects the opportunities and quality of life of dark-skinned individuals but even argues that racism in Brazil is, once again, limited to idiosyncrasies and not a significant part of the nation's everyday culture or ingrained in our public institutions.[5]

The author is not alone in coupling this belief with the notion that there is something intrinsically antiracist about *mestiçagem,* the term given to Brazil's practice of cultural and racial mixture. Although Antonio Risério's new book *A utopia brasileira e os movimentos negros* [The Brazilian Utopia and the Black Movements] (2007) is much more detailed and a bit more nuanced, it nevertheless follows along the same lines. Despite recognizing that Brazilians do not live in a racial democracy, Risério ardently claims that the country's unique forms of cultural and racial mixture are among its most positive attributes as a nation. For Risério, black activists have, for the most part, inverted this statement and tried to disseminate the idea that *mestiçagem* is, itself, a racist project, since it aims to blur the lines between blacks and mixed-race individuals, thus weakening identity discourses. In response, Risério defines as *"neo-negros"* (neo-blacks) (379) those sectors of the Brazilian black movement that seek social ascension by adopting the U.S. racial binary and the one-drop rule. He argues that it is not only unfeasible but also undesirable to import concepts and policies from the United States and apply them to the Brazilian situation. Risério criticizes what he views as the need of U.S. academics to combat the "Great Brazilian Mystification" (18) — the Brazilian myth of racial democracy — and to mobilize Brazilian blacks within the same models of struggle employed by their U.S. counterparts.

The comparison between the two countries' slavery systems, forms of racism, and racial politics is long-standing and has frequently been constructive. The contrast becomes worthless, however, or in fact harmful, when one country is depicted as better than the other, as when Brazil is considered to have experienced a "milder form of slavery," or when the United States is celebrated because its more accentuated racial division is perceived as more conducive to the mobilization of oppressed identities. This hierarchy easily informs the notion that one country should act as a model for the other.[6] Until the 1940s, African Americans looked up to what they considered to be Brazil's "racial paradise" (see Hellwig 1992). Nowadays, although many African Americans still dream about Brazil because of its alleged Africanness, we seem to have arrived at the exact opposite situation: Afro-Brazilian activists are looking up to the United States as a site of highly developed identity politics. In addition, as we saw above, affirmative-action policies, greatly informed by their U.S. equivalents, are being implemented in Brazil for the first time.

I do not find it productive to respond to Kamel's sensationalist title — "we are not racists" — by stating the reverse: "we are racists." Entire societies cannot be reduced to such sweeping generalizations or to static "models of racial relations." Although these may be useful for the sake of rhetoric or convenient as marketing strategies, they are usually detrimental for the purpose of in-depth analyses. Yet it is important to note that the title's negative mode indicates that if Brazilians are not racists, then others are. When it comes to discussing race and racism, Brazil and the United States have functioned as alter egos or, better yet, "alter-nations" to one another. If an alter ego is a second side to one's personality, an alter-nation refers to a process of change in which one thing or subject follows (or is supposed to follow) another in a repeated pattern. One of the most complicated patterns from the United States that Brazil is now expected to follow is the establishment of rigid and permanent boundaries between blacks and whites.

The EIR and the quota system call for the recognition of a well-defined racial division, which in turn requires the construction of a distinct black identity.[7] This is certainly not to say that black identities did not exist prior to the discussion of these new laws. On the contrary, they could only be proposed because specific forms of black identification were already in place. The novelty, though, is that these disconcerting discourses of difference grounded on "race" are receiving unprecedented support from the federal government and from a few state governments, such as Rio de Janeiro's. Government backing, however, has not been accompanied by widespread societal approval. While sectors of the black social movement celebrate their victories, they have been continuously challenged to substantiate the authenticity of a separate black identity in a nation that has long represented itself through metaphors of racial and cultural mixture.

In order to benefit from the new racial laws, one must disengage from *mestiçagem* and surrender one's nonblack ancestors. On a collective scale, this demands a radical transformation of *mestiços*, *pardos*, and *mulatos* into blacks, or "Afro-descendants." The term *pardo* is rarely used in individual self-classification, but it functions in the Brazilian census as an umbrella for a wide variety of mixed-race color categories, including the very popular, albeit loose, term *moreno*.[8] For the purpose of planning and implementing antiracist public policy, *pardos* and *pretos* (blacks) are counted together as "Afro-descendants." Although deemed a great accomplishment by the black social movement, this practice has generated strong opposition as well (see Maggie 1996; Fry 1995–96; Kamel 2006; and Risério 2007, among others). Granted, dark-skinned *pardos* are often subjected to the same lower standards of education, health, housing, and employment opportunities as *pretos*.[9] Yet when it comes to enjoying the newly implemented racial benefits, such as the university entrance quotas, many *pardos* are not considered "black enough," either because their skin is not very dark, their facial features are not as negroid, or because their hair is not sufficiently curly. Who knows which of these criteria was employed by the University of Brasília's selection committee to approve one twin brother's designation as black, while denying the other?

Yes, you read that right: a selection committee. Due to the complexity of defining who is black in Brazil, a committee was put together in 2004 to make that decision. According to Romilda Macarini, director of Cespe, the office that regulates entrance exams at the University of Brasília, applicants that self-classify as *preto* or *pardo* have a picture taken of their faces against a beige background. Scrutinizing the photograph, the committee examines the applicant's phenotype and skin color to see if they match "the typical characteristics of the black race" (Maio and Ventura 2005, 193). The university does not explain what these characteristics are, nor does it disclose the names of the committee members, explaining only that it consists of black activists, specialists in "race," and nonrotating members of the quota implementation project. The authority of science is once again called upon to confer the legitimacy of race, although this time stemming not from biology but from the anthropologist (the race expert) who sits on this committee. Because of its arbitrary character, and resemblance to the craniometrical studies of the early nineteenth century and to the infamous "comb tests" carried out in Apartheid South Africa, this committee has been described as authoritarian and abusive.[10]

Besides pointing to the inevitable slipperiness of racial categories, the requirement of counting *pardos* as black challenges the cliché that Brazil is the blackest country outside Africa. The importance of Brazil's Africanness, including the claim that its black population is second in size only to

Nigeria, was publicized by the Brazilian military dictatorship in the 1970s as part of its strategies to develop commercial agreements with African countries. The idea is widely disseminated today by the Brazilian tourism industry, especially in the state of Bahia. However, although 48 percent of Brazil's 170 million people are counted as Afro-descendant by the census, only 5.9 percent are self-declared *pretos*, while 42 percent employ a wide variety of intermediary color categories to classify themselves. The census then counts these categories as *pardos*. This means not only that the skin colors of these individuals vary across the entire spectrum of brown and that they have a wide assortment of hair textures and facial features. More importantly, the great number of *pardos* reveals that these individuals self-classify, and therefore self-identify, as not black, or at least not black in all circumstances (see Sheriff 2001), which explains the black movement's need to construct an indisputable black identity.[11]

This problematic form of measuring Brazil's black population has contributed to the "puzzle" mentioned by Howard Winant (1994), Michael Hanchard (1994), and others, in which Brazil is represented as a pathology: the country with the largest black population in the New World but with one of the lowest levels of racial consciousness in the Americas (Hanchard 1994, 95). Denise Ferreira da Silva, a sociologist and black activist, has offered a very insightful response to the application of this "ethnocentric universality" — a term she borrows from Chandra Mohanty (1988) — in the analyses of racial consciousness in Brazil. "Similarly to Winant, Hanchard not only forgets that this concept of 'race consciousness' emerged in a multiracial social space [the United States] where racial separation is the main strategy of racial subordination, but also bases his analysis on a fundamentally repressive conception of power. . . . Consequently, Hanchard cannot but claim that racial subordination in Brazil is the working of an over-powerful racial ideology, which in hiding from blacks their own blackness paradoxically denies that which premises modern constructions of race, that is, that racial traits produce culturally distinct peoples" (Silva 1998, 222–23).

Perhaps the major consequence of the new racial laws is the way in which they upset Brazil's hegemonic national project grounded on *mestiçagem* and racial conviviality. The establishment of a separate black identity goes against the ideal Brazilians hold of themselves as a syncretic nation that has overcome internal boundaries. This argument has been fiercely put forward in the anthology *Divisões perigosas: Políticas raciais no Brasil contemporâneo* [Dangerous Divisions: Racial Policies in Contemporary Brazil]

(Fry et al. 2007). Assembling dozens of short articles written by academics, journalists, and a handful of black activists, the book assumes an antirace, antiquota, and anti-EIR position. It grew out of a letter written by several of its authors and delivered to the Brazilian congress in June 2006, pleading with the representatives to vote against the EIR.

Although the articles vary in style and levels of complexity, the volume represents an important contribution to the current discussion of racism. It comes as an indispensable reminder that racism invented races, and not the other way around, as we tend to believe.[12] José Roberto Militão, a black lawyer, argues in his contribution to the book that the much-needed policies of affirmative action should not be implemented via a rigid and static system of quotas: "In addition to their collateral damages, quotas attack the effects [of racism] without removing the causes. Affirmative action, on the other hand, acts on the effects and attacks the causes" (2007, 330). The book is indeed very valuable in calling our attention to the deepening racialization that will result from the implementation of these projects, since official recognition by the state will contribute to having races written in stone. On the other hand, "dangerous divisions" already exist in Brazilian society. In this regard, the book's argument is absolutely, and in fact *dangerously*, mistaken in suggesting that these divisions will be *initiated* by the quota laws or by the Statute of Racial Equality.[13]

Racial Democracy, Dead or Alive

Another important, although unfortunate, outcome of the debate surrounding the new racial laws is that it has reduced the conversations about racism in Brazil to a binary discussion, leaving little space for complexity. Scholars who have argued against the EIR and the implementation of quotas have frequently been categorized as conservative or even racist. The heavily loaded epithet "neo-Freyrian" has been too easily employed by academics and activists who favor quotas, as a means to discredit those who find the use of "race" as a political tool to be problematic. The reaction against the quota system and the Statute of Racial Equality has indeed triggered a neo-Freyrian perspective, but it is at best naive and at worst disingenuous to pigeonhole the variety of opposing voices under this single label.

This burgeoning neo-Freyrianism is perhaps most strongly illustrated by the startling Movimento Pro-Mestiçagem. The movement's Web site, www.naçãomestiça.org, explains that it was founded in 2001 with the aim of valuing the process of miscegenation among the various groups that gave rise to the Brazilian nation. It hosts talks and seminars, celebrates the "Day of the Mestiço," and advocates including the category *mestiço* in the census. The movement also encompasses a surprising "Nucleus of Mulatto Resistance" that fights against what it defines as the "racial imposition of black organizations" and the "anti-*mestiço* politics of the Brazilian government." The Pro-Mestiçagem Movement claims that the wide variety of intermediary color categories (*pardos, mulatos, caboclos, cafuzos,* and so on) must be acknowledged and respected and not forced into an extreme and exclusive type of identification.

Those who celebrate *mestiçagem* have frequently argued that the existence of multiple color categories is a sign of an ambiguity that dissipates conflict. However, this logic fails to recognize that the various color categories with which Brazilians define themselves are loaded with racial notions of black inferiority and white superiority. In addition, the idea of *mestiço/a* requires the *mixture of races* and thus does not overcome the very notion of race, contrary to the Pro-Mestiçagem Movement's passionate claim.

Nevertheless, not all academics or activists who question the validity of the EIR and racial quotas and point to their pitfalls are neo-Freyrian. There are several problems with applying this label indiscriminately. First, Gilberto Freyre is not the inventor of Brazil's myth of racial democracy. The myth of a Brazilian racial paradise was formulated by Brazilian abolitionists with the help of their U.S. counterparts several decades before Freyre produced his prolific body of work (Azevedo 2003). Images of Brazil's exceptionally peaceful racial relations existed in U.S. abolitionist circles as early as the mid-1800s, as part of their leaders' efforts to emphasize the cruelty of U.S. slavery. Another problem of equating racial democracy with the work of Gilberto Freyre is that he did not even employ the term in his most famous book, *Casa grande & senzala* [translated into English as *The Masters and the Slaves*] (1989), although the idea of harmonious conviviality among the races was undeniably put forward there. Antonio Sérgio Guimarães (2006), a sociologist who is in favor of racial quotas and greater racial consciousness among blacks in Brazil, has shown that racial democracy, initially an ideological construct of modern Brazilian intellectuals, could only be transformed into a collective political commitment in the 1940s and 1950s because it gained the endorsement of subordinate sectors of society, including black activists and organizations.

Thus, the major problem with the neo-Freyrian label is that it has been based on a Manichean, and therefore simplistic, logic: one is either for the black movement or for *mestiçagem*, the latter understood, ultimately, as harmful to identity groups. Whether we are for or against quotas, enthusiastic or skeptical about the uses and abuses of "race", we need to recognize that the operations of *mestiçagem* are an undeniable and crucial part of Brazilian reality. Peter Wade's (2005) approach is very inspiring, in that it seeks neither to celebrate nor to condemn *mestizaje* and *mestiçagem* in Latin America, but rather to understand their workings and effects as processes linked to embodied identities and kinship relations. If *mestiçagem* is not inherently positive, neither is the myth of racial democracy intrinsically negative. If we do not recognize the power and pervasiveness of the myth, identity politics will inevitably fall into a void.

While it is certainly not feasible to state that Brazil is a racial democracy, it also makes no sense to claim that the myth of racial democracy is waning, as has been argued, among others, by Edward Telles. Defining racial ideas as belonging to "stages," Telles contends that "popular and elite support for the idea of racial democracy ended in the 1990s" (2004, 10). The author also dismisses as "schematic" and "anecdotal" the work of scholars who argue that myths are not mere falsehoods, since they represent powerful popular ways of thought and practice (16). Believing that only statistical work can provide concrete "evidence about race relations," Telles establishes a hierarchy between "anecdotal evidence" (which he implies qualitative work to be) and "strong evidence" (provided only by quantitative sociology grounded on statistical indicators). Rejecting such hierarchies, I contend that both quantitative and qualitative methods should be embraced in the study of racism. In addition, the myth of racial democracy is very much alive in Brazil and therefore deserves our utmost attention.

I understand myths to be powerful narratives that unify the otherwise conflicting realms of imagination, and not conspiracies, masks (Andrews 2004), or false premises (Hanchard 1994, 6) created by elites and imposed upon the masses. Analyzing the widespread acceptance of the myth of racial democracy among nonwhite Brazilians, John Burdick explains that for people to believe a myth "it must fairly describe some important part of their everyday lives" (1998, 12). While the ubiquity of interracial relationships in Brazil (including both marriages and friendships) is permeated by antiblack racist notions and does not correspond to a reality of racial harmony, it does point to an open-ended racial configuration that is amenable to transformation. Thus, although the myth of racial democracy does not accurately reflect Brazilian society, it does harbor the desire of how the reality of the nation's class and racial relations could be constituted. If dark-skinned, impoverished Brazilians embrace the myth, it is not because they are gullible or easily fooled. As agents, they chose to take on the myth of racial democracy not because they believe there is no racism in Brazil but because of the elements of hope and liberation the myth conveys.

In her analysis of racism and racial democracy in a small town in the state of Rio de Janeiro, Frances Winndance Twine investigates why Brazilians continue to believe the myth of racial democracy in face of a pervasive racist reality. For Twine (1998, 136), the nonconfrontational response to racism by underprivileged Afro-Brazilians does not challenge the myth of racial democracy, thus preserving *racismo cordial* (polite racism) and failing to alter racist practices. I contend that what Twine identifies as a failure to challenge the myth of racial democracy can only be called such if that was the intention of the response to racism in the first place. Instead of trying to confront the idea of racial democracy in order to respond to racism, Twine's interviewees, like most nonelite Afro-Brazilians, are doing the opposite: they are trying to realize the myth's promise of racial equality. As Burdick (1998) argues, researchers should not merely analyze why there is little grassroots support for the black movement's antiracist strategies but should also pay closer attention to why the black movement adopts stances that fail to reach their targeted constituency. Twine's central question poses myth against reality, when these dimensions are actually much more intertwined than many scholars are ready to accept. Myth is one way of reading and explaining the world, and not a second layer of interpretation that is discon-nected from, or somehow uncontaminated by, reality.

A second hindrance to the black movement's effort to combat the myth of racial democracy is the fact that ethnic or racial identification has a limited mobilizing effect for most black people in Brazil. Grassroots engagement in political mobilization has occurred predominantly through other, primarily class-based, forms of identification. My argument here differs from Carlos Hasenbalg's (1992) claim that, because misery is an overwhelming social reality, the themes discussed by the black movement would therefore seem abstract or even less urgent for the great mass of the black population. In my view, such hierarchy does not hold true, since race and class are not separate or independent layers. Impoverished nonwhite individuals are certainly aware of how their skin color concretely affects the material conditions of their everyday lives. However, the majority of the nonwhite population has not chosen to further emphasize racial differences in its reaction to racism. The uprising of destitute rural communities in the backlands of northeastern Brazil, the organized proletariat in the urban centers of the southeast, and the sizeable landless movements (e.g., the Movimento dos Trabalhadores Sem Terra — MST) and homeless movements (e.g., the Movimento dos Trabalhadores Sem Teto — MTST) have brought together impoverished Brazilians of all skin colors. This does not mean that race or phenotypical attributes are of no importance for the members of these organizations; they are, however, not more important than poverty, or gender differences, or unequal access to formal education. They have not carried sufficient weight to fragment the class-based elements that bind their members to one another and stimulate their joint mobilization against a common source of oppression.

The black movement's goal of confronting the myth of racial democracy is intimately connected to its effort of constructing a distinct black identity. They believe this is necessary in order to reach two major goals: overcoming the long-held belief that racism does not exist in Brazil and proving that there is a black particularity in spite of the nation's hegemonic discourse of *mestiçagem*. It is too soon to tell how much the newly implemented quota system and the possible implementation of the Racial Equality Statute will further the black movement's goals. But it is possible to assess the effects of the debate generated by these new racial laws, as I have attempted to do above. Both sides of the argument would probably agree that the public debate on racism in Brazil has been, in itself, profoundly important and necessary. Another positive aspect of the debate is that it exposes the powerful, yet frequently hidden, struggles over the open-ended meanings of blackness, Africanness, whiteness, and *mestiçagem* in the Brazilian nation.

One of the arguments employed by those who oppose quotas is that, because of centuries of cultural mixture, there is no black distinctiveness in the country. Proof of this would be the "Africanness" of Brazilian whites. Antônio Risério (2007, 148), for instance, argues that because of Brazil's intense processes of cultural mixture, hybridization, and syncretism, Brazilian whites are, to a great extent, more Africanized, and therefore "blacker," than U.S. blacks. This is a very problematic line of reasoning, filled with knots which I hope this book will contribute to untying. The culturally constructed and continuously reinvented feature that we call Africanness does not necessarily define one's degree of blackness. Another complication is that one may partake in a hybrid culture, filled with Africanisms, without recognizing the African origin of certain cultural expressions. Many of the African-derived expressions that pervade Brazilian Catholic rituals, for instance, are deemed purely Christian by most devotees. I used to tease my grandmother by telling her that the pope would definitely not approve of her samba dancing, clapping, and singing in honor of saints Cosmas and Damian. But she could swear that these rituals, as well as her offering to the saints of the palm oil–based dishes *vatapá* and *carurú*, were Catholic to the core. Instead of deliberate denial, this kind of attitude reveals that, unlike academics and activists, most people are not really very concerned with the geographic origins of their quotidian practices.

On the other hand, one may recognize, and even celebrate, the African or black origin of a given cultural expression, but within a context that contributes little to the defeat of racialism or the promotion of racial equality. This is the case when specific notions of Africanness are employed in support of totalitarian discourses, as when Getúlio Vargas's government endorsed samba as Brazil's national symbol in the 1930s. Presently, the municipal and state government's promotion of Bahia's locally produced forms of Africanness is the most emblematic example of how the recognition of an African origin not only does not contribute to the antiracist struggle but may, in fact, stand in its way. Black activists have raised concerns over origin, tradition, and purity as a means of increasing the consciousness deemed necessary for the establishment of a distinct black identity. While the classification of "things black" has proved important for the development of black identities, it has also raised problematic consequences for the antiracist struggle. Besides unintentionally favoring practices of cooptation, the process of reclaiming black culture for the black race has produced a rigid notion of blackness that has not managed to move beyond the centrality of the body as a marker of difference.

CHAPTER ONE

Bahia in the Black Atlantic

The sea: a shelter within reach.
— "Jeito Faceiro," by Jaupery and Pierre Onassis, Olodum

It is undeniable that a wide range of cultural elements brought to the Americas by enslaved Africans have endured throughout centuries of colonialism and oppression. A mere glimpse at many, if not most, Latin American cultures reveals the persistence of African features in the way people walk, dance, speak, pray, prepare their meals, and produce music. However, while we can easily identify this "Africanness" and sometimes even trace its origins back to specific African ethnicities, it is not possible to pin down the exact way in which Africanisms have been rearranged, reassembled, recycled, and ultimately reinvented in the New World. Rather than searching for the roots of what is considered black in Latin American cultures, I contend it is more important to understand the meanings of Africa and Africanness for contemporary black peoples in the diaspora.

The notion of Africa has been central in the construction of black identities in the Americas. The diaspora's longing for Africa has generated several versions of what I call the *myth of Mama Africa*. This belief has been significant in the development of diasporic discourses and representations of blackness. The search for Africa in Bahia, and specifically in the city of Salvador, the locus of Brazil's most celebrated black culture, currently led mainly by the *blocos afro*, has made Salvador even more "Africanized." In turn, Bahia's increasing aura of blackness has rendered it extremely attractive to those in search of its purported Africanness, as can be seen in the ever-growing number of African American roots tourists. In essence, the diaspora has also searched for Bahia, a search that has shaped Bahia's position within the black Atlantic network that connects the imaginaries of blackness and Africanness.

The Myth of Mama Africa

Africa has functioned as a fundamental source of inspiration for black cultures in the diaspora. Colonization of the New World and its consequent scattering of enslaved Africans prompted attachments to a lost homeland that would later become known as Africa. The Africa I speak of here is not the vast contemporary continent that is home to dozens of different countries and hundreds of different ethnic groups. Even when its heterogeneity is recognized, black communities in the diaspora still predominantly envision Africa as a unified entity.[1] Whether conceived of as tribal or as the birthplace of great civilizations, this imaginary Africa is linked to the past and to the ancestors, but is ultimately loyal to its present-day descendants, whether they inhabit the continent or not. What matters is that Africa resides in the fertile realm of Afro-descendants' imaginary.

Grounded in history, memory, and imagination, Bahian cultural producers draw cultural elements from local and transnational sources to compose the myth of Mama Africa. Among the various local producers of discourse, ranging from Candomblé temples and capoeira schools to intellectuals and politicians, the *blocos afro* are unquestionably major creators of the myth of Mama Africa in Bahia. This myth, as put forward by the *blocos*, is predominantly centered on the black body, for which it establishes an ideal combination of appearance, essence, and tendencies. As a magical entity that supposedly lives in every black person, Mama Africa feeds the body, nurtures the soul, and brings into being the inherent African character, advancing the idea that for a black appearance there is a corresponding black essence.

Representations of Africa have held great importance for the deterritorialized and reterritorialized black groups of the American continent. Initially, however, the nostalgia and depression felt by the enslaved did not express a longing for Africa itself, since this notion did not yet exist among those who only later would identify themselves as "Afro-descendants." The recurrent longing for home, which in Brazil was often called *banzo*, reflected instead the desire to return to one's village, community, the place of origin from whence one had been forcefully taken, but which for the enslaved was not yet called Africa.[2] The notion that Africans and their descendants in the diaspora shared a common "African" identity started in the mid–nineteenth century but only began to take clear shape later in that century, mainly through the writings of pan-Africanist intellectuals (Howe 1998; Gilroy 1993a). At that time, Africa was imagined almost exclusively within the limits of Pharaonic Egypt. The grandeur, wealth, and scientific discoveries attributed to Egyptian civilization is a common theme to this day, inspiring several strands of Afrocentric discourse, including those of the *blocos afro*.

Arising initially among Caribbean scholars and soon blossoming in several parts of the Americas, pan-Africanism called for the unification of the African continent and its concrete and progressive alliance with a united diaspora. Since then, Africa has existed as an "imagined community" (Anderson 1991) for dispersed blacks. We could also call it — and perhaps more appropriately — an "imaginary community," since, unlike a nation-state, and except for very specific cases such as the creation of Liberia and the migration of Afro-Brazilians to the Bight of Benin, Africa did not become a place of return for the majority of the black diaspora.[3] Nonetheless, Africa continued to be imagined from afar as a homeland and as a central ingredient feeding the imagination and cultural production of diasporic Afro-descendents.

In the 1910s and 1920s, the ideas proposed by the Jamaican leader Marcus Garvey influenced blacks in Jamaica, the United States, and Africa, giving birth to a transnational alliance and creating a black movement of global proportions. Garvey had a worldwide impact by defining a universal connection among dispersed blacks. He contended that black people, regardless of where they live, are all children of Mama Africa and are thus siblings who share the same African affiliation. Among his objectives, Garvey wanted Africa to become a black nation with international power, a place to which blacks could return (Barret 1988). As dispersed Afro-descendants strove to both restore and regain Mama Africa, they would simultaneously strengthen their own position in the world: "Sons and daughters of Africa, scattered though you may be, I implore of you to prepare. Prepare in all ways to strengthen the hands of Mama Africa. Our mother has been bleeding for centuries from the injuries inflicted upon her by a merciless foe. The call is for a physician to heal the wounds, and there can be no other physician than the dark hued son of the mother, and there can be no other nurse as tender and kind as the daughter of this afflicted mother" (Garvey 1919, cited in Hill 1983, 159–61).

The 1930s was also marked by a transnational movement that not only nurtured black peoples' affiliation to Africa but also established an "African character" purportedly shared by all Afro-descendants. This movement became known as *négritude*, and had followers in Europe, Africa, and the Americas. Among its many assertions, *négritude* reclaimed the values of the African civilization and the recovery of an African memory in order to bring pride to black peoples in the African continent and in the diaspora. *Négritude* emerged first in the field of literature as a reaction to the dominance of European canons and as an attempt to return to what were deemed the "primordial tenets" of the "black race," which were imagined as "African" (E. Nascimento 1981). *Négritude*'s values spread from literature to other cultural realms, adapting to local specificities and influencing black discourses to this day. The belief in an African character, for instance, is very much alive in the myth of Mama Africa circulated by Bahia's black organizations.

In the 1960s, the bond between black diaspora cultures and Mama Africa was further strengthened. Soul music produced in the United States became the soundtrack for the civil rights movement, while Martin Luther King Jr. and Malcolm X raised the racial consciousness of black people around the world. Among the many black organizations responding to that call was the Afro-Bahian group Ilê Aiyê. As stated by one of the group's directors, "Ilê Aiyê was founded and heavily based on black Americans — Black Power, Malcolm X, Martin Luther King Jr., Mandela, and many other Africans who fought for the freedom of their country. So we make it a point to remember these people, because they are a force, a way of showing that blacks have fought around the world to free their people."[4] In a similar vein, the publication of Alex Haley's bestseller *Roots* in 1976 was a great driving force behind the movement for diasporic blacks' search for Africa. Before this, although more restricted to intellectual circles, Richard Wright's *Black Power* (1954) had already inspired black Americans in the 1950s to look again, and in a new manner, at Africa. Symbols harking back to Africa popped up all around the United States. African maps were printed on clothing and accessories, and African-inspired hairstyles became increasingly fashionable. Aesthetics, as well as music, became an important means of circulation of new and proud forms of black identity in the African diaspora.

Forgotten connections were once again established in a new and creative manner, producing identities based on the myth of a unifying Africanness that would coalesce dispersed blacks. In this transnational imaginary, Africa was conceived as a sign of coherence in the face of experiences of dispersion and fragmentation. As Stuart Hall explains, the triangle of the African diaspora is centered on Africa as the mother of many different civilizations: "Africa is the name of the missing term, the great aporia, which lies at the centre of our cultural identity and gives it a meaning which, until recently, it lacked" (1993, 394). Diaspora language is created by people who feel, live, and invent a connection with a primordial home. This sense of connection changes through processes of forgetting, assimilation, and oppression. For William Safran (1991, cited in Clifford 1994), diasporas are "expatriate minority communities" dispersed from an original center to at least two peripheries: they preserve a memory, vision, or myth about their original homeland; they believe they are not totally accepted in the country to which they were taken; they see their ancestral homeland as a possible place of return; they believe they are committed to maintaining and recovering their original land; and they believe that their consciousness and solidarity are chiefly defined through the continued relationship with their original mother country.

Diaspora is derived from a Greek word that means dispersion. For a long time it was used mainly to describe the dispersion of Jews or to refer to Jewish groups relocated beyond their original homeland. At the end of the nineteenth century, the expression began to be employed to refer to the Africans spread around the world as a result of slavery. Edward Wilmot Blyden, a Caribbean scholar considered to be one of the pioneers of pan-African thought, has been credited as the first to refer to an African diaspora. In 1880, Blyden asserted that there were many similarities between the dispersion of Jews and Africans, even though Jews had moved around as a free and economically independent people, while Africans were taken as "things," comprising the largest model of a forced diaspora. The expression *African diaspora* or *black diaspora* only became widespread, however, in the mid-1960s, initially in the United States and the Caribbean, and then throughout the entire diaspora after it was amply endorsed by black scholars and black political movements (Salzman et al. 1996, 762).

Achille Mbembe states that African and Afro-descendant thinkers adopted elements of the Jewish model of reflection and construction of their own history, such as the notions of suffering, contingency, and finitude, and have used these as building blocks for the creation of images about African history and identity promoted in the greater public eye (2000). Through constant repetition, a set of dogmas and dreams were imposed on the modern discourse produced about Africa by *insiders*, generating two main currents of thought: an instrumentalist one, which by affirming itself as radical and progressive attempts to manipulate and determine the supposedly authentic African discourse; and a reductionist current, which emphasizes difference and the native condition to promote the idea of a single African identity founded on the concept of belonging to the same "black race." For Mbembe, both currents are based on myths and perpetuate fantastical notions about Africa.

While carrying their own contradictions and underlying risks, myths can be significantly productive for groups who have been historically oppressed and socially excluded. This is even more important for communities that define themselves as being part of a diaspora. Diasporic groups cultivate myths about their original homeland, and for this reason they are committed to its symbolic restoration, feeding the imaginary constructed around the motherland. The concept of diaspora thus presupposes long distances, a separation similar to exile, and the taboo of return, connecting multiple communities of a population that is geographically dispersed. James Clifford (1994) points to the curious fact that many minority groups that did not previously identify themselves as diasporic are now claiming diaspora origins and affiliations. The transnational connections produced by diasporic discourses create, especially for underprivileged groups, a sensation of the expansion of the boundaries of the nation in which they are minorities. Membership in a diaspora strengthens concepts such as W. E. B. Du Bois's "double consciousness," developed in *The Souls of Black Folk* (1990 [1903]), because its discourse reflects the feeling of belonging to a transnational network that includes the motherland not as something left behind, but as a place through which one can connect with modernity. This concept expresses the hybrid culture of black Americans and the permanent tension of being simultaneously *black* and *American*. By signaling the multiple and diverse natures of black people, Du Bois demonstrates the interconnections between Africa, the Americas, and Europe that gave rise to the modern black person.

In the 1950s, Frantz Fanon (1991 [1952]) studied the nature of this in-depth quest for Africa by blacks in the diaspora and connected this passionate search to the need to overcome self-hatred and condemnation. He viewed the rediscovery of Africa as part of a rehabilitation process for blacks in the diaspora. According to Stuart Hall, this rediscovery is the *production* of Africa itself and of the many identities that reinvent it, "not an identity grounded in the archeology, but in the re-telling of the past" (Hall 1993, 393). In this invention of the past, traditions have played a central role, but have been understood mainly as "one-way transmission belts" (Hall 1995, 207) which can safely and solidly connect us to our origin. Recovering traditions has thus been predominantly understood as a goal, when it should be seen as a never-ending creative practice.

As Eric Hobsbawm states, invented traditions, "taken to mean a set of practices, normally governed by overtly or tacitly accepted rules and of a ritual or symbolic nature, which seek to inculcate certain values and norms of behaviour by repetition," are attempts "to establish continuity with a suitable historic past" that nevertheless "is largely fictitious" (1983, 1). Such "responses to novel situations . . . take the form of reference to old situations, or . . . establish their own past by quasi-obligatory repetition." This mandatory repetition explains why invented traditions frequently require the belief in the existence of national, ethnic, or racial essences. One of the textbooks produced by Ilê Aiyê clearly indicates the connection between inventing traditions and defining what is "essentially African": "Some values are essential to African peoples' lives: family is the essential nucleus; to know and respect one's ancestors is a sacred obligation for the African family; each society has its beliefs, its customs, its traditions; solidarity is an essential trait of traditional African communities—people help each other in all moments of life" (Ilê Aiyê 2000, 4).

In this imagination of the African past, the importance attributed to family and tradition is closely connected to an understanding of fixed and essential gender roles. It is no wonder the title of the textbook produced by Ilê Aiyê is "África: Ventre fértil do mundo" [Africa: The World's Fertile Womb]. The child-bearing and -rearing vocation of this fantasized entity probably explains why the myth establishes a "Mother" instead of a "Father Africa," although the notion of a fatherland was, in the past, also employed to define Africa from afar. Martin Delany, an African American journalist and physician considered one of the pioneers of black nationalism, argued that black Americans should migrate to a *fatherland*, even if that territory was not located in Africa. Nicaragua was, initially, the location of his colonization project. Classifying Delany as "the progenitor of black Atlantic patriarchy," Paul Gilroy (1993a, 26) associates Delany's inclination for a fatherland—compared to his counterpart Robert Campbell's preference for the term "motherland"—with the interconnected relationship between nationality, citizenship, and masculinity that permeated

Delany's writings. Whether referring to motherlands or fatherlands, racial discourses are always gendered and sexualized. The choice of feminizing or masculinizing the imaginary homeland or concrete place of return is indicative both of the kind of relationship established with that land and the configurations of blackness that inform the myth of Africanness.

In the gendered discourses of the African diaspora, the fatherland has usually been conceived of as a place where the concrete actions of its male children will serve as a modernizing agency to help renew Africa's position in the world. The motherland, in contrast, imagined in a more abstract manner, is a place of symbolic — not actual — return, where Afro-descendants can recover from the difficulties encountered in the New World. Michelle Stephens argues, when describing Caribbean imaginations of Africa, "As both the new national state and the older imperial governments get figured as masculine 'fatherlands,' women remain, seemingly contradictorily, the figures for more open-ended, sentimental, affective, and relational dimensions of both imagined national and diasporic communities — the imaginary homeland as a motherland" (2005, 16). The motherland today, with its comfortable and generous lap, stands for the affective dimension of the diaspora, while the fatherland was perceived in the late nineteenth century as a site of action, "an image of the consolidated, racially unified, sovereign black nation" (Stephens 2005, 16).

While most of Stephens's arguments about Caribbean diasporic discourses on Africa apply to the context of Bahia, there is an important differentiation to be made. In Bahia's myth of Mama Africa, racial hybridity is not mapped onto an imagined female body. Instead, the metaphysical body of Mama Africa is conceived as a source of purity where one can recover from *mestiçagem* and disentangle oneself from the trappings of Brazil's narrative of racial democracy. Mama Africa's wholesomeness is further imagined through representations of her large, generous, accessible breasts, continually dispensing the essence of black life. In this aspect, paradoxically, Bahia's myth of Mama Africa shares characteristics with other representations of black womanhood that are far from liberating. It is similar to the mammy figure of the U.S. South, and to Gilberto Freyre's idealized *negra velha*, a romanticized depiction of the elderly female black house slave whose hands magically flavored the food she cooked and whose fingers offered the master's family members the pleasures of *cafuné*, an Afro-Brazilian version of "oiling the scalp."[5] Like the *negra velha*, Mama Africa does not have ownership of her body. On the contrary, her body exists for others: it is there for the taking. The bighearted *negra velha* is quintessentially represented as big breasted. In Freyre's depictions, her large breasts are sagging because she has spent her life nursing not only her own children, but any child that is close by, including, of course, the master's children.

Sharing traits with the *negra velha*, the myth of Mama Africa is largely centered on stereotypical notions of black motherhood. Her existence is grounded in the satisfaction of others. The magic that supposedly emanates from her being reinforces the notion of black women's natural servitude. Held responsible for raising and educating her children, Mama Africa complies with the traditional role set up for women and is thus manipulated as a static, unchanging entity from which black wisdom and truth can be drawn. Her daughters and sons will also follow established gender roles believed to be innate to their being. This black essence plays out differently in female and male black bodies. While racialized discourses seek to defy prejudice and overcome racism, they cannot be radical unless they also challenge gender hierarchies.

This production of an African past not only requires that black gender roles be established and African traditions be invented; it also demands the production of the very concept of Africa. We should not forget that the concepts of black, white, race, and African — so pervasive in our understanding of the world — are, in fact, modern inventions. Pan-African discourse, created by diaspora scholars back in the late nineteenth century, was fully impregnated with the Western ideals of the time, which preached the existence of "races" and the belief that the "black race" was different from the white one. Africa was then considered the birthplace of the "black race," while Europe was seen as the cradle of the "white race." Pan-African scholars believed that all blacks throughout the world belonged to the same common entity and shared a common African essence (Appiah 1992). For Appiah, what pan-Africanist pioneers did not seem to realize, however, was that Africa was, in and of itself, a Western construction, and that the large variety of people who inhabited the continent before European colonization did not conceive of themselves as belonging to a single geographical or racial unit. They were people who frequently did not even know about each other's existence.

The myth of Mama Africa should be assessed both in its positive and liberating grounds, and in its paradoxical outcomes. Although it is a powerful narrative that unites dispersed peoples, the myth of Mama Africa, like all myths, touts exaggerated notions that essentialize blackness. Several black studies scholars have warned us against the traps contained in these emotional attachments to an Africa that exists solely in the imagination. Femi Ojo-Ade (1995) criticizes the conquerors of Africa who tried to reduce the African ethos to the instinctive reactions of savages. To this day the idea persists that Africa is synonymous with backwardness and savagery. The problem, according to Ojo-Ade, is that those who purport to defend Africa and who should produce a new discourse that would protect them from the aggressions of the colonizers end up proclaiming Africa as a type of paradisiacal or idyllic monolith. "If the first point of view is scandalously false and racist, the second one is not any less scandalous in its simplistic and superficial nature, for in reality both end up reaching the same goal: proving that African culture is exotic, otherworldly, lacking dynamism. . . . It may sound unbelievable, but in fact Africans [and Afrodescendants] themselves have — consciously or not — helped and facilitated the past and present situation of confusion and cultural degradation" (Ojo-Ade 1995, 37).

Writing about the mythification of Africa from within the African continent, Achille Mbembe states that since the nineteenth century, a threefold fiction of race, tradition, and geography has been used to bolster the argument that Africans have a unique identity. Supporters of this view hold that "there is a specific African autochthony," and they "have sought to find a general denomination and a place to which they could anchor their prose. The geographical place turns out to be tropical Africa, defined by a thoroughly fictional boundary" (2000, 10). Stuart Hall's theoretical considerations of those diasporic cultural identities that project Africa at their center also follow the same line of thought: "The original 'Africa' is no longer there. It too has been transformed. History is, in that sense, irreversible. We must not collude with the West which, precisely, normalizes and appropriates Africa by freezing it into some timeless zone of the primitive and unchanging past" (1993, 399). Of course, members of the diaspora must take Africa into account, but they cannot recover it. It belongs to an imagined history and geography (Said 1978), with value that we can feel and name, like an imagined community. "It is not once-and-for-all. It is not a fixed origin to which we can make some final and absolute Return" (Hall 1993, 395).

In Brazil, the idealization of a mythical Africa and the establishment of links with other points of the diaspora are central components of the discourses of black cultural organizations. The search for Africa as a basis for recreating Brazilian black traditions is evident in several spheres of the country's cultural life. In music, mythical Africa is present in samba lyrics and *música popular brasileira* songs, as well as those of *afoxés* (Carnaval groups that take the sacred music of Candomblé to the streets) and *blocos afro*. Afro-Brazilian aesthetics has been steadily producing new elements through clothing, accessories, hair styles, and fabric patterns. Recently, ethnic toys have appeared on the market, exemplified by dark-skinned dolls dressed as "Africans." Religion is also witnessing a re-Africanization movement that recreates the symbolic relationships between Brazil and Africa. In Bahia, this movement is led by Mãe Stella de Oxóssi, of the Candomblé temple Ilê Axé Opô Afonjá, who defends the rupture with Catholicism and the dissociation between *orixás* (Yoruba gods and goddesses) and Catholic saints, as part of a strategy to re-Africanize and "purify" Candomblé from its syncretic forms.[6] Music, aesthetics, and religion have served as cultural realms for the development of the myth of Mama Africa and its underlying belief in an Africa as the source of all knowledge.

Bahia in Search of Africa

After this quick journey through the routes of the black Atlantic, during which we anchored at sites of the diaspora where Africa has been constantly resignified to serve as a reference for the construction of not only local but also transnational black identities, we will dock in Bahia to understand its role as a producing locus of black ethnic symbols within this important system of symbolic exchanges. Among the many regions in the diaspora which are marked by a strong African cultural presence, Bahia has stood out for its immense legacy of Africanisms. In the 1940s and 1950s, anthropologist Melville Herskovits, delighted with the arsenal of African "reminiscences" and "cultural retentions" in Bahia, ranked it highly on his "scale of Africanisms." Candomblé, musical rhythms, capoeira, and palm oil–based cuisine are the main examples of cultural expressions with African origins reassembled on Bahian soil and used to characterize the state as black and African.

In addition to the usual stock of Africanisms that ensure historical continuity with the motherland, Bahia's aura of blackness has also resulted from the search for and affirmation of its ties to Africa, through a movement that began in the 1970s, inspired by cultural and political events with transnational impact. The 1970s provided fertile ground for the emergence and strengthening of black political movements in several parts of the world. The civil rights movement that gained strength in the United States beginning in the late 1950s; the black musical genres of soul, funk, and reggae that became global rhythms beginning in the 1960s; and the world-wide fame of black boxers Muhammad Ali and George Foreman were some of the most important factors that elevated the self-esteem of blacks all over the Americas and in the Caribbean (Risério 1981).

In Bahia, perhaps even more important than these events were the struggles for independence on African soil, news of which reached Afro-Brazilians and provided tales of heroic feats that augmented the imaginary about Africa and its peoples. One of Ilê Aiyê's texts in particular reveals the importance of the anticolonial struggles in Africa for the imaginary of blacks in Bahia: "The long list of African countries that have been able to achieve independence, some through revolution — such as Guinea-Bissau, Cape Verde, Angola, Mozambique, Zimbabwe, and Ghana — fostered change in the image that black Brazilians, and especially those in Salvador, have of black Africans and therefore of black Mama Africa, making it clear to this group that to be a black African was not to be passive, careless, underdeveloped, despite the distortions by the mass media, and that the experience of the African struggles could be reproduced here, since we comprised the majority of the population" (Ilê Aiyê, 1982, 36).

Ilê Aiyê is a key representative of the Brazilian black community, and its discourse has had a profound influence on the lives of those whose identities are forged based on the *bloco*'s "African" mold: both directly on the young members of the group and more indirectly, yet no less effectively, on those individuals seeking "African" elements for the construction of their black identities, including residents of the city of Salvador, who consider the *bloco* to be a type of guardian of blackness, and African American visitors who contact the group in search of what they believe to be their lost Africanness.[7]

Influenced by the times and revolted by the constant discrimination in their lives, a group of young blacks from the neighborhood of Liberdade in Salvador founded *bloco afro* Ilê Aiyê in 1974. The following year, the so-called blackest city of Brazil witnessed a Carnaval parade that included a group comprised entirely of blacks, all dressed in "typically African" outfits and brazenly singing, "White man, if you knew the value of blacks you'd dip yourself in tar and turn black too." Although several *blocos afro* have emerged in its wake, Ilê Aiyê has held the honor of being the pioneer throughout its three and a half decades of existence, and it is considered "the most African" of the *blocos afro* of Bahia. Ilê Aiyê is deemed the main example of African genuineness — one which guards and protects identity and traditions.[8]

The so-called re-Africanization of Carnaval, initiated by Ilê Aiyê in 1975, has grown ever since and persists to this day, continuously updating the myth of Mama Africa. In Bahia, the *blocos afro* that emerged in the midst of the development of a contemporary international black culture have since been the main conduits of this connection to Africa. Through their song lyrics, Afro costumes, and hair styles, and the production of a rich identity narrative, the *blocos afro* recreate and perpetuate the myth of Mama Africa, the motherland of blacks in the diaspora, where foundation and originality supposedly lie. Ilê Aiyê's choice for its 2001 Carnaval theme, "Africa: The World's Fertile Womb," confirms the belief in this female entity that emanates wisdom: an Africa as the source of all knowledge. The study packet produced by the group to inform and guide the composers about the year's chosen theme states, "Africa is born in Egypt and in the interrelationship between North Africa and South Africa; the great kingdoms of TASETI, in NUBIA and KENET in Egypt, which means BLACK CITY or BLACK COMMUNITY, meet and clear paths for civilizations of the entire world. It is the pyramids of Egypt; the temples of Zimbabwe; . . . the art of combining words, creating stories, songs, legends, histories, and proverbs; the oral tradition that organizes itself and creates legitimacy as a voice and tradition of the ancestors. All of this is Africa, producing and spewing forth life, knowledge, spirituality, rhythm, music, from its Fertile Womb to the entire world" (Ilê Aiyê 2000, 1, emphasis in original).

Once again, Africa is imagined as a generous mother whose womb breeds life. As a female magical entity, Mama Africa does not produce knowledge, since she is not capable of transcendence, or what Simone de Beauvoir (1993 [1953]) defined as the activity that produces rupture, which is expressed mainly by men. For Beauvoir, oppressed peoples such as slaves and women do not freely choose values, customs, and laws, thus their lives have little possibility of transcendence. Imagined as a black woman, Mama Africa has been conceived as endowed with the repetitive and uncreative life of immanence, naturally and spontaneously spurting forth knowledge, in the same way that milk naturally seeps from her breasts. The myth of Mama Africa, and its underlying belief in an Africa as the source of all knowledge, are central in the discourse of the *blocos afro*. Bahia's version of the myth shares several tenets about the African past and the preservation of traditions with other diaspora-created beliefs about Africa, and contains commonalities which bring together diasporic Afro-descendants. The myth of Mama Africa represents the basis of the history of foundation and assumes a central role in identity narratives. This has led to the production of an African past in which desire and longing have shaped the memory of Africa.

The discourse of young *bloco* members contains several important elements concerning the Africa they imagine. The idea of Africa etched in the imaginary of these members juxtaposes, sometimes in a single statement, two main images: on the one hand, an idyllic, paradisiacal Africa, a land in which only blacks live and where traditions are still preserved; and on the other hand, a place marked by pervasive poverty, hunger, and racism, just like in Brazil. The younger interviewees, especially those 15 and under, tend toward the paradisiacal Africa, while the older ones, 16 and up, generally hold a more realistic view of the social state of affairs of African countries, although they also believe in a tribal, traditional, and homogenous Africa. The first group defines Africa as a place where blacks are freer and happier, where there is more harmony and no racism, and for this reason a highly desirable place they dream of visiting:

"Sometimes the 'teach' asks us what dreams we want to achieve, if we could go anywhere, where would we dream of. Everyone answered it was to go to Africa to see blacks, to see how blacks are treated [there]." "I imagine it's beautiful. We've never been there, but one day there's going to be a trip to go there. . . . It's a place where blacks aren't discriminated against like they are here." From this perspective, Africa is defined in a very generic manner: "It's the place where blacks and religion come from, where there are many different black hair styles." They believe that all Africans dress the same: "People in Africa wear big shirts with sleeves like this, like a loose shirt and pants. There's some [of that] here, but it's pretty rare to see that here. 'Cause these clothes come from Africa and people make them to send here." The young *bloco* members believe that among Brazilians, only Ilê Aiyê members use such clothing, and even then, only on special occasions: "Performance outfits are only used during concerts, not on a daily basis. In Africa, you see those people, every day, with the big tunics, with those baggy pants underneath, and the head wrap. You always see that, on most people. People take their clothes off and put on others that are the same. The next day you wear another outfit that's the same as the last one. But not here, we only use the clothing — in this case the Afro-style clothing — when it's time to show the happy part of Africa, the part of Africa that we're honoring with that type of outfit."

The second set of interviewees, comprising mostly older teenagers and young adults, recognizes that there are vast afflictions and social inequalities in Africa. One of the band leaders of Band'Aiyê states, "Africa is almost the same as Brazil. In everything! In terms of suffering, discrimination, in terms of blacks not having their own freedom in some places, because in a certain sense here in Brazil we are free and welcome to do some things, and there they aren't. So, see, I think Africa, that African people are very repressed, despite the fact that they fight [against it]." Although these interviewees recognize the suffering that exists on the African continent, they nevertheless give Africa credit for remaining "tribal." In the words of one of the most active young female members of Ilê Aiyê, "tribal Africa" seems static and frozen in time:

> The culture, the ritual they had in Africa [is] connected to dance, connected to food. The ritual they had for eating, and they all ate together . . . the schedule they had for harvesting the crops, and they'd take the women and the men and divide them up to work, the type of work where men and women live together but only women do the work, you know? A macho society. . . . One that gathers hog-plums, which are served for breakfast, lunch, and dinner. So these times of the day they have them down pat, everyone's born knowing the stories. They already know how it's done. They wake up early, I don't remember what the ritual is that they do, they go to bed early, and the older ones do the ritual, I don't know if it's a salutation, a salutation to nature, for one more day of life, and then a harvest comes and goes, and then they plant and then they harvest and split it up among the families and then they eat together. And then there's the dance ritual, a salutation in gratitude for the food. There are still some tribes that do that; others don't. So that's the history I know about Africa, and that I dare to tell, and that I have read about — it's basically that. I think it's interesting. In some homes they still do that. My family is one that still has the habit where the children ask for their father's blessing to go to bed, to wake up, to leave the house. My family still has this ritual, of getting up early and saying 'my blessing, mother.' Oh, that comes from Africa for sure. That's proof that some families are able to preserve [traditions]. Others can't. Mine still does that thing of asking the elders for their blessing. So yes, this culture, which we know exists, and which we inherited, and which we put into practice, and it still works. [In] some families that I know, it still works. This respect for elders, not in and of itself, not because they are part of your family, but respect for elders because of their life experience and their information about life, so that we don't fail in the same way they already did, for the experience they've already lived.

The habit, still common among many Brazilian families, of asking for an elder's blessing is highlighted as part of the African heritage. Even though it is most likely a Catholic tradition, it has been resignified as an Africanism that has been preserved only by some black families. For the young woman, everything inherited from the past must have an African origin. Not only is the past generalized as African, but as stemming from a homogenous and unchanging Africa. Throughout her interview, the young dancer expressed knowledge about the current conditions of the African continent, learned not only through books but also by means of her travels to several African countries. She also critiqued the sexist representation of her own mythic Africa. Nonetheless, she constantly referred to a generic Africa, filled with African traditions that are mechanically reproduced by a nonspecific "African people." These ideas are in tune with the teachings of the older *bloco* members, the founders, who formulate and transmit the images of Africa described by the young ones. In addition to being tribal and a source of traditions, Africa is also depicted as a homogenous block, eliding the reality of its hundreds of different peoples and cultures. This tendency to mythicize Africa is not, however, a new or exclusive characteristic of the discourse produced by Ilê Aiyê or by the imaginary of Bahia's *blocos afro*. In most countries where there is a great presence of Afro-descendants, African traditions have been reinvented through a strong desire to rediscover the "missing link," tracing the routes that lead back to one's roots.

This mythical Africa offers a much more comforting memory of an imagined past than does the history of the pain and suffering endured on the slave ships or sugarcane plantations. As Gilroy asserts, "Blacks are urged, if not to forget the slave experience which appears as an aberration from the story of greatness told in African history, then to replace it at the centre of our thinking with a mystical and ruthlessly positive notion of Africa that is indifferent to intraracial variation and is frozen at the point where blacks boarded the ships that would carry them into the woes and horrors of the middle passage" (1987, 189).[9] In this same vein, the discourse produced by the *blocos afro* does not emphasize the horrors of slavery, opting instead to invoke the greatness of Egypt and Ethiopia and the traditionalism of "tribal Africa," as illustrated by the lyrics of these hit songs by Olodum and Ilê Aiyê, respectively:

Pelourinho is a small community
Yet one which Olodum will unite with bonds of fraternity.
Wake up to the Egyptian culture in Brazil,

Instead of braids we'll see Tutankhamen turbans
And heads will be filled with freedom.
Black people demand equality, setting aside divisions.
Where's Tutankhamen? Oh Giza, Akhenaten,
Oh Giza, Tutankhamen, oh Giza, Akhenaten oh,
I said Pharaoh, oh Pharaoh

Ilê Aiyê's theme this year is Congo-Brazzaville,
Another African country.
In the fifteenth century, the powers of the Old World
Turned their eyes toward the continent
Seeking more in-depth knowledge[10]

As indicated in the lyrics of both songs, the myth of Mama Africa developed by the *blocos afro* in Bahia is centered on two main subsets: on one hand, the magnificent ancient civilizations of Egypt and Ethiopia, and on the other, the foundational knowledge of "primitive" Africans. Describing what he calls the "lure of Egypt," Stephen Howe explains that "for more than two centuries, black scholars and publicists made the claim that civilization was African in origin, a centrepiece of their efforts to vindicate the reputation and enhance the self-esteem of African-descended peoples. Identification of Pharaonic Egypt . . . or of 'Ethiopians' . . . as the originators of arts, sciences, technologies and political organization became a centrepiece of the fight back against white aspersion" (1998, 32). Although Egypto-mania frequently dismissed other African nations or ethnicities as less important, or even inferior to Egypt, this is not the case in the imaginary of Bahia's *blocos afro*. Relying on oral testimonies as much as on academic scholarship, creators of the *blocos'* discourses have celebrated the "places of origin" of Afro-Brazilian ancestors. Thus, African ethnic groups brought to Brazil as slaves are revered in song lyrics alongside contemporary West African nation-states that subsequently developed in these same regions.

Besides these specific representations of Africa, the Bahian myth also includes some countries of the African diaspora, thus envisioning Jamaica, Cuba, and the United States as branches of Mama Africa. An example of this ramification of Africa is found in *bloco afro* Muzenza, which Africanizes itself by way of Jamaica. Even though Jamaica is not located in Africa, the group considers it one of the elderly mother's extended arms sheltering her black children. Muzenza was created in 1981 by Olodum dissidents. The *bloco* has several emblematic African themes, but none is as important as

Bob Marley and the Rastafari movement.[11] For this reason, Muzenza is also called "Reggae Muzenza" and attracts a special type of reveler who forms a unique wing within the *bloco*: the Rastafari, Jah's warriors who parade carrying a huge Ethiopian flag above their dreadlocks.[12]

Olodum, the most famous of Bahia's *blocos afro*, also appropriates reggae and Rastafari themes, yet from a different perspective than Muzenza: more than exalting Bob Marley and Jamaica, the group goes directly to the Rastafari myth of origin, celebrating Haile Selassie and Ethiopia (Gomes da Cunha 1991). Olodum was founded in 1979 by former members of Ilê Aiyê. Like every *bloco afro*, Ilê Aiyê and Olodum are characterized primarily by their costumes and music. Both groups create their own outfits, based on bibliographic research about a given black African community or country, according to the theme chosen for each year's carnaval (Risério 1981).

Much has been written about the black musical rhythms produced in Bahia. While in the past the focus of these studies was on the capacity to retain African cultural traditions (Herskovits 1943; 1966b [1948]; Frazier 1942), more recent studies have emphasized the modern and globalized character of Bahia's musical production, even when coupled with a discourse grounded on tradition. The works of Christopher Dunn, Ari Lima, and Osmundo de Araújo Pinho (in Perrone and Dunn 2001) have defined Brazil as both a receiver and a producer of musical forms in the black Atlantic world.[13] In *Brutality Garden*, Dunn (2001, 180) underscores that the new Afro-Bahian music produced by the *blocos* was, from the very beginning, diasporic and transnational both in terms of its rhythms and its values. I position my work along the lines of these scholars who have identified modernity and transnationalism in the music of the *blocos afro*. Yet, I contend that greater attention should be paid to the adamant appeals for tradition within the *blocos'* modern discourse and to the insistent myth of a fundamental motherland which coexists with a diasporic narrative. It seems to me that even though the term *diaspora* inevitably conjures up a large, unrestricted universe characterized by infinite possibilities of communication and exchange, this same word — as inevitably is the case for all signifiers — can acquire meanings that are quite distinct and even contrary to the transnational, multicentered concept of the diaspora as used by poststructuralist scholars. While the idiom of the diaspora abounds in the lyrics of the *bloco afro* songs, it is still very much connected to a static understanding of Africanness.

The music produced by the *blocos afro* is a central means for the production and circulation of their discourses. This music has made its own incursions throughout the African diaspora, even if such journeys have occurred solely in the realms of poetry and imagination. My approach here focuses on the lyrics created by the *blocos'* poets and composers, rather than the musical rhythms per se, such as *afoxé*, *ijexá*, samba-reggae, samba-afro, and myriad other beats that present themselves as either old and traditional or new and current, but which are all unquestionably *modern*. My analysis of the *blocos'* lyrics weaves in phrases and expressions that have been sung so often they became slogans. While they sound very familiar and may even arouse particular memories and emotions for Brazilians, I do not anticipate that the same would happen with an Anglophone readership, unfamiliar with the songs of the *blocos afro*. Although a lot is lost in translation, I have retained the phrases from the *blocos'* lyrics in the hope that they will provide a sense of the atmosphere of the Africanness created by the *blocos* in Bahia.

As Antônio Risério (1981) indicates, the African past recovered by the *blocos* is often found in books and encyclopedias. The groups' lyrics and outfits are created based on research in which academic literature is among the main sources of information for the invention of traditions. The Africanness flaunted by *bloco* members is inspired by the desire to affirm a recently produced Afro-referenced sense of blackness. The knowledge sought in encyclopedias is reflected in the lyrics, which are often similar to bibliographic entries, highlighting elements of the geography and history of African countries, describing the location of rivers, mountains, deserts, forests, and even providing statistical information about the population, such as ethnic groups, economic activities, and predominant religions. For example, in one song we learn that "the Congo region has many wetlands and rivers; its main rivers are the Congo, Motaba, and Ubamgui; its highest peak is Mount Leketi; and its inhabitants subsist mainly from agriculture."[14]

During the Carnavals of the late 1970s and the 1980s, the history and geography of countries such as Egypt, Ethiopia, Madagascar, Senegal, and the Republic of the Congo (referred to generically as "the Congo") were heralded along the streets of Salvador, informing the local population about the legends of Osiris, Tutankhamen, and the pharaohs of Egypt, or leading Bahians to repeat refrains asserting "Senegal borders Mauritania and Mali," that in Madagascar, "alienated because of his powers, King Radama was considered a true Meiji, who led his kingdom to dance," or "Bantu, Indonesians, and Arabs assimilated into Malagasy culture," and that Osei Tutu was the king of Ghana's Ashanti Empire, with its gold and cacao wealth, and that "Menelik II won the battle, expelling the Italians from Axum."[15]

The emphasis on nature (rivers, deserts, and so on), as well as heroic feats of the African peoples—who not only expelled their colonizers but also invented metallurgy and the foundations of mathematics—confirms the predominant belief in an Africa as source of all knowledge. By transforming encyclopedia entries into poetry, *bloco afro* songs exalt chiefly the greatness of African peoples and the origin—and therefore affiliation—of black Bahians to Mama Africa. Yoruba origin (*origem nagô*) is the affiliation preferred by the poets who write these lyrics, transforming the Yoruba adjective into a distinguishing term that labels blackness and at the same time produces an imagined Yoruba Bahianness (*baianidade nagô*).[16]

The discourse of Salvador's *blocos afro* conceives of the diaspora as a panorama of the black race mythology. Their songs invoke the magnitude of the great civilizations of Egypt and Ethiopia, and the fundamental originality supposedly inherent to "tribal Africa." The foundation and base of tribal Africanness are sung in lyrics that extol the Congo, Dahomey, Ghana, Togo, and Benin, while simultaneously dipping into the contemporary U.S. Afrocentric discourse to exalt the nobility of the great African civilizations, as seen in Olodum's lyrics cited above. This song incites Bahians to awaken to the "Egyptian culture in Brazil / instead of braided hair, we'll see Tutankhamen turbans."[17] Aimed at strengthening the ideal of blackness, the *blocos'* lyrics also celebrate black beauty, which is associated mainly with the bodily features of skin color and hair texture. Songs include such themes as the beauty of black women, who are praised as "goddesses of ebony," and the "jet black silhouette that blackness created," with "braids brimming with originality." Lyrics emphasize that "blacks are filled with the song of their beauty," and that blackness "consists of a universe of beauty, explored by the black race."[18]

The awareness of blackness itself is usually associated with the need to preserve African traditions, and therefore the *blocos'* songs describe the archetypes of the *orixás* and tell of the legends of Candomblé, always emphasizing that the gods traveled from Africa to Bahia along a preestablished and unidirectional route. The lyrics "Pelourinho is a small community that Olodum nevertheless unites in bonds of fraternity" and "Salvador became more alert with Afro Olodum's singing" highlight the role of the *blocos afro* as "cultivators of blackness and Africanness."[19]

At the end of the 1980s, Afro-Bahian music exploded on radio stations around the country, albeit interpreted much more frequently by white singers and *trio elétrico* bands—who then began to invest in this niche—than by the voices of the *bloco afro* singers and composers who had been writing such music for over 15 years.[20] At the time, young, predominantly white, middle-class Bahians were bellowing out the refrain, "I'm very black [*negão*], my heart is in Liberdade."[21] And even if they lived in Itaigara or Caminho das Árvores — wealthy neighborhoods of Salvador — they would repeat, "I'm from Curuzu, Ilê, that's my truth."[22] Curuzu and Liberdade are impoverished city neighborhoods, inhabited mostly by blacks and stigmatized as dangerous "hoods" that middle-class white Bahians almost never venture to visit. Even though it was interpreted by people with little or no connection to the *blocos*, the success of Afro music consolidated Salvador as the Mecca of Brazilian blackness. Many *afoxés* and *blocos afro* began to crop up in São Paulo, Rio de Janeiro, as well as other northeastern states, sending their leaders on apprenticeships with the original *blocos afro*, especially Ilê Aiyê, which is unanimously considered the "guardian of African traditions in Bahia."

During that same period, *blocos afro* began writing songs extolling the greatness of other countries marked by a strong black culture yet located outside Africa. The network of countries with large black populations, especially those in the Caribbean, began to be defined as "*latinamente* black," uniting "black people *latinamente* in song, uniting a people *latinamente* in common thought," even if these were English-speaking countries.[23] Jamaica is once again molded by the lyrics, becoming not just African, but also Latin. Cuba, the subject of many songs, was praised in Olodum's lyrics for its black people and culture as much as for its socialist revolution and its leaders Fidel Castro and Che Guevara. While most *blocos afro* began to expand their lyrics to include other countries in the diaspora, Ilê Aiyê opted for a more traditionalist stance and remained loyal to the countries located within the physical boundaries of Mama Africa. Olodum, on the other hand, assumed a vanguard position, signaling the connections of the diaspora in a more dynamic fashion. It informed its audience, for example, that "Haile Salassiê — Rastafari — emerged in Ethiopia and became a philosophy that Jamaica embraced."[24] In conjunction with Malê de Balê, another important *bloco afro* founded in 1979, Olodum was dazzled by Cuba and the similarities that the group believed united the people of the Caribbean island with those from Bahia. And in consonance with Muzenza, Olodum celebrated Jamaica and the Rastafari movement, paying tribute to the fighting power of "Jah's warriors." The notion of Africa proffered in the songs of Bahia's *blocos afro* therefore included the African diaspora of the Caribbean and the United States.

Nevertheless, despite the fact that these countries located outside Africa began to be celebrated in the *blocos'* songs, and although such terms as *black diaspora* and *African diaspora* started to be frequently used in the *blocos'* overall discourse, their choice was based on what was considered most African in such countries, selecting them as sites that retained Africanness. Thus, the concept of the diaspora continued to privilege Africa as the unifying center of blacks throughout the world, either for its ethnic particularities (Africanisms), or as an "African nation" that unites blacks universally.

If diaspora is conceived as based on movement, dynamism, multiplicity, and communication, black identities should be explicitly antinationalistic. However, understanding the diaspora in the opposite sense — as a static set of sites endowed with Africanness — reduces the idea of Africa to an "African nation." In this sense, the discourses that glorify the African past disseminated by the movements that define themselves as explicitly Afrocentrist reveal a nationalist ideology that has little relation to diaspora.[25] Michelle Wright has pointed out that even among academics, the term *diaspora* has been used as a synonym for nation. "Using these terms does us little good, especially when one considers how nationalism necessarily relies on a mythic concept of homogeneity, of Others, and of women as passive helpmates to the male subject. As a multivalent, international, intranational, multilinguistic, and multicultural space, diaspora suggests a movement away from homogeneity and exclusion toward diversity and inclusion" (2004, 133).

Bahian *blocos afro* emerged during a time marked globally by the desire to reclaim Mama Africa, and therefore the basis of their discourse emphasizes the need to preserve traditions. This inevitably leads to an intense process of creating and inventing what is imagined to be African. The search for, and the consequent invention of, traditions in contemporary Afro-Bahian culture created a new demand for information and symbols from Africa, strengthening generalizations about the "nature" of African/ black peoples and solidifying essentialized pieces of a supposed — and absolute — "African culture." Even when the metaphor of the sea is used in *bloco* songs, references address the *coast* (of Bahia and the Ivory Coast) or the *gulfs* and *bays* (of Todos os Santos and Luanda) much more than the *ocean* that connects the continents. In this conception of diaspora, land — perhaps because it represents the solidity of a culture that is wished to be homogeneous — is prioritized more than the sea and its constant and incessant movement of transformation and mixture.

Black cultural movements in Brazil have blended roots with interna-

tionalism, and black expressions from the United States have been important references (Vianna 1988). In Salvador, soul and funk music led to an
important development, perhaps the biggest dream of black movement
ideologues: it brought awareness to the black masses.[26] Antônio Risério
argues that organized funk dance parties (*bailes funk*) set the stage for a
revitalization of Bahian *afoxés* and the birth of the first *bloco afro*. One of Ilê
Aiyê's founders, Jorge Watusi, told Risério, "In Rio de Janeiro, the impact
[of funk] was more commercial, apparently alienated, because [blacks]
didn't have such an intense relationship with black cultural roots. Here in
Bahia things were very different. Awareness first arrived in the form of
fashion, of course. The sound, the clothing, etc. Then, with time, we
realized that this whole fashion thing wasn't so important. That's when Ilê
Aiyê emerged. I think it was with Ilê Aiyê that the transformation occurred; we went from one thing to the other. Because with Ilê we started
manifesting ourselves during Carnaval with more real, Afro-Brazilian
tones" (Risério 1981, 31).

Paul Gilroy (1993a) contends that black music has gone hand-in-hand
with black struggles and that it has the power to communicate information, organize awareness, and express individual and collective subjectivity.
Hip-hop culture, for example, emerged among impoverished blacks in the
United States and from there became a youth movement that reached
several countries around the globe, including Brazil. Hip-hop's musical
components are hybrid forms based on social relations in the South Bronx,
to where the Jamaican culture of sound systems — street parties where MCs
played music on trucks loaded with a generator, turntables and speakers —
was transplanted during the 1970s, creating new roots. In conjunction
with specific technological innovations, this Caribbean culture reterritorialized in the United States initiated a process that transformed black identities in this country and had a decisive influence on popular music.

As Gilroy has indicated, the style, rhetoric, and moral authority of the
U.S. civil rights and black power movements traveled to other sites of the
diaspora, where they were adapted to different places with similar needs.
The appropriation of these forms, styles, and histories of struggle was
possible in spite of great physical and social distances. Its adaptation was
facilitated by the common backdrop of urban experiences and by the effect
of similar — yet not identical — forms of racial segregation, as well as memories of slavery, a legacy of Africanisms, and a stockpile of religious experiences. Taken from their original conditions, the elements of this African
American culture nurtured a new metaphysics of blackness, elaborated in

public spaces through an expressive culture dominated by music. The political language of citizenship, racial justice, and equality became one of the narratives present in the transfer of political and cultural forms across the black Atlantic.

Gilroy employs the term *black Atlantic* in explaining the transnational structures that are developed and expressed through a system of global communication, comprising influxes that transport black images, ideas, and symbols throughout the entire Atlantic region. The visual metaphor of ships moving between Europe, America, Africa, and the Caribbean is crucial to understand the black Atlantic. The ship — a living microcultural, and micropolitical system in motion — is an especially important image for theoretical and historical reasons. The ship also represents the exchanges that occurred within the circulating systems ranging across the black Atlantic, whose origin coincides with the period of slavery, when black men and women of different ethnic groups started to be generically referred to as "Africans."

Gilroy argues that the process that produced blackness generated its own specific contradictions. Thus, black music, black art, and radical black thought — whether political or religious — are expressions of the countercultural critique of the black Atlantic, which generated a counter-interpretation of modernity. This perspective has its own genealogies and can be historically mapped, reconstructing links and points of articulation. One of the main aspects of this counterculture is the fusion of ethics with aesthetics, stimulating a counter-discourse that positions itself beyond the Western presumption of duality between art and politics. Diaspora musical and cultural practices of African origin are bearers of both the utopia of a better world and of deep criticism of capitalism and the West. What is manifested in many forms and in many places of the black Atlantic, then, is an interpretation based on the separation between politics and culture, stemming from European thought yet distant from the reality of the diaspora.

The Caribbean, Africa, Latin America, and the United States contributed to the development of a transnational black racial identity. Their cultural expressions were created in an urban context that favored the stylistic appeal on which local ethnic identifications are based. The creation and transnational exchanges of black ethnic symbols represent fundamental building blocks in the narratives and discourses on blackness with which black groups express their struggles and experiences (Gilroy 1993). Within this international exchange system of symbols, ideas, and images, there are several centers — in addition to Africa and the hegemonic United States —

disseminating blackness. Although it is still restricted to a small sphere of influence, Bahia has emerged as a fearless center for the production of black symbols, and it has slowly earned a space and affirmed its position along the routes of the black Atlantic.

The Diaspora's Search for Bahia

Bahia emerged as one of the centers of the black Atlantic during the colonial period, when the international slave trade definitively placed Brazil inside the networks of transatlantic commerce. Recent analyses have shown that Brazil's development occurred more as a result of its relationship to Africa than to Portugal. Luís Felipe de Alencastro (2000) demonstrates that Bahia and Rio de Janeiro were more connected to Luanda and Benguela than to other Brazilian cities of the period. Bahia's ports did business with foreign ships long before Dom João VI, then prime regent, officially opened the Brazilian port system. By the end of the eighteenth century, Brazilian merchants already had the upper hand in the slave trade, which began at that point to be managed from Bahia rather than Lisbon. In addition to benefiting from its geographical position, which allowed for great autonomy from Portugal, Bahia was the only state in Brazil that produced tobacco, one of the main currencies used in the slave trade at the time.

The name Bahia has been used by both Brazilians and foreigners to refer to the city of Salvador da Bahia de Todos os Santos, the capital of the state of Bahia. Its name refers to the bay around which the Recôncavo area is located, and to All Saints' Day, November 1, 1501, when it was first encountered and christened by the Portuguese.[27] For people living in both the interior of the state and outside the country, Salvador became known as Bahia, according to Pierre Verger (1999a) "as if other bays did not exist." Based on this previously established designation, I take the liberty here in this book to use the name Bahia to refer to the city of Salvador and the other black cities of the Recôncavo. Thus, the terms Bahia and Salvador will be employed here interchangeably.

Travelers and explorers who visited during the eighteenth and nineteenth centuries noted the region's black majority and nicknamed it "New Guinea" and "Negroland" (Verger, 1999a). Later, Bahia also received the titles "Black Rome" and "Mecca of Blackness," underscoring its central status within the network of circulating black people and symbols. The two latter epithets clearly emphasize the character of Bahia as a world city, highlighting its centrality within the black Atlantic and its role as a point of convergence, contact, and peregrination.

I believe that Bahia can be considered a world city because during the colonial period it was an urban space of central importance to the political economy of the world system. World cities are centers of cultural and political power in the development of the modern world system; they have several meanings and a wide variety of roles, but they are, above all, contact zones where various groups meet and experience exchange and conflict. Unlike global cities (Sassen 1991), a concept that emphasizes the economic roles of megalopolises, world cities are characterized by their capacity to intervene in the global hierarchy of the concentration of power and production of knowledge, which Anibal Quijano (2000) calls coloniality of power. Moreover, while the term *global city* is used to define the economic centers of the current phase of globalization, marked by the increase in financial capital since the 1970s, world cities have been central to the modern world since the early stages of capitalism.

Throughout the nineteenth century, several emancipated black Bahians began participating in commercial trade with Africa. Among the many products brought from the Gulf of Benin to Bahia were the products used in Candomblé such as red feathers, dyes, and fabric. Along with these material items, personal messages and religious secrets connected people from the two sides of the Atlantic. The transatlantic exchange initially carried out by merchants gained new mediators when researchers entered the scene. Pierre Verger became the best known of them, carrying in his luggage an endless stream of gifts, messages, objects, and secrets. As an interlocutor between Bahia and West Africa, Verger pleased Candomblé purists who were eager to reconnect with the original African source, and at the same time displeased the equally purist researchers, who believed that the legacy of African survivals in the New World should be carefully preserved so it could be discovered and mapped by their research. Melville Herskovits, for instance, was quite bothered by Verger's travels and dissemination of traditions from one side of the Atlantic to the other, thus messing up the pieces of Herskovits's giant puzzle — his laboratory of cultural retentions and survivals. Currently, many *mães* and *pais de santo* (priestesses and priests of Candomblé) take their own journeys back to Africa in search of lost traditions. Meanwhile, religious individuals from the African continent, especially those involved in Bantu forms of worship, also travel to Bahia to find traditions supposedly lost in Africa yet preserved in Bahia's Candomblé temples.[28]

According to Vivaldo da Costa Lima, the label "Roma Negra" arose from the expression "Roma Africana," coined by Mãe Aninha, the founder of *terreiro* (temple) Ilê Axé Opô Afonjá. The famous *ialorixá* (Candomblé priestess) had declared to anthropologist Ruth Landes in the 1940s that Bahia was the African Rome, not only because of its great number of Candomblé *terreiros* but mainly because of its centrality within the transatlantic worship of the *orixás*. The metaphor, inspired by the *ialorixá*'s Catholic faith, hinted that if Rome was the center of Catholicism, then Salvador was the center of Candomblé, and therefore an African Rome. The term was translated into English by Ruth Landes in *City of Women* (1994 [1947]) as Negro Rome and then back-translated into Portuguese as Roma Negra.[29]

The title Mecca of Blackness is also due in great part to Candomblé and not, as it might appear, to the large presence of Muslim slaves that once inhabited Bahia. This more recent coinage has been promoted mainly by black activists and cultural producers from other states of Brazil who consider Bahia to be the main source of the country's African culture. *Pais* and *mães de santo* from São Paulo and Rio de Janeiro frequently link the ancestry of their temples and their religious initiation to Bahian *terreiros* and *ialorixás*. The same is true for several capoeira schools, whose masters associate their training with old Bahian capoeira masters as a way of legitimizing their practice. Similarly, the founders of the first *blocos afro* have shared their knowledge of Afro-Bahian culture by providing consulting services to black cultural groups located in other Brazilian states. The aura of blackness surrounding Bahia, despite its early colonial origins, has been constantly and intensely reelaborated. In the 1970s, the re-Africanization process emerged in the realms of Carnaval, music, dance, and aesthetics, establishing Bahia as the Mecca of Blackness, and thus updating its significance as a cultural center in the black Atlantic.[30]

In order to understand Bahia's place in the black Atlantic, we must consider it as both receptor and transmitter of the objects, symbols, and ideas that circulate throughout these routes. The *blocos afro* provide a good example of this two-way path, for they arose from the process of forming a contemporary international black culture, whose historical and symbolical references were the independence struggles of African nations and U.S. popular culture. While initially positioning themselves at the receiving end of these exchanges, the *blocos* are also producers of a black culture that attracts to Bahia those who seek Africanness. The *blocos afro*, as well as several other black cultural producers, import symbols from the international arena in different ways, updating their meanings and modifying their messages. In this sense, the peripheral neighborhoods of Rio de Janeiro are connected to the black ghettos of the United States through soul and funk music, and reggae similarly unites Jamaica and Salvador. Reggae, like other locally selected transnational elements, inspires the identity construction of young blacks and *mestiços*, tuning them into the global flows of this diasporic counterculture.

Olodum's Web site demonstrates the arrival of transnational symbols at the ports of Afro-Bahian culture. The site highlights the public figures celebrated by the group, along with brief biographies of each one extolling their contributions to a transnational black culture. Among these people are Zumbi dos Palmares, leader of Brazil's most famous Quilombo (community formed by runaway slaves); Gilberto Gil, Brazilian singer and composer who has, since the 1970s, connected Brazil to the black Atlantic though his music; Antônio Agostinho Neto, the first president of Angola; Marcus Garvey, the Jamaican leader who founded the Universal Negro Improvement Association (UNIA); Samora Machel, former president of Mozambique, who died in 1986; and the reggae singer Alpha Blondy from Côte d'Ivoire. According to the site, "Alpha Blondy has a lot in common with Olodum: his political struggle for a better world, his tough militant music, his attachment to an Africanist modernity, his appreciation of black history and identity."[31]

Among the group's many objectives is the intention to "promote cultural exchanges between Olodum, and black people and cultural groups in Brazil and the world; . . . to internationally disseminate the street culture of Salvador . . . and of Afro-Brazilians, connecting the local culture to new trends in art and culture around the world."[32] The circuit of transnational symbols heralded by the *blocos* is integrated in the broadest network of the symbolic imaginary. And while their cultural production is located along the diaspora routes of the black Atlantic, the *blocos afro* create objects and symbols that simultaneously reinforce their connection to Mama Africa, thus updating Bahia's African cultural expressions.

It is precisely what seems to have been preserved of Africa in Bahia that attracts an ever-growing number of African American tourists. Since the 1970s, African Americans have traveled to Bahia in search of Africanness. What started as an informal trip by a group of friends has transformed, over the decades, into a structured and organized market that includes travel agencies in Brazil and the United States. I call this phenomenon roots tourism because it is developed by people who travel to find their African roots, whether these be located on the African continent or in countries of the diaspora with large black populations. African American roots tourists seek knowledge about black cultures of the diaspora and connections with Afro-descendants from other parts of the diaspora.

Although Afro-descendants began their symbolic — and often physical — search for Africa in the nineteenth century with the pan-Africanist movement, it was only in the 1970s that African American tourism to Africa gained popularity. By the late 1970s and early 1980s, African American tourism expanded to include countries of the diaspora. Salvador and the cities of the Recôncavo, recognized for their African heritage, have been visited with increasing frequency by black militants from other states in Brazil and by African American tourists carrying out roots trips. Many African Americans visit Bahia in order to experience, up close, what they see as their lost traditions. They can be regularly spotted wearing Africanized clothing, braids, and turbans, at *bloco afro* rehearsals, Candomblé *terreiros*, and other public sites of Afro-Bahian culture.

While the African Americans who visit Bahia are a heterogeneous group, there is a common thread that permeates their discourse. All the tourists I interviewed stated that they came to Bahia with the intention of finding their African roots, which exist not only in Africa but in all the diaspora sites where Africa has been preserved. In describing her visit, Rachel Jackson Christmas, an African American scholar, depicts the African pulse that Bahia offers to African Americans: "We felt the African pulse in the beat of samba, known as *semba* in Angola; swallowed it with the spicy food, made with nuts, coconut milk, ginger and okra also used in African cooking; witnessed it in Candomblé ceremonies, rooted in the religion of the Yorubas of Nigeria; heard it in the musical Yoruban accent of the Portuguese spoken in the state of Bahia. . . . Today Bahians seem far more aware of their origins than African-Americans" (Christmas 1992, 253–54).[33] Christmas described the *blocos afro* as comprised of people linked to her by a common African past, and who knew the importance of rescuing it: "Their hands flying up and down on drums that stood in neat rows, members of one of the city's *blocos afro* set many hips in motion. In preparation for the annual festivities, members study Bantu, Yoruba or another African cultures to be incorporated into their music, songs and dance" (256–57).[34]

The *blocos afro* create a mythical Africa that becomes a reference for constructing a narrative of ethnic identity, further enhancing the myth of Mama Africa. Mama Africa generates the traditions, gives birth to the Africanisms, and radiates the "African" character of the cultural objects and symbols produced by the *blocos*. The impact of the cultural production of the *blocos afro* is certainly not limited just to their members or to the spaces where they meet and rehearse for Carnaval celebrations. By symbolically appropriating Mama Africa and recreating its meanings, the *blocos afro* create traditions and produce new concepts of being and feeling black, conferring joy, pride, and a sense of authenticity to those who define themselves as black and Afro-descendant.

Through their cultural production, the *blocos afro* play a fundamental role in the new forms adopted by the contemporary black movement, helping to mold the image of their city and functioning as an important reference point for other black organizations in Brazil and other parts of the world. The aesthetic production, musical rhythms, and many other elements that comprise the groups' narratives were certainly influenced by discourses and symbols that crossed the black Atlantic, but it is crucial to note that just as they receive influences, the *blocos afro* also re-create, resignify, and produce new elements that participate in the contemporary international black scene. The *blocos* are creating objects of blackness that, despite their modernity, have a taste of the past, of tradition, of Africanness, immediately corresponding to what is sought by African American tourists.

Even though Ilê Aiyê, the oldest *bloco afro,* has only been around for a little over 30 years, its headquarters have acquired the same reputation of traditionalism as the centuries-old Candomblé *terreiros*; these are a sacred pilgrimage site for African American visitors, as are Afro-Bahian restaurants and capoeira schools. Visitors especially seek out the entity or practice seen as representative of the most traditional of each subset of Bahian Africanness: Ilê Axé Opô Afonjá, among the Candomblé *terreiros*, Angolan capoeira versus regional capoeira (the latter is seen as more mixed), and Ilê Aiyê, the *bloco afro* that is the most "faithful to African traditions."[35]

It is important to remember that Bahia not only imports elements of shared black culture in order to incorporate and give them new meanings but also creates and exports black ethnic symbols. The city of Salvador has thus become a reference point of Africanness for blacks from other countries of the African diaspora. Bahia, we might say, is both a buyer of international black modernity and a seller of black tradition.[36]

If we look closely at roots tourism in Brazil, we note that these travelers are more interested in visiting Bahia than they are in the rest of the country's states. These tourists view Rio de Janeiro, for example, as a place where African culture has strayed from its origins, whereas Bahia still is home to African reminiscences and a more preserved African culture. It is therefore believed that Bahia produces black symbols bearing an African seal of authenticity.[37] Brazilian scholars in the 1920s and 1930s contributed to a popular understanding that associates Rio de Janeiro with a miscegenated Afro-Brazilian culture and Salvador with a pure one. Some elements selected from Rio's black cultural expression, such as samba, Carnaval and *umbanda*, are used to represent Brazilianness. Thus, many black *cariocas* (residents of Rio) seek the source of black purity in Bahia. "In turn, in the representations of Afro-Bahian culture made both externally and by a select group of black community members who play the role of representatives and spokespeople, what is considered ingenious and beautiful is the capacity to relate to Africa ostensibly, and more generally, to be loyal to traditions" (Sansone 2000a, 3). These spokespeople try (quite successfully) to make Bahia the Black Rome of the Americas.

The increasing ubiquity of roots tourists in Bahia can be considered one of the most important networks for the circulation of black material culture and discourses, for they confer modernity and ethnic status upon the expressions of Afro-Bahian culture. Some expressions have become more ethnic than ever because of the seal of approval provided by these tourists, thirsty to find their roots. They bring in new forms of dress, talk, and thinking that seduce many black Brazilians, and several African Americans explicitly state that they take such trips with the intention of exchanging their modernity — represented chiefly by the victories obtained in the realm of U.S. civil rights — for Bahia's African tradition — found in Afro-Bahian cultural expressions.[38]

African American tourists usually come to Bahia after having made several trips to the African continent, and sometimes to other countries of the black diaspora, such as Jamaica or even Cuba. Thus, it is possible to draw a map of Africanness in which each place visited is endowed with different meanings: Egypt is the site of black pride, the great evidence that blacks had produced a civilization more important than Greece or Rome, and therefore the starting point for replacing the Eurocentrism with an Afrocentrism based on the wealth and grand discoveries of the Nile. West Africa is the site of origin from whence black ancestors forcibly departed, only to encounter the horrors of the middle passage. Travelers more often use the regional term instead of the names of specific countries (Benin, Togo, Ghana, Nigeria, and so on), because African Americans do not know their exact ancestors, only that these had come from somewhere in West Africa. In these countries, roots tourists visit the dungeons where enslaved Africans were kept in inhumane conditions until it came time to cross the Atlantic. Bahia holds specific meaning among the routes traveled by these tourists. Like Cuba, but much more accessible, Bahia is a site to find African traditions — traditions considered to have been preserved among black Brazilians and lost among black Americans.

Despite the fact that the various countries visited by African American tourists should be seen as complementary parts of the same map of African-ness, there is, however, a fundamental distinction between the roots tourism developed in Africa and the one developed on the other side of the Atlantic. This difference involves pain and joy. The experience of visiting the dungeons where slaves were confined and the terrible doors of no return invokes the horrors suffered by the ancestors. Confronted with this experience, tourists undergo catharsis and cry out in pain, remembering the past of those who preceded them. Inversely, when they visit Brazil, and more specifically Bahia, tourists feel the joy of reconnecting with a culture that, in their view, dared to survive, having been capable of resisting oppression and maintaining cultural ties with Africa. However, despite the joy and contentment, African American tourists also experience frustration and disappointment during their visits to Brazil, especially when they realize that black Brazilians conceive of blackness and Africanness differently.

Unlike what occurs on the African continent, where tourists are confronted with the painful fact that many locals actively participated in slave trafficking, in Brazil they find themselves among African descendants who, like themselves, were enslaved and brought by force to the American continent. The history of Brazilian blacks' participation in slave trafficking, especially during the nineteenth century, is thus completely erased, leading African Americans to think of black Brazilians as brothers and sisters in destiny, a term I am creating here to represent the sensation these tourists describe when they meet other blacks of the diaspora who have been marked by a common trajectory of abuse and oppression. The idea that blacks in the diaspora form a sort of family is nothing new and is reflected in the rhetoric of pan-Africanism, Marcus Garvey's UNIA, and the *négritude* movement. African American tourists in Brazil frequently comment that they could just as well have been born in Brazil or in the United States. The unpredictability of their ancestors' destiny is conceived in conjunction with the certainty of their shared destinies, marked by slavery, oppression, struggle, and resistance.[39]

The tourists' joy is certainly mostly promoted by the travel agencies that have little or no interest in informing visitors about the enormous social and racial disparities in Brazil. Although there are agencies in other parts of Brazil that specialize in exploiting the country's poverty, carrying out favela tours, the persistent motto is that Bahia rhymes with *alegria* (joy), thereby constructing a public image in which black culture plays a central role. A symptomatic example of this is the manner in which Pelourinho, a historic neighborhood named after the pillory that was once located there, is currently represented by the tourism industry. With the exception of a few cases, such as Gilberto Gil and Caetano Veloso's song "Haiti," Pelourinho is rarely associated with the place where slaves were punished. Dotted with souvenir and trinket shops, Pelourinho today is the most popular tourist attraction in Salvador. Ironically, Bahians and visitors join each other in dance, literally and metaphorically stepping on top of "negro heads," the local term for the rounded stones that pave the streets where slaves were whipped a little over a century ago.

Some agencies specialize in this type of tourism, taking advantage of the existing market of travelers in search of their roots by promoting trips to the many sites of what I am calling the map of Africanness. Agencies offer group tours — often geared toward travelers with a common background, such as retirees, university professors, or university students.

Travelers are frequently guided to the city of Cachoeira, in the interior of Bahia, to participate in the Festival of the Irmandade da Boa Morte (Sisterhood of the Good Death), or to the Voodoo Festival, held on the beach of Whydah, Benin, by the traditionalist faction of priests and kings.[40] Anthropologist Peter Sutherland (1999), who conducts research on this event, states that it seeks out the support of African Americans to emphasize the local value of voodoo tradition. In order to accomplish this, the festival projects the culture of voodoo in a transnational context, representing Benin as home to African brothers and sisters who live in the diaspora, and as the African source for diaspora cultures of the Americas.

This reconstruction occurs through the veneration of ancestors and through a two-way flow of people and gods across the Atlantic, promoting roots tourism. The festival reinforces the idea of transatlantic unity among voodoo practitioners. The symbolism enacted in the festival encourages brothers and sisters of the diaspora to return to their motherland, both in the form of ancestral spirits and as tourists in search of their roots. Sutherland first heard of the festival through an African American who told him that it represented a ritual of atonement performed by Africans asking forgiveness from their brothers and sisters in the diaspora for the Africans' cooperation with slavery, as a way to "purify the Benin people of the guilt incurred by their historical involvement in the sale of slaves to European merchants" (Sutherland 1999, 196). However, while researching the ritual, Sutherland realized that it was a power play by the priests and kings, who by exploiting the tourism angle were trying to preserve their traditional authority in the face of the neocolonial values of the Benin government. This discovery reveals the contradictions that exist between, on the one hand, the ideas of the African American tourists eager to find their roots and prove that their African brothers and sisters regretted having cooperated with slave trafficking, and on the other hand, the voodoo priests' concern with preserving their political power in the country. The festival thus acquires distinct meanings for each group, an incongruity that lies buried under the projections made by the African American tourists.

Similarly, contradicting views surround the Festa da Boa Morte in Cachoeira. Meanings are and always will be different for each group, since they partake of different realities and have distinct worldviews, but the tourists' discourse indicates a desire for a homogeneous blackness, since they believe that as "black siblings" they should all share the same perspectives. An example of this dissonance — permeated by Manichean binary thinking — is the lament by many African American tourists that the elderly black sisters of the Boa Morte worship a white saint, Our Lady of Glory. Most tourists are unaware that this saint has been worshipped by the sisterhood since the beginning of the nineteenth century and that such worship occurs in a context of religious syncretism which, in and of itself, represents a strategy for the struggle and survival of the slaves' beliefs. To understand the festival, one must also understand the very formation of Candomblé in Brazil, a religion that bills itself as universal and nonexclusionary and that accepts converts from all ethnic groups. Its gods and goddesses are essentially comprised of energy and do not choose the skin color of those whose bodies they possess. "To be appointed as a symbol of genuine African heritage, as some wish to do, Candomblé would have to deny its own history, as if it recognized the 'mistaken' nature of the established alliances or saw them as a mere imposition by dominant groups, without considering the possibilities of choice and the actual choices made throughout time and that allowed, within the realm of the political game, the resignification of the encounter of religious universes" (Silva and Amaral, 1996, 209).

To believe that the sisters should worship a black saint is quite a narrow way of understanding history, and in my opinion it reflects the limited manner in which blackness, and the Africanness that supposedly forms its foundation, have been understood. The racial interpretation of Africanness has imposed a restrictive definition of what can and cannot be considered African or to be endowed with Africanness. Such a belief denies that the "original African" can have diverse and multiple ancestries — since, as the template for blacks in the diaspora, it is understood as something that must be maintained pure. This belief also denies a fact so obvious and widely recognized that it forms the basis of the very notion of diaspora: that the descendents of Africans uprooted by the slave trade have necessarily produced hybrid cultures. As Mbembe asserts, "One result of the slave trade is that blacks live in faraway places. How should we account for their inscription within a nation defined racially, when geography has cut them off from the place where they were born and from the place where they live and work?" (2000, 12).

Africans and Afro-descendants are understood as people who should necessarily be black and bearers of an absolute Africanness; this implies that their culture is automatically and purely black and African, and therefore one that would reject the worship of white saints. "The African will henceforth be not someone who shares in the human condition itself, but a person who was born in Africa, lives in Africa, and is black. The idea of an Africanity that is not black is simply unthinkable. In the logic of this assignment of identities, non-blacks are relegated to a place that does not exist. In every case, they are not from here (autochthonous) because they come from somewhere else (settlers). Whence the impossibility of conceiving, for example . . . that Africans might have *multiple ancestries*" (Mbembe 2000, 11).

Seeking "African purity," African American roots tourists travel to several radiating centers of Africanness, projecting their desires and expectations upon the local black cultures. In his description of Benin's Voodoo Festival, Sutherland shows how the figure of the slave has been fetishized through the marketable transformation of the slave trade into slave tourism. Along the same lines, Bahia's black cultural production is also being transformed into commodities, paving the way for its appropriation, commercialization, and consumption. African American tourists are important receptors/consumers in this process and, for this very reason, can influence the format and content of cultural production by favoring some elements over others. Each year African American tourists become more visible at the Festival of the Good Death, not only because they are the main source of profit for hotels, restaurants, and cultural producers, but also because their expectations create new demands for the event.

There is certainly no ready consensus about how to remember the past and represent histories of suffering. There are significant discrepancies, for example, between the manner in which African Americans and Ghanaians interpret the preservation of sites where slave trade activities were carried out and that recently have become pilgrimage and roots tourism destinations (Bruner 1996; Finley 2001). Another emblematic example of the differing interpretations of the past is the number of competing representations of U.S. slavery proposed as part of a new Disney theme park that was being considered in the 1990s; some versions were viewed as part of a strategy to convert a past of pain into mere entertainment (Trouillot 1995). As Vron Ware indicates (2001), in the midst of so much disagreement and divergence, negotiations about the past are part of the political process of transforming the racialized thinking of the present.

The dissonant and frequently contradictory perspectives about how the past—and those places considered to embody the past—should be represented must be understood in connection to the hierarchy which has thus far permeated the black Atlantic world. In this unequal exchange of objects, symbols, and ideas, Brazil imports black objects that have the aura of modernity and exports black objects that have the aura of tradition. Capitalist-driven globalization is centered more on vertical than on horizontal exchanges. Lívio Sansone states, "In terms of the global flows of symbols and commodities based on international black culture, Salvador holds a peripheral position. In relation to the other centers of production and transmission of most of these symbols and commodities, Salvador is located on the extreme end of reception, in the vast hinterlands of the black Atlantic. The centers are located in the Anglophone world" (2000b, 14). The main reasons for this, Sansone argues, are Brazil's weak position within the world economy and the geography of power, and U.S. and European dominance over the global circulation of scientific paradigms about race, in a globalized system where Brazil still represents mostly a consumer periphery.

Criticizing unicentered perspectives, Paul Gilroy (1993a) argues that the diaspora does not have a single center in Africa as its motherland or in the United States as an exporter of models of ethnicity; instead, it has several centers spread around the black Atlantic. This multicentered black diaspora contains infinite variations of black culture that cannot be reduced to ethnic or national traditions. Thus, he rejects the paradigms of what he terms ethnic absolutism while also contesting the centrality of African American discourses for the black diaspora, asserting the importance of the Caribbean and Europe in the context of the black Atlantic. One of the main contributions of Gilroy's theory is his liberating understanding of the diaspora as a dynamic system that allows for the emergence of counter-powers that have challenged territorial sovereignties and beliefs in absolute identities. This notion of diaspora offers an alternative to the restrictions imposed by the belief in a primordial kinship and a rooted belonging, rejecting the metaphysical idea of a "race" that determines a culture supposedly innate to the body (Gilroy 2000, 123).

The exchanges and influences triggered by the black diaspora result in political expressions and struggles that are capable of transforming local black groups into a broader transnational community, connected not only by the celebration of a common origin but also by similar histories and experiences. Thus, the myth of Mama Africa can be useful in redefining groups that find themselves in a historical context of exclusion, strengthening cultural identities and favoring dynamic and lucid political interventions. The diaspora discourse articulates roots and routes, to construct what Gilroy (1987) describes as alternative public spheres: forms of community awareness and solidarity that preserve identification beyond time and national boundaries, allowing for transnational forms of belonging, despite local differences.

On the other hand, while the images associated with the myth of Mama Africa may represent utopian and liberating ideas, they are not exempt from generating frozen understandings of both Africa and the diaspora. The myth of Mama Africa may contribute to a liberating process for historically oppressed peoples, but it can also contribute to a limiting process that reduces blackness to fixed notions. In Afro-Bahian culture, both processes occur simultaneously within the same historical and political context, never achieving a balance. Depending on which process is hegemonic, it is possible to know who is reaping the benefits and who is carrying out the work. I have opted to conceive of the diaspora as Gilroy (1993a) has defined it because I believe this definition allows for a much broader meaning of blackness, freeing culture from the obligatory nature of roots and territory and releasing it from the prison of the body.

The critique that the black Atlantic theory privileges the Anglophone world over Latin America and its vast Afro-descendant population (Clifford 1994; Sutherland 1999; Martinez-Echazábal 1999) — a critique that is quite justified — does not undermine the relevant and necessary premises put forward in Gilroy's work. As a heuristic project, the black Atlantic theory offers invaluable routes to be pursued by those of us who refuse to give in to the increasing ethnic absolutisms and essentialist notions that continue to freeze blackness. In this book I have both followed those routes and sought to open up new paths that may expand the map of the black Atlantic. My analysis of Bahia as a black world city is carried out with this goal. I look at Bahia's position in the black Atlantic through a perspective that takes into account the elements of continuity and rupture in relation to the modern hierarchies of power, wealth, and recognition, analyzing how these elements affect the specific contexts in which black communities live.

The study of transnational black relations should be concerned with how global configurations of power influence the relationships between blacks who live in the superpower and those who live in the peripheries and semiperipheries of the world. For this very reason, when I analyze the relationship between black Brazilians and U.S. African Americans, I take into consideration the dominance of the United States as the main transmitting center of black forms, objects, and ideas in the diaspora, and I bear in mind the unequal access to power of those in the center and those in the peripheries of the world system. On the other hand, roots tourism is a channel of communication and exchange that challenges, at least partly, the supremacy of the United States in the African diaspora, since it promotes the existence of alternative centers of blackness and Africanness. Consequently, Salvador da Bahia, situated in a Lusophone country of the global South, reemerges as a world city, expanding the black Atlantic map while at the same time challenging the hierarchy of its configuration.

One of the main contributions of the black Atlantic theory has been to reveal that the black diaspora does not have an exclusive transmission center of symbols, images, and ideas. In addition to the nobility of Egypt and Ethiopia and the foundational knowledge of the "tribal" peoples of West Africa, there are other poles of Africanness and blackness located outside Mama Africa and beyond the hegemony of the Anglophone world. New paths are being opened up, and new communication and circulation channels are constantly being created. In the new routes that have been cleared by those who seek signs of blackness to build their identities, Bahia confirms its position as a transmission center of black culture in the African diaspora, updating a position that, as we saw, began as early as the colonial period.

The myth of Mama Africa both fosters the construction of racial and Afro-referenced black identities and informs the relationship between black culture and local politics in Bahia. This book tackles three central issues in the ongoing creation and effects of the myth. The first is the formulation of black identities in the midst of an intense black cultural production which has been promoting the place of Bahia in the black Atlantic. Based on a very specific notion of blackness, these identities are founded upon the centrality of the black body and its alleged appearance, essence, and tendencies. This brings us to the second question, which is the construction of blackness itself. Black particularity is recognized here as playing a central role in the formation of black subjectivities, but it is seen at all times as socially and historically constructed. The third issue that permeates this book is the notion of "race" and its employment in the struggle against racism. I examine black "race," black culture, and black identities in relation to local and global politics, looking at the meanings of blackness within the current ruling order defined by the official discourse of Bahianness and the meanings of Bahia within the recently produced transnational discourses of the diaspora. The next step of our journey will be to locate Bahian forms of blackness within the trajectory of Afro-referenced black identities produced in Brazil.

Afro Identity Made in Bahia

Identity becomes a "moveable feast": formed and transformed continuously in relation to the ways we are represented or addressed in the cultural systems which surround us. It is historically, not biologically, defined.

— Stuart Hall, "The Question of Cultural Identity"

There is no doubt that now . . . an African identity is coming into being. . . . This identity is a new thing; . . . it is the product of a history. . . . The basis through which so far it has largely been theorized — race, a common historical experience, a shared metaphysics — presupposes falsehoods too serious for us to ignore. Every human identity is constructed, historical; every one has its share of false presuppositions, of the errors and inaccuracies that courtesy calls "myth," religion "heresy," and science "magic." Invented histories, invented biologies, invented cultural affinities come with every identity; each is a kind of role that has to be scripted, structured by conventions of narrative to which the world never quite manages to conform.

— Kwame Anthony Appiah, *In My Father's House*

The myth of Mama Africa can only be understood in connection to the identities that it generates and by which it is generated. The contemporary effects of racism, discrimination, and social exclusion on black subjectivities shape the myth of Mama Africa and its Afro-referenced identities. The work of scholars who have pored over the issue of identity has helped not only to systematize the concept but also to bestow on it the importance it currently enjoys in the fields of social sciences and cultural studies (Barth 1969; Cohen 1974; Eriksen 1993; Hall 1996a; 1996b; 1996c; 1997a; 1997b; Brandão 1968; Cardoso de Oliveira 1975). Although the *blocos afro* do not fit neatly or precisely into the definition of an ethnic group as conceived by Frederick Barth (1969), their members strive to produce a clear-cut ethnic identity by partaking in a myth of origin as well as a common—albeit imaginary—lineage and ancestry. Phenotype is also an indispensable element of the black identities meticulously constructed and idealized by the *blocos*.

In Bahia, as elsewhere in the diaspora, there are many competing black discourses and forms of identification. The focus here is on the Afro-referenced black identities that are inspired by the cultural production of the *blocos afro*. By situating the Afro-referenced black identities produced in Bahia within the wider trajectory of black identities constructed in Brazil in different historical moments and geographical contexts, we can understand blackness as a "structure of feeling" that developed socially and historically and not as an automatic consequence of a previous, essentially defined form of identification. Akin to other Afrocentric black identities in the diaspora, those inspired by Bahia's myth of Mama Africa are centered on the body as a locus of affirmation of an Afro-referenced blackness. With the purpose of manipulating physical appearance to enhance black distinctiveness, the *blocos afro* have engaged in a process of inventing "Afro" elements that both informs Afro-Bahian black culture and contributes to the production of body-centered black identities.

Theories of Identity in the Social Sciences

Identity is one of the most ubiquitous, passionate, and disputed topics in the world today. As globalization advances, identity gains greater importance both as a scientific model for interpreting societies and as a political influence on individuals and groups throughout the world. Yet while it seems to be one of the greatest signs of our times, the issue of identity is much older than we can imagine, although it was shrouded behind other labels for a long time. The concept of identity, as used in philosophy, is based on the idea of *noncontradiction* or *nondifference*, that is, a theory of unity. An important example of this is Hegel's analysis of German unification. He felt the main obstacle to this process was the absence of sufficiently strong links of solidarity capable of fomenting the consolidation of a national state (Ruben 1986). The issue of nationality attached to the notion of a unifying identity also occupies a central place in the works of African American leaders Alexander Crummell, Martin Delany, and Frederick Douglass. This important group of post-Enlightenment thinkers shared the Hegelian belief that a combination of Christianity and nation-statehood could overcome internal antagonisms (Gilroy 1993a). In other words, in order to exist, a nation requires a sense of identity that can allow its inhabitants to feel like a single people. The underlying message shared by these different examples is that identity is also constructed as a feeling.

The emotional weight of identity possibly explains why it was long the subject of psychological studies. Until the 1960s, identity was seen predominantly through a psychological prism and was therefore considered impervious to cultural transformations (Cardoso de Oliveira 1975). Surpassing the limits of individual identity, which had been widely studied in the fields of psychology and philosophy, anthropology initiated an analysis of collective identities, which later came to be called ethnic identities. While psychologists had focused on self-consciousness and individual recognition, anthropologists and sociologists were concerned with understanding the role of identities in social conflicts (Brandão 1986). Several scholars have underscored the difference in perspective that distinguishes the analyses of identity within different academic fields (Brandão 1986; Cardoso de Oliveira 1975; Hall 1995; 1997a; 1997b). These authors concur that the study of individuals and their mental processes has been undertaken mostly in the field of psychology, while anthropology and sociology consider individuals as located within collective norms and processes that shape their subjectivities. The latter perspective understands identity as constructed in connection with collective representations and examines it accordingly.

There is no consensus in academia about the precise origins of the modern theory of identity, but its systematization certainly emerged together with the need to define ethnic groups. Therefore, *identity* and *ethnicity* were initially conceptualized in connection to one another. Many scholars agree that the term *ethnic identity* was coined and defined by Norwegian anthropologist Frederik Barth, in the now classic work *Ethnic*

Groups and Boundaries: The Social Organization of Culture Difference (1969).[1] Theoretical foundations for analyzing identity were drawn not only from Barth's pioneering formulation, but also from that of other scholars dedicated to this topic, including Abner Cohen, Ronald Cohen, and Charles Keyes, whose works explored many of the topics that still concern anthropologists and sociologists today. Among them is the understanding of ethnic groups as "interest groups" who employ their ethnicity as political and economic tools, as Abner Cohen suggested in the early 1970s. While my discussion is grounded on more complex theories of identities developed by more recent scholarship (Yúdice 2003; Alvarez et al. 1998; Wade 1999a), the uses of identity and ethnicity by oppressed groups is still a central topic in these studies.

Many Brazilian social scientists agree that the modern origin of identity theories is found in the work of Barth, who characterized ethnic groups as social organizations in which people both include themselves and are included by others (Cardoso de Oliveira 1975; Carneiro da Cunha 1985; Ruben 1992, among others). For Barth, the concept of ethnic group was not limited to a "culture-bearing unit" but was defined, most of all, as "an organizational type," designating a population that "(a) is largely biologically self-perpetuating; (b) shares fundamental cultural values, realized in overt unity in cultural forms; (c) makes up a field of communication and interaction; (d) has a membership which identifies itself, and is identified by others, as constituting a category distinguishable from other categories of the same order" (Barth 1969, 10–11). Social actors employ ethnic identities not only to categorize themselves and others but also to define the type of interaction they will establish with those who belong and those who do not belong to the ethnic group (13–14).

Barth's choice to prioritize social relations and interactions in the analysis of ethnic groups and identities was the biggest flaw in the ethnic studies of the 1960s. Because these studies focused excessively on social relations, they did not pay sufficient attention to the representations and ideologies generated within interethnic relations. Roberto Cardoso de Oliveira (1975) states that in order to define an ethnic group one must add to "cultural peculiarity" the "ethnic identification of its members." In other words, while the emphasis should be on the social (or collective) dimension of identity, it should not overlook the personal (or individual) and the fact that these two dimensions are always interconnected. This interconnection between subject and collectivity sheds light on the way the myth of

Mama Africa plays out in the bodies and souls of those who partake in the ethnic identity produced by the *blocos afro*.

One of Barth's main contributions was the assertion that identity is expressed as a system of oppositions and contrasts, and that the ethnic identity of a given group can therefore only exist in contrast with other groups. The affirmation of *us* versus *others* thus establishes the outer limits of identity as sameness and alterity. Identification occurs through inclusive boundaries, where the group defines who can and cannot belong to it, and exclusive boundaries, based on the perceptions that others have of the group. In this process, several elements are used as mechanisms for identification: values, traditions, ancestry, a common past, and phenotype. For each of these elements, contrast plays a crucial role, functioning as a starting point in the construction of identity.

By discussing boundaries, Barth certainly captured one of the main dimensions of identity. However, he defined boundaries as stable and continuous, in a way that froze identity. Ronald Cohen (1974) took this issue a step further when he stated that the boundaries of an ethnic group are not stable but instead represent sets of overlapping multiplicities. He argued that the process of identity formation is marked by both objectivity and subjectivity, which together produce the dichotomies of inclusion and exclusion. More recent studies on the topic (for instance, Roosens 1994) have questioned Barth's emphasis on boundaries, positing that boundaries do not produce identities, but instead that identities construct and reinforce boundaries. The construction of boundaries, therefore, does not constitute identity, but neither should an identity be seen merely as a boundary-producing entity.[2]

The boundaries of identities are not just unstable — they are also porous. Individuals frequently cross identity boundaries. One way of doing so is by choosing to share cultural values, myths of origin, a common past, and even certain "biological" commonalities. This is the case of subjects who "discover their blackness" during adulthood, usually in response to racial awareness campaigns carried out by black organizations. In the case of the *blocos afro*, the recent process of "blackening" has allowed individuals to traverse boundaries and to both view themselves and be viewed by others as black. One can "become black" by manipulating one's appearance and by learning how to perform skills that have been defined as black. Ultimately, one can become black by apprehending and performing the myth of Mama Africa.

Yet, while porous and flexible, the elasticity of identity boundaries has a limit which is defined both by those situated inside and outside of the group, in a dialectic manner. In the case of Bahia, the delimitation of blackness, and, thus, the definition of who can enter or leave blackness, is provided greatly by the meanings attributed to phenotype, and above all to skin color. In other words, a light-skinned *mestiço/a* will not be allowed to "become black" no matter what effort might be made in that direction. Hence, Barth was right to say that an ethnic group has to have some kind of "biological self-perpetuation," although he failed to explain what is currently a commonplace notion in the study of identities: biology, phenotype, skin color, and other physical attributes of "race" are culturally, and not objectively, defined.

Besides sharing a supposedly common phenotype, members of an ethnic group share a common origin, whether concrete or imagined. Thus, it is necessary to add to the metaphor of boundaries the metaphor of origin: that is, the feeling of belonging to a group whose members claim common ancestry and cultural tradition. For Eugeen Roosens (1994), the common origin alone suffices to construct ethnic identity, since he believes that ethnicity is defined from within, and not externally through the relationship of "us" and "others." In other words, the formation of ethnic identity depends upon the belief that a previous "us" existed before the encounter with the "other." In my view, while the metaphor of origin is fundamental for comprehending the construction of ethnic identities, one should not lose track of the importance of contrast in this process. The belief in a previous "us" can only be triggered by the distinction brought about by the contact with "others." It is not possible to imagine or conceive of blackness without the advent of whiteness, and vice-versa. Blackness and whiteness require one another in order to exist. It is important to examine how this interconnection takes place in the case of Brazil, where an intense process of racial mixture and formation of multiple racial categories is believed to have erased the extreme poles of black and white.

As porous and flexible as they are, boundaries are a central component of the discourse of identity groups because they serve to minimize the effects of internal differences. With the intensification of the processes of globalization, marked by multiplicities, discontinuities, and ruptures, the internal fragmentations of identity groups have become the target of greater internal control and surveillance. Identity groups are internally divided by differences based on gender, class, age, and access to formal education. The stronger these internal divisions become, the weaker the group's external boundary. This may represent a threat for group cohesion, since it serves as an uncomfortable reminder of the frailty of the coherence provided by identity. In Bahia's case, the dominant producers of the myth of Mama Africa have been struggling to keep the external boundaries in place by suppressing internal fragmentations within the *blocos afro*. The surveillance of the body, and its obedience to "correct" forms of blackness (e.g., dressing, styling, and acting "black") has been an important mechanism in this process.

It was expected that affiliations based on ethnicity and nationality would weaken under the intensification of globalization processes and increased communication among peoples situated in different parts of the world, giving way to a more cosmopolitan and universalistic understanding of humankind. Instead, as Stuart Hall (1997a) indicates, it has become increasingly evident that the processes that globalize the world have resulted in varying and contradictory tendencies that have had a significant influence on the configuration of identities. On the one hand, identity referents have become more open and hybrid. On the other hand, and concomitantly, globalization has led to the "reemergence of nationalism, the return to fixed forms of identity and other cultural and ethnic particularisms, as a defensive response" (60).

Many scholars consider black ethnic identities that revolve around myths of Africa to be among the most essentialist, because they aim at constructing complete subjects, previously established according to purported "African" standards (Gilroy 1993a; 2000; Hall 1995; 1996a; 1996b; Appiah 1992). The essentialist perspective clashes with the pluralist position that upholds blackness in all of its variations and recognizes the internal divisions among blacks themselves, acknowledging that there are distinctions of class, gender, age, and sexuality that fragment black subjectivity. Paul Gilroy (1993a) criticizes the essentialist perspective for its emphasis on ethnic absolutisms, according to which origin is not only a mark of distinction but also ends up acquiring a sense of priority over the other dimensions of black identity. Yet he criticizes antiessentialism as well for its equally simplistic standpoint of attributing to black cultures an automatic tendency toward plurality that denies their specificity. Even though black identities are constructed within specific historical and social contexts, this does not mean that we should dismiss as inappropriate the unifying structures that underpin feelings of identity in contemporary black cultures. There is such a thing as a black particularity that connects dispersed blacks to one other. Analyses of black culture must therefore transcend the bipolar and simplistic opposition between the rigid perspectives of essentialism and antiessentialism, thus adopting an anti-antiessentialist stance.

In order to understand the existence of a black particularity, we can evoke the concept of "structure of feeling" coined by Raymond Williams (1961). Williams defined these as social experience in process, always imbedded within a historical period and cultural context through which it transforms itself. As residue distilled from lived experience, the structure of feeling stimulates the formation of a shared subjectivity through which people feel or imagine their connection to the group and based on which the group defines itself in relation to society's institutional and ideological organization. This concept points to a definition of culture as something that one learns and that can be apprehended, in a fluid and often unexpected manner, while it simultaneously molds the thinking and the reactions of the group in regard to the world that surrounds it.

The reemergence of ethnic particularisms or absolutisms has brought about a new understanding of the notion of difference. Internal differences are frequently suppressed within identity groups for the purpose of strengthening the external differences that supposedly set one identity group apart from the others. High modern societies are characterized by the recognition or even excessive celebration of difference. Thus, the cohesion of societies transformed by globalization does not stem from unification, as Hegel had imagined in the early nineteenth century, but from an articulation of their different elements. As much as identity groups strive to produce a sense of internal homogeneity, it is not possible to fully control the effects of difference in creating subject positions within their boundaries. Fragmentation has socially positive effects, because it opens up the possibility of new articulations and consequently the formation of more plural or versatile subjects, surpassing the concept of a stable subject with a fixed identity. In this sense, our focus as researchers should not be only upon relations *of* and *between* groups formed around an identity, but also on the internal relations and divisions existing within identity groups. My analysis of the embodiment of the myth of Mama Africa in Bahia looks at how the *blocos afro* supervise the internal fragmentations—generated by differences of gender, class, and age—among their members with the purpose of preserving the unity formed around blackness.

Nowadays we have an explosion of referents that enable and influence identity processes. We have been witnessing accelerated growth in the production of identities and in the affirmation of differences, as well as an unexpected—and at times desperate—increase in feelings of belonging. Globalization's syncretism does not fuse cultures in order to homogenize them. Instead, they are bottomless sources of new identifications, which in turn instigate future differentiations. Globalization creates instability, and the axes around which identity pivoted—such as class, gender, ethnic group, and nationality—are undergoing profound transformations. As a consequence, "identities are being de-centered, that is, dislocated or fragmented" (Hall 1997a, 4). Consequently, the study of identities has become an increasingly complex task, demanding a wide-ranging vision capable of addressing its dynamics, interrelations, and representations.

The analysis of the effects of globalization on the increasing instability of identities should take into consideration the notion of *identity as a feeling* and its intrinsic connection to a search for fulfillment. For Hall, "identity arises not so much from the fullness of identity which is already inside us as individuals, but from a lack of wholeness which is 'filled' from outside us, by the ways we imagine ourselves to be seen by others" (1992, 287). This psychoanalytic argument points to the sense of plenitude that identity encompasses. This sense of pleasure, of satisfaction, of overcoming the internal divisions of the subject, should be closely studied by social scientists, since the notion of a shared subjectivity is fundamental for the connection between subjects and the identity group. Gilroy (2000) provides several examples of the dimension of pleasure embedded in identities. The process of identifying oneself (as black, gay, or even neo-Nazi—any identity that fulfills a sense of belonging to a group) on the one hand recreates the comforting ideals of fraternity and solidarity, but on the other hand can transform the values contained in the notions of "race," nationality, culture, and history into mystical and metaphysical qualities. Along the same lines, Kwame Anthony Appiah (1992) states that there is not much room for reason in the construction of identities. Because they generate and are generated by emotions and feelings, identities are complex and multiple— never stable, fixed, or exclusive.

To account for the increasing complexity of identities in an ever more globalized world, it is necessary to contextualize identity groups in time, place, and space. Besides examining the historical conjuncture that stimulates the formation of a specific identity, it is indispensable to analyze *place*, or the specific location where the group's representations of identities develop, and *space*, the power structure where a ruling order shapes the production of meanings. In the case of the Afro-referenced identities examined in this book, the place is Bahia, a growing center in the black Atlantic world, and which in the last decades has also become an important reference for the development of black identities constructed in other points of the diaspora. The space is marked by a hegemonic discourse of *baianidade* (Bahianness), which paradoxically draws from the ever trendier symbols and objects of blackness produced in Bahia by those who are aiming to construct oppositional identities. The local political establishment and the tourism industry have promoted the dominant discourse of Bahianness by commodifying selected symbols of black culture, through a process that I call "milking Mama Africa."

We can better understand the emergence of Afro-referenced black identities in Bahia if we situate them in the broader history of Brazilian black organizations. In order to respond to racism and racial inequality, black identities that emerged throughout Brazilian history had to transform the existing demeaning representations of blackness into new and dignified forms of identification. As Kim Butler argues, since the early twentieth century Afro-Brazilians have employed ethnicity as a strategy of social and political advancement: "The development of empowering ethnic identities became a critical avenue to power for a people systematically denied that power by the societies in which they lived" (1998, 48). If identities are expressed as articulations of power that act in relation to dominant representations, the process of resignifying is even more conspicuous in the case of the identities of oppressed groups. Therefore, to analyze identity, we must cast a new eye on the very concept of representations and consider them as *constituting* and not merely *reflecting* reality (Hall 1997a). Until the early twentieth century, Afro-Brazilians often looked for dignity, respect, and self-esteem in references of whiteness, but a profound shift occurred starting in the 1940s, when black organizations began to seek these invaluable elements in diacritical representations of Africa, Africanness, and blackness.

Afro-Referenced Black Identities in Brazil

Africa was already a crucial reference for Afro-Brazilians long before the 1940s. Candomblé *terreiros* and Afro-Catholic sisterhoods and brotherhoods had, from their very inception, their own special connections to Africa. Besides their concrete organization as African nations (Geje, Nagô, Bantu, etc.),[3] these institutions have also created more abstract, but no less important, links with Africa through their ongoing process of inventing traditions. However, as significant as these connections with Africa have been, they were also, for a long time, quite secretive. Both for fear of repression as well as due to the magical powers attributed to secrecy, these religious-based organizations opted to conceal rather than display their Africanness. Thus, it is not possible to draw a linear understanding of the ways Afro-Brazilian organizations have used references to Africanness. My emphasis on the 1940s as a period in which Africanness replaces, or at least significantly challenges, whiteness as a source of dignity, respect, and self-esteem for Afro-Brazilians is due to the diacritical character of the uses of Africa since then, especially by the Teatro Experimental do Negro (Black Experimental Theater, TEN). Previous uses of Africanized iconographies, music, and dance were met with intense repression by a light-skinned elite desperate to look, and make Brazil seem, "European." This is exactly what happened when Africanized black cultural associations decided to parade in the streets of Salvador during Carnaval in the late nineteenth century, dressed as "Africans," under such names as Pândegos d'África (African Revelers) and Embaixada Africana (African Embassy).

Countless black organizations have emerged throughout Brazil's history to respond to social disparagement and to confront racism and exclusion. Throughout this long history, black organizations in Brazil attempted not only to promote a better quality of life for blacks in a society marked by racial inequality but also to produce new meanings of blackness. Combining delicate forms of negotiation with instances of direct confrontation, Afro-Brazilian reaction to oppression and exclusion has ranged from the famous *quilombos*, communities formed by runaway slaves in several parts of Brazil during the colonial period, to present-day *blocos afro* in Bahia. This replete history of resistance also includes the Frente Negra Brasileira (Black Brazilian Front, FNB) of the 1930s and the Teatro Experimental do Negro of the 1940s and 1950s, among several other important black organizations.

While the TEN can be credited with the first explicit invocation of Africanness for Afro-Brazilians beyond the secretive limits of religion, the FNB was the first well-known organization to speak in the name of a "black race." Thus, the 1930s can be considered the beginning of the Brazilian black movement. I use "black movement" to refer to the black organizations that emerged in Brazil and have mobilized and organized themselves around the idea of a "black race." I am not referring, therefore, to any specific organization, but to Brazilian black organizations in general, including the *blocos afro*. The movement has undergone many transformations since its inception, and, according to Maria Angélica Motta Maués (1991), its trajectory can be divided into three main moments: the entire 1930s (marked by the emergence of the FNB), the period from the mid-1940s to the end of the 1950s (marked by the emergence of the TEN), and from the second half of the 1970s, when the Movimento Negro Unificado (MNU) emerged, until today. I would add that we have entered a fourth period in the trajectory of the Brazilian black movement, marked by the discussion and initial implementation of affirmative action policies by both the government and private initiatives. Despite its division into decades, this description of the Brazilian black movement is not meant to be linear, especially because elements that emerge in one specific historical period (such as references of Africanness and the "black race") have poured over into organizations founded in subsequent decades.

Although the FNB protested against the unprivileged position of blacks in Brazilian society, its discourse indicates that the group had assimilated the ideology of whitening and the ideals of integrationism. Spouting xenophobic and nationalist notions, the FNB defended the idea that President Getúlio Vargas's government should lock Brazil's doors to forbid the entrance of any further immigrants so that blacks could reclaim their rights in the country (Andrews 1991b).[4] Darién Davis explains that although the FNB campaigned for additional opportunities for blacks, it placed the burden of change fully within the black community (1999, 185). FNB leaders thus defined their goal as the promotion of education and family values among blacks. The leaders also believed that blacks should overcome their "inherent difficulties" in order to participate with dignity in Brazilian society. An excerpt from the organization's periodical *A Voz da Raça* clearly illustrates this: "And we shall win. Prevail over ourselves: prevail over the passions that dominate us; the bad traits, alcohol, the raging samba, the unwarranted discrediting, . . . the disrespect that confirms the infamous saying by [José do] Patrocínio—the enemy of blacks are blacks themselves."[5]

Thus, while it promoted a specifically black form of identification, as can be noted in the organization's name, the FNB simultaneously attempted to integrate blacks into Brazilian society. Kim Butler (1998, 63) defines the FNB's approach as "alternative integrationist," since it sought to become part of society by using alternative mechanisms. In tandem, Darién Davis contends that the FNB never espoused rebellion, only integration through reform consisting of "four major aims: undermining the traditional racial domination by openly attacking color prejudice through demonstrations and publications; encouraging racial pride and competition with whites on all levels. . . . ; fighting against apathy and indifference in the black community; and re-educating whites in order that they see the importance of the Negro to *brasilidade*" (1999, 184).

Thus, the FNB aimed at constructing an identity that combined the recognition of difference (blacks vs. whites), based on the perception of the unequal treatment given to blacks, especially in the labor market, with the search for acceptance. The FNB argued that blacks should make themselves viable in the labor market through the manipulation of their appearance and control of their tendencies. Like all identities, the one constructed at the heart of the FNB was founded on contrast — in this case with whites (Brazilians and foreigners) — yet this contrast was to be minimized as much as possible according to the FNB's ideals.

The recognition of identity boundaries, the control of internal differences within the group, and the management of black appearance, essence, and tendencies have been important components of most Afro-Brazilian organizations, as we can see by comparing the perspectives of the FNB and the *blocos afro* regarding control of the black body.

In the 1940s and 1950s, the Brazilian black movement retained some of the characteristics established in the previous decade, continuing to believe, for example, that blacks needed to "search within themselves" for the qualities that would help them overcome the difficulties imposed by society. Unlike the FNB, however, organizations in these decades believed that the "natural tendencies" of blacks were positive — joy, spontaneity, and creativity — and should therefore be extolled. Heavily influenced by the *négritude* movement, the Teatro Experimental do Negro, founded by Abdias do Nascimento, emphasized black values and invoked qualities that belonged to black people: "innate" emotiveness, passion, and theatricality. The TEN contributed to the establishment of a black intellectual elite, hailing education as a means of social promotion for excluded blacks. Based on the ideals of pan-Africanism and on their own version of the myth of Mama Africa, the TEN prioritized teaching African history as a way to celebrate blacks' grand origins, giving its members reasons to feel good about their own blackness and thus stimulating a black identity based on pride for one's Africanness.

Davis shows that the TEN benefited from the work of the FNB. Although these organizations were quite different in form and content, some of their methods were similar, including the education of the black masses by black intellectuals: "Similar to the leaders of the Black Front, TEN assumed a didactic role within the black community which some writers have confused with elitism. Unlike the Black Front, TEN was vigorously pan-African, although in the tradition of black Brazilian organizations unequivocally affirmed its *brasilidade*" (1999, 193). Yet TEN encouraged blacks to participate in the nation at the same time that its leaders made clear the need to redefine the dominant national myth. Creating new myths of liberation, grounded on mythical notions of Africanness, the TEN represented Africa as a symbol of transnational black affiliation.

Although the notion of Africa was already present in the pan-African discourses of the early twentieth century, in the 1960s it blossomed as a referent in the formation of black identities in the diaspora. During this decade, the ideal of "black is beautiful" started to spread in the United States and have an impact in the rest of the world. This movement to reclaim black self-esteem reversed the bodily symbols associated with blackness (dark skin, kinky hair, large buttocks), which until then had been coded as predominantly negative, turning them into a positive sign. Stokely Carmichael, one of the movement's biggest proponents, called for the use of braids and Afro hairstyles, and the adoption of African dashikis and head wraps as part of the "correct" appearance of conscious black Americans. That period's inspirations, in conjunction with the repercussions in Brazil of the independence struggles in several African colonies, led to the emergence of the Movimento Negro Unificado contra a Discriminação Racial, or MNUDR (Unified Black Movement against Racial Discrimination), later shortened to MNU. Founded in São Paulo on July 7 1978, the MNU's predominant influences were the black movements in the United States and the idea of the return to African roots. It openly denounced Brazilian racism, leveling a sharp criticism of the myth of racial democracy. Gilberto Freyre's work, especially *The Masters and the Slaves*, has since been repudiated by some factions of the black movement, because its author has been considered one of the main promoters of the myth of Brazil's harmonious racial relations.

The process of racial miscegenation, which Freyre had depicted as an indication of Brazil's racial harmony, was then redefined by the MNU as the result of the violent exploitation of black women by white men. The MNU, as well as the other movements and organizations that emerged in its wake, deeply altered the national discourse on "race," rendering it an explicitly political theme. Intentionally disrupting the widespread acceptance of the myth of racial democracy, the black movement of this period denounced it as a project employed to mask and perpetuate Brazilian racism. This condemnation of the myth of racial democracy was combined with renewed and exalted pride in the "black race," grounded on the need to render explicit and irrefutable the differences between blacks and whites in Brazil.

This context triggered the construction of black identities that were deliberately contrasted with whiteness and defiantly opposed to the hegemonic notion of Brazilian racial relations as harmonious. Sharing the TEN's outraged disapproval of the treatment afforded to blacks in Brazil, and drawing on the FNB's notion of a "black race," the MNU sought to establish a racial, ethnic, and Afro-referenced black identity demarcated by solid boundaries that were supposed to be impermeable to racial mixing in both "biological" and cultural terms. Yet while the MNU's counter-discourse has been extremely important in exposing the intricate practices of Brazilian racism, it has not been capable of overthrowing the myth of racial democracy.

One of the reasons for this failure is the fact that the myth of racial democracy, as much as the myth of Mama Africa, is not a mask; it is a powerful narrative that unifies the otherwise clashing realms of the imagination of Brazilians of distinct classes and skin colors; it is Brazil's dominant national narrative. Although it does not accurately reflect Brazilian reality, the myth of racial democracy represents, and therefore puts forward, a national project of harmony and equality. If the majority of blacks in Brazil have embraced the myth, it is not because they believe that racism no longer exists, but because they are trying to achieve the myth's promise of racial equality. A second obstacle to the black movement's attempt at challenging the myth of racial democracy is that social mobilization has coalesced around poverty more than ethnic and racial identity, and grassroots engagement in politics has been carried out primarily through class-based forms of identification.

Several black organizations, including some *blocos afro*, are involved in the production of a discourse of blackness as ethnicity, although this phenomenon is still largely restricted to intellectualized sectors of the black population and is far from establishing a counterhegemony. Because Ilê Aiyê was founded in 1974, only four years before the MNU, both organizations share many similarities, among which is the search for, and thus invention of, Africa. Africanness is therefore once again called upon not only as a reference to construct blackness, but to further congeal the boundaries that separate blacks from whites in Brazil. This process has boosted the tendency to seek in Africa and in African values the references for affirming a delimited and distinct black identity. Thus, when I contend that the process of black identification developed at the core of the *blocos afro* is ethnic, I am referring not to a reality in which individuals spontaneously mobilize around ethnicity, but to an intentional and to some extent calculated intervention made in the Brazilian context of racial identification by members (especially leaders) of the *blocos afro*. While for MNU and other less explicitly "culturally grounded" black organizations Africa is usually a background or secondary reference — something that inspires, for instance, hairstyles and clothing — for the *blocos afro*, and particularly Ilê Aiyê, Africa is the key element around which identity is organized, informing not just appearance but also essence and tendencies.

Evidently, this distinction between "cultural" and "political" organizations does not correspond to the cultural studies perspective adopted in this book. It has become commonplace for social scientists to recognize that culture and politics are intertwined and overlapping realms. Social organizations are both expressive and instrumental, since their struggles for material conditions occur simultaneously with their struggles over meanings. Peter Wade (1999a) argues that the distinction between culture and politics, or between practice and discourse, only exists for researchers, and not for those who are producing identities, cultures, and meanings. These separate realms are created by the observer, and not inherent to the object of analysis itself. While I agree with Wade that the production of culture unquestionably takes place in the realm of power, I find it necessary to acknowledge that from the standpoint of many organizations, the distinction between "cultural" and "political" does exist and is frequently employed in a strategic manner.

My acknowledgment of the distinction between "culturally" and "politically" oriented black organizations does not signal agreement with Michael Hanchard's (1994) argument that Afro-Brazilian organizations have been predominantly "culturalist," as opposed to "cultural." Defining culturalism as the excessive valorization and reification of cultural production, Hanchard (1994, 9) contends that culturalist groups have been largely apolitical — without focus or direction — and incapable of producing counterhegemonic political activities, because they reproduce tendencies found in the ideology of racial democracy. While Hanchard recognizes (and praises) the *blocos'* "race-first" strategies, he does not acknowledge their important and tireless confrontation of Brazil's notions of racial harmony. The *blocos'* very effort to produce a distinct black identity challenges the myth of racial democracy.

The *blocos afro* aim to produce a specifically black form of identification, as had been done by early black organizations, such as the FNB in the 1930s. Kim Butler (1998, 57) explains that the FNB was the first organization to aggressively employ the term *negro* (black) and to invert its pejorative meaning into a positive one. Unlike the FNB, however, whose model of black identity was a mirror image of whiteness, the black ethnic identity proposed by the *blocos* is based on an interpretation of Africanness. Another important distinction between the FNB and the *blocos afro*, especially Ilê Aiyê, is that while both organizations recognize the existence of boundaries between blacks and whites, the former believed these boundaries are due to the unequal treatment offered to blacks, and that they would gradually disappear as blacks became integrated into Brazilian society. For a *bloco afro* such as Ilê Aiyê, as well as for several sectors of the contemporary black movement in Brazil, the boundaries that separate blacks from whites should be strengthened, since blacks should strive to further differentiate themselves from whites.

Like the FNB, contemporary black Brazilian organizations concur that the maintenance or dissolution of a group's boundaries is intrinsically connected to the management of internal differences, as well as to control over members' essence, tendencies, and appearance. The main difference is that the FNB hoped the management of these elements would lead to the dissolution of identity boundaries as blacks became equal to whites. On the other hand, for organizations like Ilê Aiyê, the management of internal differences and control over the black essence, tendencies, and appearance are geared toward solidifying identity boundaries. For the FNB, blacks were supposed to supersede their "essential characteristics," which were considered flawed, and they should manipulate their appearance to look "whiter," because a black appearance was deemed repulsive. For the *blocos afro* in general, but even more so for Ilê Aiyê, blacks' supposed inherent essence and natural tendencies need to be enhanced in order to strengthen black ethnic identity. Accordingly, black phenotypes, no longer defined as ugly but instead beautiful, should be manipulated to look even "blacker."

The black ethnic identity that *blocos afro* established not only responded to local forms of racism and racial exclusion but also connected to a transnational consciousness-raising movement among the black diaspora. Similar to the TEN, which was influenced by the *négritude* literary movement, the MNU and the *blocos* receive, adapt, and re-create information arriving from other points of the black diaspora. Ilê Aiyê's importance within Afro-Bahian culture should be stressed here; the group is considered a guardian of African traditions, and is seen as not only "the most beautiful of all" but also "the oldest of all *blocos*."[6] As the first *bloco afro* to open the paths to re-Africanization, Ilê Aiyê also represents the "most African" of the Afro-Bahian *blocos*.

Other Afro-Bahian cultural expressions, such as Candomblé, capoeira, Afro-Bahian music, and locally produced versions of hip-hop, reggae, and Rastafarianism are also sources for the construction of identities, since they, too, inform and are informed by the myth of Mama Africa. By emphasizing Candomblé as one of the main sources for constructing black identities in Bahia, I do not mean that this necessitates direct participation in Candomblé *terreiros*. Candomblé is a fundamental source for establishing blackness in Bahia because of its iconography, legends, archetypes, and myths, as well as its examples of historical and cultural resistance that reach beyond the walls of the *terreiros* and influence the mainstream black and Bahian imaginary. The emergence of the *blocos afro* in the 1970s further strengthened the importance of Candomblé as a central element for reconstructing blackness and Africanness in Brazil. It is important to stress that while some of Bahia's black movement activists had previously been Candomblé devotees, many other activists throughout Brazil, especially those informed by Marxist principles, were not enthusiastic about religion and did not envision Candomblé as an arena for political organization and resistance. Until the 1970s, many black activists were also critical of Candomblé because of its connections to right-wing politicians and the large number of whites participating in the religion. The transformation of Candomblé into a symbol of black resistance occurred mainly in the 1980s, when, during the process of "becoming black," many activists adopted this religious practice as a means of reconnecting with their ancestors' history. In this context, many began to see Candomblé as the "correct" religion for blacks.[7]

Some *blocos afro* already had an intrinstic connection to Candomblé. The Ilê Aiyê founders, for instance, were already Candomblé devotees before creating the *bloco*. Vovô, cofounder and lifetime president of Ilê Aiyê, is the son of a *mãe de santo*, Mãe Hilda, the head priestess of the *terreiro* Ilê Axé Jitolu, located only a few steps away from the *bloco*'s headquarters. Mãe Hilda is simultaneously a symbol of black motherhood and a sign of Africanness. She plays a major role in Ilê Aiyê's educational project, acting as a type of griot for the young children that attend the school supported by the *bloco*. Her religious knowledge also provides the *bloco* with information — such as the legends and archetypes of the *orixás* — that influences the composition of songs, costumes, and accessories.

Yet while Candomblé is a central reference for *bloco afro* identity narratives — a source of tradition and connection to Mama Africa — it does not provide the *blocos*' discourse with reference to modernity. *Blocos afro* arose out of a need to connect tradition to modernity, a need that also accounts for the increasing exploration and acceptance of cultural elements produced in other parts of the black diaspora. Explaining why *blocos afro* adopt and re-create musical styles from other countries, João Jorge, cofounder and director of Olodum, stated, "Reggae gave us the modernity that young black Bahians were seeking. Tradition alone was not fulfilling us any more" (Guerreiro 2000, 58). Although this explicit search for modern references of blackness is one of the main features that distinguishes Olodum from the more tradition-oriented Ilê Aiyê, all *blocos afro* produce modern identities based on a retelling of the past and on a deliberate manipulation of the body in the present.

Striving to produce a distinct black ethnic identity capable of disrupting the notions of Brazil's racial harmony, since the 1970s Afro-Brazilian organizations have sought to strengthen their ties to Africa, although this has occurred more in the realm of imagination and cultural production than in the sphere of international politics or diplomacy. Afro-Brazilian cultural elements, which had become associated with the dominant narrative of the Brazilian nation, have been resignified as black, with the intention of reaffirming the connection to Mama Africa. The exaltation of Africanness which *blocos afro* promoted via a "cultural" standpoint and the MNU promoted in the more explicitly "political" arena has produced elements considered Afro in order to conjure up a positive African-oriented identity for blacks in Brazil. In Salvador, the *blocos afro* have been the main creators and disseminators of such Afro symbols.

What Is This "Afro" in Afro-Bahian Black Identities?

The movement to *re-Africanize* Bahia's Carnaval, initiated in the 1970s, sowed the Africanizing symbols that have gained evermore significance in the city. Antonio Risério (1981, 16) describes the moment at which previously hidden Africanized elements were not only displayed but transformed into a source of black pride in Salvador: "Everyone perusing the streets, alleys, and parks of the Carnaval circuit would come face-to-face with several *afoxés* and *blocos afro*, people sporting varied and intricate braids, wearing fabrics and tunics, [showing off] torsos and turbans, necklaces and cowry shells, to the sound of drums and *baianagô* ballads. They were true Afro-Bahian tribes, usually bearing . . . Yoruba names: Ilê Aiyê, Araketu, Olorum Babá Mi, Malê Debalê, Obá Dudu Agoiyê, Olodum."

Risério included the prefix *re* in *re-Africanization* due to the fact that a previous attempt at performing Africa in the streets of Salvador had already occurred on the cusp of the nineteenth and twentieth centuries. Nina Rodrigues, in *Os Africanos no Brasil*, described how black cultural associations then used Africa as a reference for expressing their blackness: "Bahia's Carnaval festivities have been reduced lately to almost solely African clubs organized by a few Africans, Creole blacks, and *mestiços*. Characters and themes are taken from the cultured peoples of Africa, Egyptians, Abyssinians, etc. . . . Sometimes the intent is to relive traditions. . . . African dances and ballads that were successfully performed during this carnaval are Candomblé dances and songs from the Gege-Yoruba denomination" (1935, 270–71).

These Africanized Carnaval groups were met with intense repression at a time when the elites were trying to promote a Europeanized and "civilized" way of celebrating Carnaval: the Parisian-style masquerade balls that had been imported in the mid-1880s to replace the *Entrudos*, a pre-lent festival held on the streets of Brazil's largest cities. The *Entrudo* had become an inconvenience for the upper classes because its irreverent nature had fostered increased intimacies across "race," gender, and class lines. The masquerade balls, on the other hand, brimming with elegance and good manners were held indoors in private clubs, thus keeping the masses at the margins (Pessanha and McGowan, 1991). Between 1905 and 1914, Africanized organizations were banned from participating in Bahia's Carnaval because of their allegedly "primitive" aspect. The exposure of black bodies decorated to "look African" caused shock and repulsion among the prejudiced light-skinned elites who were striving to promote a white and modern nation.

Seven decades later when Ilê Aiyê paraded for the first time in Salvador in 1975, the *bloco afro* was also met with a fierce reaction from mainstream Bahian society. This time, however, the disturbance caused by an all-black Carnaval group was not due to its "African-looking" configuration. Rather, it was the *bloco*'s appeal to an unambiguous black identity that generated such stern response. According to a much-cited newspaper article of the time, Ilê Aiyê was portrayed not only as an annoyance to Bahian society but also as an antiwhite racist group:

Racist *Bloco*—A Note That's Out of Tune: Carrying signs with phrases like Black World, Black Power, Black for You, etc., the *bloco* Ilê Aiyê, nicknamed the *Bloco* of Racism, provided an ugly spectacle during this Carnaval. In addition to inappropriately exploiting the theme and imitating the United States, which reveals a huge lack of imagination—since in our country there are endless topics to be explored—Ilê Aiyê members, all of color, even went so far as to mock whites and others who observed them from the official podium. Because of the very prohibition of racism in the country, it is expected that Ilê Aiyê members parade in a different way [than this] in the next Carnaval, and use the natural liberation of instinct, typical of Carnaval, differently. Fortunately, we do not have a racial problem. This is one of the great good fortunes of Brazilian people. The harmony that reigns among sectors of society originating from different ethnicities constitutes, obviously, one of the reasons for the inconformity of the agents of annoyance who wish they could add, to the goals of class struggle, the spectacle of race struggle. But they cannot do this in Brazil. And every time they come into view, they reveal the ideological origin to which they are attached. It is very unlikely for anything different to happen to these "good guys" from Ilê Aiyê.[8]

The article's very title, "A Note That's Out of Tune," points to Ilê Aiyê's dissonant nature and interprets its attitude as one that disrupts the mythical harmony of racial democracy. The article not only argued that Brazil did not have a racial problem; it condemned the *bloco*'s stance of adopting U.S. black identity references, such as slogans and diacritical forms of manipulating bodily appearance. What is defined as "lack of imagination" and an "imitation of foreign ideas" is, in fact, Ilê Aiyê's refusal to play the game of embellishing the nation with black cultural expressions. Instead, the *bloco* believes that symbols of blackness should be employed to assert a clear-cut and oppositional black identity. In order to do so, not only would existing black symbols (such as Candomblé iconography) be resignified as ethnically "black" rather than mainstream Brazilian, but new Afro symbols had to be invented. In order to produce new Afro symbols, the *blocos afro* followed two main directions: they dived deeply into the existing iconography of Candomblé to find its roots, and they navigated through the most accessible routes of the black Atlantic, adopting and adapting U.S. forms of black identification.

Despite this initial criticism, ironically, today *blocos afro* are one of the key components of Bahia's Carnaval. The "tribal" look of its members' black bodies, adorned with "African" and sometimes intentionally "primitive-looking" clothing, accessories, and hairstyles, which had previously caused embarrassment and repulsion among the middle and upper classes of Salvador, was later resignified as a trendy and exotic attribute endorsed by both the tourism industry in its eagerness to attract foreign tourists, and by the state government in its construction of a discourse of Bahianness grounded on blackness. This intentional fusion between Bahianness and blackness had begun in the 1930s, when black cultural expressions previously despised by the higher classes, such as those linked to Candomblé and Afro-Bahian cuisine, started to be employed in regionalist and nationalist discourses. However, hyper-black symbols, produced since the 1970s to support a deliberately ethnic and contrastive identity, have also been gradually incorporated into the discourse of Bahianness.

Many recently produced or resignified hyper-black symbols are connected to an Afro-aesthetics centered on clothing, hairstyles, and accessories meant to "look African." What is termed *Afro* in Brazil is based on a certain sense of Africanness attributed through impression or intuition. Objects considered Afro are not so labeled because they were produced in Africa, but primarily because they are produced to refer to Africa. What matters is the sense of Africanness that these objects supposedly carry. The term *Afro* refers to those objects that, despite having been produced outside the borders of the African continent, still serve to invoke Africanness. They thus reveal how this imaginary homeland is conceived. The Afro that characterizes this aesthetics represents the desire to connect one's body and soul with Mama Africa.

Although it is grounded on a notion of a bygone past, the valuing of one's own Afro traditions and of a specific Afro identity is, in fact, a product of modernity. Salvador's traditional black culture is mined in the production of ethnic symbols that are used to create a budding black identity. Lívio Sansone (2000b) points to the example of sacred Candomblé bead necklaces (*contas*), previously worn exclusively as religious symbols underneath one's shirt, which have now acquired the status of ethnic symbols and are openly displayed to explicitly indicate black identity. Another illustration of the public display of previously concealed Candomblé objects that I noticed among *bloco afro* members is the use of raffia fiber (*palha da costa*) for making bracelets, ankle ornaments, and headbands. Before it became a secular symbol of Africanness, raffia fiber was used to manufacture important Candomblé symbolic objects, especially those meant to separate what can and cannot be seen, such as the long costume that covers Omolu, the *orixá* of health and sickness, from head to toe. Loaded with Candomblé Africanness, *palha da costa* has been resignified as a mundane Afro object when used for the *blocos'* Carnaval costumes.

The search for Africanisms initiated by historians and social scientists in the 1940s and 1950s as they sought to define what could or not be considered genuinely African outside Africa (Herskovits 1941; 1943; Frazier 1942; Verger 1991) has also occurred within the Brazilian black movement, in its desire to find African values that could confer dignify and pride on its members. *Bloco afro* members are constantly seeking this Africanness, as revealed by their colorful clothing, intricate braids, and the Afro accessories that further blacken their bodies. Little does it matter if their pants and shirts are made of imported Balinese fabric or that their hairstyles often include synthetic weaves, or that their Africanized necklaces and bracelets are produced by local artisans. The *palha da costa* interwoven with colorful beads or cowry shells to form their bracelets is a locally grown raffia fiber (*palha*), and does not come from the Guinea coast (*costa*), as its name suggests. Regardless of where they are made, these Afro objects function as diacritical signs believed to be endowed with infinite blackness, with an Africanness impossible to find even in Africa.

In one of our interviews, one of Ilê Aiyê's young female dancers expressed the importance of Afro objects for her sense of self-confidence and belonging. She recalled, with great emotion, an episode in her life with the *bloco* in which Afro clothing, accessories, and hairstyles made her feel like a real African:

> We had all these clothes on, made from colorful fabrics, we had all this *palha da costa*, all these cowry shells and beads on our necks, loaded with necklaces—and that's different. That's what shows that Ilê Aiyê, that samba, is not vulgar. That Afro dance is different. That's what's so positive about Ilê Aiyê. That's what makes me feel more confident, like I really have my feet on the ground! Not afraid to be happy. That's what happened at a reception when we were in Kenya, in Africa. We were all there, the women, all dressed up in white, in real white linen, wearing necklaces and braids, dreadlocks, and tunics that reach down to here, down to the leg, with the Ilê fabric, and with a wrap on our heads made of Ilê fabric. People were looking and clapping, and they sure were clapping! That's what moves us and makes us feel this difference. . . . They were looking at us as if we were African . . . it looked like we were from some place in South Africa, Guinea, Senegal. . . . Never from Bahia!

Besides pointing to a globalized, generic, and aestheticized blackness, this statement makes it clear that Ilê Aiyê is thought to have an Africanness that transcends even Bahia's own Africanness. The *blocos'* myth of Mama Africa is employed not to sustain regional or national discourses but rather to produce symbols that are specifically ethnic. The need to establish this contrastive and oppositional black identity explains the emphatic corporeal use of hyper-black symbols. Some analysts (Appiah 1992; Hall 1997a; Ojo-

Ade 1995) question whether such exacerbated attempts to "become African," both in Africa and the diaspora—by rendering blacks as exotics, draped in folkloric outfits and copious amounts of Afro accessories— reinforce the persistent idea of blacks as the "other." If that is the case, the term *ethnic* risks becoming synonymous with *exotic*, and in a consumption-driven world the exotic is the one to be gazed upon, to be consumed, thus reflecting the power relations between those who dominate and those who are dominated. "We run the risk of an ersatz exoticism, like the tourist trinkets in the Gifte Shoppes of Lagos and Nairobi" (Appiah 1992, 72).

While this is an important concern, it is necessary to analyze the role of agency in embracing Afro aesthetics. To "dress black," adorning one's body with objects of black culture, means more than just manipulating the visual surface, since it has deep political meanings and can be a liberating force in the face of oppression. In his analysis of the cultural production of young blacks in a reggae group in Cali, Colombia, Peter Wade (1999a) states that black representations constitute an attempt by impoverished black youths living in marginalized neighborhoods to gain control over their own lives. On the one hand, they are constantly involved with representations of their culture as an object, as a set of symbols, which include Rastafari dreadlocks, Afro clothing, and rapper outfits. On the other hand, they experience culture as a way of life, in a unified manner. The group's black identity is both lived and objectified.

The incessant search for African origins has led these young Afro-Colombians to conceive of reggae, rap, salsa, and blues as "African rhythms." In a similar vein, one of Ilê Aiyê's young female dancers stated that her *bloco* plays a very important role in the dissemination of Africanness, not only in Brazil but also in other countries where blacks live. She referred specifically to the United States, where African Americans, who in her words "might be quite ahead of black Brazilians in terms of the rights they have secured," are "very behind with regard to Afro culture." Therefore, when Ilê Aiyê goes to the United States, as this young woman once did to teach a dance course, it does so to "bring this Africanness," this "African foundation" sought by African Americans. "There [in the United States] I still see more jazz, ballet, even classical dance. But Afro dance, Afro culture is still pretty scarce. . . . Ilê Aiyê does a different samba—the original samba, samba from Cachoeira, the sound of the *terreiros*. So when [African Americans] watch our performance, they see it's really Afro, based on Candomblé *terreiros*, that it has a foundation."

Afro-Brazilians and African Americans interviewed on the topic of roots tourism believe that black Bahians and Brazilians possess a tradition to be exchanged for the modernity enjoyed by U.S. blacks. On several occasions I have witnessed Afro-Bahian activists refer to jazz and blues as modern and European (or Europeanized) musical forms that have lost their connections to Africa. In recent interactions between Afro-Bahian members of ACBANTU (Associação de Preservação do Patrimônio Bantu, Association for the Preservation of Bantu Heritage) and African American college students on a study tour that I led to Bahia in June 2007, jazz and blues were more than once cited by the Afro-Bahians as proof of African Americans' disconnection from Africa.

The members of the group Wade studied in Colombia, as well as the younger members of Ilê Aiyê and Olodum and of so many other black groups in the diaspora, Africanize their identity through a generic, globalized, and commodified Africanness made available to them through the global circuits of exchange. Only some symbols are selected as relevant, such as the social injustice addressed in reggae songs. The groups' young members construct their social identity as a lived reality, as a way of being and situating themselves in the world, while simultaneously constructing their culture as representations that can be disseminated and embodied by other young people in other parts of the diaspora. As Wade shows (1999a), the dreadlocks adopted by several of these young blacks are a good example of an embodied engagement that is both material and symbolic. Culture is thus produced through the use of objects and artifacts to transmit notions of identity. These sources of identities sustain the structure of feelings that organize and confer meaning upon individuals' lived experience.

The term *Afro* not only labels the objects that make their bodies "blacker" but also represents, for the young *bloco* members, everything that comes, or is believed to come, from Africa: rhythms, dances, aesthetics, religion, and the overall forms of expressions learned and apprehended within the *bloco*. When asked about what they define as Afro, most young members of Olodum and Ilê Aiyê interviewed employed the term to describe the cultural expressions produced by the *blocos*, associating the word *Afro* with some element of black culture: dance, clothing, hairstyles, or rhythms. "What's Afro? I think Afro is a mixture of Africa with rhythm," stated one of the band leaders of Band'Aiyê.[9] One female dancer said that the word *Afro* reminded her of "Ilê's dance, which is Afro dance"; another responded "Afro? Dancing . . . Afro to me is anything that means a lot to us. It's Africa, it's African."

For the young members of Ilê Aiyê, Afro represents the originality, the "tribalism" that in Bahia only Ilê Aiyê possesses and values, because other *blocos afro* have supposedly lost track of their Africanness, thus "losing their identity" and distancing themselves from traditions. According to one of the young women interviewed, "Afro comes from the Candomblé *terreiro*. It's the *Ijexá* [an African rhythm played in Candomblé ceremonies], which is the so-called tribal, you know?. . . . The only similarity between Afro, reggae, and *afoxé* is that they all descend from what's African. But Afro is tribal." Such words echo those of the young Afro-Colombians that Wade interviewed, thus confirming the notion of a globalized and generic Africanness. Despite their appeal to tradition, Afro elements employed to transform diasporic blacks into "Africans" are perceived as essential building blocks of a contrastive, oppositional, and modern identity intended to challenge long-established negative representations of blackness.

Essential for supporting an Afro-referenced understanding of blackness, the "Afro" in Afro-Bahian identities unmistakably embodies the myth of Mama Africa. The colors of Ilê Aiyê's fabrics (black, white, red, and yellow), chosen by the founders just a little over three decades ago, have already come to be perceived as "traditionally African" and have been defined by the young members as Ilê's traditional colors, or more generally as the colors of Africa. The young members also know that the colors are important because "white stands for the peace required in all of Ilê Aiyê's work," "red is a reminder of the blood of all the blacks that has been spilled over the centuries," "yellow is gold, it's the life that Ilê Aiyê is, it's the discovery of Ilê Aiyê," and "black is Ilê Aiyê's symbolic color, blacks are the members, it's blackness being beckoned."

Besides Ilê Aiyê's specific colors and the unmistakable combination of red, green, and yellow as the colors of Olodum, in Brazil colorful fabrics in general have become associated with Africanness. Osvalrísio do Espírito Santo, one of the directors of Ilê Aiyê since the second year of the group's existence, argues that Africans have a natural appreciation for colorful costumes: "Blacks in Africa always wore colorful clothing. First the colors of the *orixás*; the *orixás* wear different colors — and bold, bold — and blacks always dressed according to the *orixás*. When they came here to Brazil, they were only given white clothing. So they had to wear the white clothing. So later on they continued wearing white because it was put in their heads that it was ugly to wear any other color." John Burdick (1998, 59) found the same association between bright colors and Africanness in his research among Catholic black activists in Rio de Janeiro, where many laypeople and clergy stated that Brazilian blacks had a natural preference for vibrant colors. This idea parallels the belief that black people have an "inner joy" that should no longer be repressed. Once again, appearance (dressing in colorful clothes) is connected to essence (allowing inner blackness to flow).

The "Afro" in Afro-Bahian black culture is grounded mainly in objects that are signified as hyper-black symbols: that is, symbols that are not amenable to becoming national symbols, but rather are invented to support a clear-cut and oppositional black ethnic identity. They are signs of pride, dignity, and proof of one's conscious connection to Mama Africa, while simultaneously and reflexively connecting to other versions of Africanness produced in the black diaspora. Serving to both figuratively and metaphorically embody Africanness, the Afro objects fulfill the task of blackening (instead of whitening) the body.

In his much-cited essay "What Is This 'Black' in Black Popular Culture?" Stuart Hall (1996b) argues that the repertoire of diasporic and postmodern black popular culture has been based on the centrality of style, music, and uses of the body. Although this repertoire is inescapably hybrid, since it has been overdetermined by its African inheritance as much as by its diasporic condition, it has been employed in ways that seek to essentialize difference. Inserted in the same historical and diasporic configuration described by Hall, the "Afro" in Afro-Bahian culture nicely fits this description, since it is also centered on producing difference through manipulation of the body, a process in which style and music have played a fundamental role. Commenting on the reflexive use of the body as cultural capital and analyzing the predominance of creativity over the slaves' material deprivation, Toni Morrison states that black art can be produced from found objects, which are apparently used effortlessly, without breaking a sweat, resulting in a final product with no visible hems or stitches (Gilroy 1993b, 181). Cultures produced by the descendants of slaves are thus marked by high levels of aestheticization.

Although it fits Hall's account of diasporic black cultures, the "Afro" in Afro-Bahian culture has also been able to challenge, at least partially, one of the general coordinates that Hall identifies in this postmodern moment of black popular culture: the fact that it is marked by the emergence of the United States as a superpower, as "a centre of global cultural production and circulation" (Hall 1996b, 465). Because of its association with tradition and purity, the Africanness of Bahia has become increasingly sought by Afro-descendants from the U.S. superpower. For Hall, the global postmodern is also marked by the fact that marginality "has never been such a productive space as it is now" (467). Even though he is referring to "centers" and "margins" within specific societies, I believe we can apply that notion to understand how the cultural production of the peripheries of the world system has also affected identities produced in the core countries. African American roots tourism in Bahia is an example of this process. The "Afro" in Afro-Bahian cultural production is the main attraction for these tourists and represents, for them, the gateway into Brazil's African world.

Discourses about heritage and tradition are frequently articulated to legitimize a black political culture produced in contexts marked by racism and social exclusion. The idea of tradition frequently becomes a refuge for communities that define their identities in racial or ethnic terms, and it can have a hypnotizing power in black political discourse, serving to unify the diversity of black experiences. In many aspects, the appeal to tradition has turned out to be an antithesis of modernity, in part as a response to the threat that modernity represents for the stability and coherence of black identity (Gilroy 1993a). Nonetheless, despite their constant appeal to tradition, black diasporic discourses, whether intentionally or not, are producing modern identities that allow for black groups to re-narrate their past and shape their current insertion in the mainstream societies to which they belong. More than reinventing an African past, Afro elements employed to construct modern black identities produce new representations of blackness in the present.

This search for coherence, stability, and homogeneity explains the fixation with the past, the origins, the traditions, and the preservation of the heritage. Thus, the "Afro" in Afro-Bahian identities stands for tradition (such as the rhythms believed to originate from Africa, even if they were crafted in Bahia) and purity (such as in Ilê Aiyê's ability, and Olodum's inability, to remain "faithful to its African roots"). This is true even if a great deal of deliberate selection, exclusion, and unacknowledged hybridity are involved in producing the Afro components of these identities. No matter which routes were followed in time or space, Afro objects symbolize African roots, as seen in the fabric imported from India and Bali to further endow the black body with Africanness. The creativity employed in producing the great variety of Afro objects is undermined by a process of internal control and surveillance deemed necessary to guarantee a homogenous form of blackness. The inventive production of an Afro-aesthetics is thus put at the service of the construction of difference and opposition, a process in which the body is understood as the vital arena of intervention.

Afro-Centricity and Body-Centered Black Identities

All forms of identification make strategic use of the body as a site of expression. Gender, age, class, "race," and nationality are continuously articulated in dress, hairstyles, poses, and body language. Yet some identities are more explicitly and deliberately corporeal than others. This is especially the case for those groups who have had to resignify the meanings of their own existence. Responding to racism, discrimination, and negative representations, black communities in the diaspora have consciously employed diacritical signs in order to represent themselves in a new light. This process has produced renewed identities that have required the manipulation of physical appearance and the control of the essence and tendencies believed to be inherently attached to the body. The *blocos afro* are among the black organizations in the diaspora who are engaged in the process of creating a positive identity for Afro-descendants. Combining tradition with modernity, and narrating a common past and present history, the myth of Mama Africa has functioned as one the *blocos'* main sources of inspiration. The myth's emphasis on origins, purity, and preservation of Africanness indicates a carefully crafted black identity that is meant to have precise contents and tightly controlled boundaries.

Hence, Ilê Aiyê's discourse producers (the *bloco*'s directors, instructors, and composers) justified the need to talk about Africa as a way to ensure that blacks would not lose sight of their origins. As Espírito Santo, one of the directors, explains, "Do you know the difference between African people and other peoples? It's that they don't lose their point of reference. Because they're centered on their [traditions] without losing their reference." Juracy Silva, an Ilê Aiyê composer, explains why the *bloco* constantly refers to Africa: "We know that Africa is the oldest continent, and we know that the eldest, regardless of whether we want to or not, the eldest always has more experience to pass on. We talk about Africa because we know that without roots a tree cannot stand up straight." In one of his beautiful compositions, Silva exalts the connection with Africa:

Africa, door to the world
Black, shining the light, the natural lantern that guides us
Mama, African Mama
Gave Ilê Aiyê the genesis of Bahian blackness
Treetop, base, and roots
She wanted freedom, the tree of Afro-descent

Ilê Aiyê, the difference project

The garden of our history irrigated by new *quilombolas*[10]

Eating African roots, the template, Ilê Aiyê continues to be noble and
   happy

It keeps going, advancing its trajectory, to station Curuzu, the site of the
   guardian of memory

Ebony body, African uniform, black whistle, Ilê Aiyê preserves memory
   in its own way

It whistles to the past, making history, Ilê Aiyê preserves carefully, it
   preserves memory.[11]

Loyalty to the African origin explains the centrality of Africa in the
blocos' discourse. When asked why Africa is important to Ilê Aiyê, most of
the *bloco's* young members' confirmed the opinion of the *bloco's* older members: the need for blacks to know their origins and maintain a connection
to them. "Because in Africa, they are black and so are we, and they know
about our origins," replied a young male member. A young female member
answered: "We were actually born and raised here, but we know that we
descend from there. We also have to know our origins. That's our purpose
— knowing where our people come from, where our people came from. . . .
It's crucial that we know about everything from there. It's our people, you
know? We were actually born and live here, but we are of African descent.
Those who know about our origins are also our people, our ancestors,
where they came from." The young members explained that it is important
for blacks to talk about Africa because "the black color came from there,"
"because Candomblé is African," and "to remember that Africans were
brought by force." In addition, the young members praised Ilê Aiyê's initiative to talk about Africa because they say it is the only black entity in
Salvador undertaking this task, which legitimizes its role as guardian of
Africanness. "I think it's great, it's neat. Because if you look around, if you
pay attention, there isn't any other movement that talks about Africa except
Ilê Aiyê, which is always researching, always doing everything related to
Africa: the outfits, the rhythm. So that's why everything we do is geared
towards Africa."

Several other *blocos afro* that emerged with proposals similar to that of Ilê
Aiyê are not considered as "faithful to their African roots." In this comparison, Olodum is constantly cited as an example of a *bloco afro* that has
"deviated." "One of the differences is the rhythm. The other difference is
that Ilê Aiyê is a *bloco* geared toward blackness. Olodum opened and opens

itself up. They're [open to] everyone, you see? Europeans, Chinese, Japanese, whoever wants to can parade with Olodum. Here at Ilê Aiyê we try—and this has been going on forever—to only work with blackness. That's the difference. One of the differences. There's another difference, now, that has to do with percussion. In Ilê Aiyê it's all percussion, namely, *repique, marcação, timbau, caixa*. In Olodum it's not that way, oh no. Look at what Olodum uses: keyboards, guitars, they use saxophones, brass instruments—that's also the difference," explained one of Ilê Aiyê's young musicians.

In the statements above, Olodum's "musical promiscuity" reflects its "ethnic promiscuity," as opposed to the musical and ethnic purity claimed by Ilê Aiyê. These notions of purity and impurity reveal what is perceived as more or less authentic. Such polarized constructions are present in several versions of black culture in the Afro–Latin American world. Most of the statements given by Ilê Aiyê's young members include notes of fondness for Olodum, since the *bloco* also talks about blacks; however, Olodum is depicted as not having the same depth or authority as Ilê Aiyê to address the issue of Africanness, because it is believed that the latter group is really the original and traditional one. As one young Ilê Aiyê member put it, "Now, loud and clear, I'll tell you: Ilê Aiyê is the best, without a doubt. It started everything, you see? It conceived of everything, you see? The first *bloco afro*, in Bahia, in Brazil. It's the one that started to get blacks to rebel. It's the only *bloco afro* that still continues to this day. It preserves and practices Bahian Afro culture in Salvador. . . . I don't think Muzenza exists any more. Malê [Debalê] is around, but it's really struggling. Olodum opened up and lost itself."

Arguing that there is a correlation between allowing nonblacks to participate in the *bloco* and an inevitable "loss of identity," Vovô, Ilê Aiyê's president, justified why it remains a blacks-only organization: "What happens with mixed organizations [*blocos afro* that accept nonblack members] is that blacks start to lose their reference as people of another ethnicity. And we in Ilê try to think that blacks are beautiful if they assume their blackness and band together. Our posture is part of a pedagogy of reeducating black people so that they can accept themselves. So, either because they don't understand our purpose or because of meanness, some people start saying we're racists." Vovô explained the reasons for the presence of light-skinned people in the *bloco* in 2000:

"In the beginning, only dark blacks, real dark blacks, participated in Ilê. Blacks who have lighter skin tones, those we actually barred. . . . Now, for some years there's been infiltration, like there was this year, and I think it's a total lack of respect. People who aren't black, who received costumes, who sent their employees, even their friends, to come buy the outfit and this is what happens. . . . That's the reason. If blacks did that in a *bloco de trio*, they'd be banned! And this year we let things go. We looked, we looked closely at their faces, their hair. . . . There's a screening we used to do every once in awhile and that next year we are going to do again, if only as a matter of safety. This year our security team failed. They didn't provide our safety; we hired four hundred men and there were only two hundred. So it didn't work. Next year we're going to have to do that screening."[12]

Composer Juracy Silva also believes in the centrality of Ilê Aiyê for constructing blackness in Bahia, although he acknowledges the efforts of other *blocos*.

They use different readings. Now both of them, like even Ara Ketu [a *bloco afro* founded in 1980], which despite its distortion in terms of music develops social projects there in [the neighborhood of] Periperi with children. I mean . . . so Malê de Balê, all of them, use different readings with a single objective, which is to work for the visibility of blacks, to work for the citizenship of blacks, to advance blacks, to work against racism. Because as soon as you start educating people, they try to equip themselves and confront prejudices, confront everything. So Ilê Aiyê, in my view, is inserted precisely in this project of difference and it's this project of radicalism on top of difference that makes me have closer ties to Ilê Aiyê.

The idea that Ilê Aiyê is the "most Afro" of the *blocos afro* permeates the imaginary not only of its members, but also of members of Salvador's other cultural groups. The same correlation between the openness to new musical rhythms and the openness to welcoming members from other ethnic groups, described by some young members of Ilê Aiyê, was also cited by young Olodum members. "In Ilê only blacks participate because Ilê is a *bloco afro*. I mean, Olodum is also a *bloco afro*, but Olodum plays reggae, jazz, blues. Ilê doesn't. They've been playing the same Afro rhythm for the last 25 years. It's tradition, so you can't change it." Once again, jazz and blues are employed as illustrations of less African musical rhythms. Stating that Ilê Aiyê preserves blacks' traditions, another young member of Olodum said that this justifies Ilê's ban on the participation of nonblacks: "For

25 years, Ilê has only paraded with blacks. It doesn't make any sense to open up the *bloco* now, because it has to preserve the traditions of blacks. If only blacks can participate, it's because that came from somewhere and it has to be maintained. If Ilê changes now, people here from Olodum, from all the *blocos*, will be very upset." Along the same lines, another young member told me, "Ilê has its reasons for not letting whites in: it's the oldest *bloco afro* in Bahia. So it has to preserve this blackness. I think it's great that Olodum is a mixture of colors, but Ilê Aiyê should remain a *bloco* for blacks, because it's beautiful. It preserves the legacy of blacks."

The view that Olodum's young members hold of Ilê Aiyê as the guardian of Bahia's blackness reflects, in great part, the discourse of the *bloco*'s leaders. This can be perceived even in the statements of those who have a more dynamic notion of blackness. One of the coordinators of Olodum, Nelson Mendes, a long-time activist in Salvador's black movement, defends the proposal of moving beyond boundaries, both in terms of holding Africa as the exclusive point of reference and in terms of reducing blackness to skin color. "Traditionally with *blocos afro* in Bahia, each *bloco* honors an African country during Carnaval, for the sake of reclaiming, of cultural identity, of the return to Mama Africa. Olodum starts to break away from this when it paraded honoring Cuba during a difficult political moment, one of isolation. But there are black Afro-Cubans, so why not build this bridge between the Caribbean and Latin America? Of course, the main point of reference is Mama Africa, but we don't have to limit ourselves to that." On this issue of color, he said, "Olodum has grown a lot, it's expanded its proposal, so it couldn't remain restricted by skin color. We've already moved beyond that stage."

However, this same individual, who defends the increasing openness of his group, also defends Ilê Aiyê's position in terms of maintaining traditions:

> We respect Ilê Aiyê's stance [of not accepting nonblacks], if only as a matter of preservation. Here's a fact that might seem strange, but by including people of any ethnic group in Olodum, it's lost a little bit of its dynamic as a *bloco afro*. What is dynamic as a *bloco afro*? People sing and dance to African rhythms. That's a format, that's part of its nature. It came about like that. I've been participating in *blocos afro* for many years. I like it, I reflect on it. I noticed that when Olodum started opening up so that everyone could participate, I stopped to look at the *bloco* on the street and I felt it had lost a little bit of its force. Not that the other people weakened

the *bloco*, but it lost its dynamism. It drags its feet, it doesn't have any dynamism, people weren't singing in unison. So, for that aspect, I agree that Ilê should maintain the tradition. It's not exclusion; it's tradition. Because then it preserves the power of African culture. When you feel that power of Ilê Aiyê singing, with its turbans . . . it's fantastic, it's incredible, it's the force of a culture that needs to keep itself alive. It's the maintenance of cultural elements that have to be preserved. Ilê Aiyê is our heritage.

If on the one hand, the affirmation of identity based on a supposed Africanness has allowed for the creation of new and positive representations in a sociohistorical context where blacks are frequently linked with pejorative images, on the other hand, the reinforcement of the idea of Africa as a magical entity that emanates authenticity weakens the internal diversity of the black experience and of black particularity itself. The Afrocentricity and Afro-references that black movements produce in response to today's hegemonic Eurocentrism follows an inverted, but similar, logic: that there is a single center from which all truth emanates. Emphasizing a single center foregrounds some experiences and marginalizes others, because it is based on the principle that there are an essential origin and ancestry defining identities. Unicentered ideologies operate under a Manichean logic that juxtaposes tradition and modernity, black and white, purity and mixture, genuineness and illegitimacy. By placing Africa at the center of this logic, Afrocentricity reduces Africa to a set of frozen and confining representations of blackness centered primarily on the body. The search for African genuineness is translated into the notion that to *be black* one must act, behave, and dress *black*, thus perpetuating the notion that blacks are all alike. Stuart Hall argues that this homogeneity is one of the properties of racism: "You can't tell the difference because they all look the same" (1997b, 444).[13] While it is an important metaphor for modern and postmodern black political discourses, the mythification of Africa, of its supposed traditions, and of its bonding essence forges static representations of blackness. A discourse that intended to transform instead ends up upholding a system of ideas that differentiates blacks and whites and creates a hierarchy between them.

As researchers are increasingly engaged with the cultural production of grassroots movements, we must actively take on the task of reminding those around us that identities are not *things*, but *processes* that are constantly undergoing renegotiation. This demands that we challenge the reification and essentialization of identities and renounce the idea that a given group has a basic identity defined by a previously established essence. To do so, we must shatter the fixed connection between place, people, and culture that has persisted for so long as a premise (Gilroy 2000), and we must counter the notion that a given territory—in this case Africa, even as an imagined territory—produces a specific culture, which in turn molds black peoples and their identities.

What unites blacks transnationally is the experience of racism and oppression, but even that takes place in different manners, creating distinct consequences for the construction of black ethnic subjectivities and identities. To forge a common black identity, or even an Afro-referenced one, for all blacks of the world is to overlook the trajectory traced since slave times to this day, ignoring the system of cultural creations and symbolic exchanges that have and will always exist—not just between blacks but between all people throughout the history of humankind. To warn against these dangers is both a challenge and a duty for academic pursuits on identity.

The concepts of "blackness" and "race," so dear to the groups that construct their identities as ethnic and Afro-referenced, are social constructs that do not exist independently. Although they have organized individuals for the past several centuries, these concepts can no longer be understood as fixed and must be always analyzed in context. Emphasis should be placed on representations, on the distinct meanings that concepts such as "race" and "black" acquire according to the location, space, and time they inhabit. For this very reason, black identities cannot be reduced to their supposed origin, as if they were immutable entities. The notion that there is a radiating source of blackness in the world does more harm than good for those who define themselves as blacks. The most persistent representations of blackness are based on a quite limited notion of the black body. Since slavery, negative values, such as unsightliness and laziness, have been associated with the black body, stigmatizing people identified as black and consequently determining their place in society. As a response to this, black ethnic groups have frequently played a game of inversion that aims to replace negative images with positive ones, associating the latter with the black body and helping create increasingly aestheticized representations of identities.

As in other parts of the diaspora, the history of racial relations in Brazil has clearly divided the attributes of the body as being stronger in blacks, and the attributes of the mind as being nearly the exclusive characteristics of whites. However, these physical attributes — which until recently represented negative characteristics, since in the Western hierarchy the body is inferior and subordinated to the mind, and which to a certain extent animalize the image of blacks — have acquired a new prestige in our postmodern context. Physical appearance is hyper-valued today through images that increasingly exploit both male and female black bodies. Dominant strands of U.S. hip-hop culture, which increasingly focus on female buttocks and male chests and abs, are currently the most evident example of this body-centered blackness.

Although they might seem celebratory of ideals of strength and beauty, body-centered representations of blackness reinforce stereotypes and, consequently, are not capable of transforming predominant racist images. After all, what is the advantage of being a superhuman in sports, dance, and music, and subhuman in every other realm? Why not have the right to be simply human, to be humanly normal? The generalization and policing of the black body ends up unifying it, freezing it in certain standards that differ little from the racist conceptions forged during slavery and colonization.[14] Paradoxically, black identities in the diaspora, which have developed as a response to racism and oppression, have frequently employed self-regulation and normatization in the construction of the self and the group (Foucault, 1978, 1988). In the following chapters, we shall see how black identities in high modernity use the body as a privileged space for regulation, vigilance, and discipline.

Oppressed groups construct ethnic identities to manipulate their own representations, either to challenge dominant discourses within the society they live in or to legitimize what has already been in circulation. Black identity groups, like many others, have transformed representations and replaced negative images with positive ones. Nevertheless, these presumably positive images may also attach static and exclusive meanings that can forge a supposed essence based on appearance. Reacting to racist depictions created by those located outside of the boundaries of blackness, members of the black diaspora in various parts of the world have attempted to construct fixed and stable black ethnic identities. In general, the more essentialist black identities hover around two basic axes: the idea of a "black race," in which phenotype, especially skin color and hair texture, plays a fundamental identifying role; and the myth of Mama Africa, which propagates the belief that all blacks in the world are unified by means of an essence originating in Africa and transported in black bodies and souls. Although researchers no longer agree that subjects carry a fixed, permanent, or essential identity, for the groups that ground their existence upon the awareness of a specific identity, the idea that culture is something that is not only owned, but also bound to the body, persists. In Bahia, the embodiment of black identities is conceived of as occurring simultaneously on physical and metaphysical levels.

CHAPTER THREE

Africa on the Body

> The word [diaspora] comes closely associated with the idea of sow-
> ing seed. This etymological inheritance is a disputed legacy and a
> mixed blessing. It demands that we attempt to evaluate the signifi-
> cance of the scattering process against the supposed uniformity of
> that which has been scattered. Diaspora posits important tensions
> between here and there, then and now, between seed in the bag, the
> packet, or the pocket and seed in the ground, the fruit, or the body.
> — Paul Gilroy, *Against Race*

The body has occupied a central place in black cultures of the
diaspora. Because it was one of the main resources of the
enslaved and to a certain extent their descendants, strategic
use of the body has been of great importance in the Afro-
diasporic production of culture. The dominance of Eurocentric standards of beauty in the Brazilian media and the
cruel forms of racism that have associated black bodies with
ugliness, stench, and criminality have contributed to an ongoing stigma and sense of low self-esteem, especially among
the black youth. Afro-Brazilians, however, have defied such
demeaning notions of blackness through an inventive production of aesthetic elements that refer to Africa, or to what
Africa is believed to be. The emergence of the *blocos afro*
contributed to the growing trend among Brazilian blacks to
search for references of beauty in idealized images of Afri-

can aesthetics. African-inspired hairstyles, such as synthetic weaves and dreadlocks, colorful fabrics from India and Bali, together with locally produced jewelry and clothes, are just some of the elements used to invent an Afro-aesthetics in Brazil. Black and Afro-referenced racial identities constructed in Bahia under the influence of the cultural production of the *blocos afro* use the body as the central locus of affirmation and inscription of blackness. The black body, endowed with an Africanness identified previously as negative and backward, and associated with ugliness and undesirability, is reinvested with an Africanness that is now resignified to confer pride and beauty. Thus, Africa is reinscribed in the body, or better yet, onto the surface of the body. The visual, the tactile, and the senses of smell and color of the black body have been used to reinvent Africanness, and therefore Africa itself, in order to produce beauty and restore dignity.

Inventing Blackness and Its Stigmas

Observed from the outside through the recurring images of Carnaval, samba, and soccer disseminated worldwide, Brazil is usually perceived as a black country. It not only has the largest black population outside Africa (at least according to official census data), but has absorbed black culture into its narration of the nation. Black cultural elements also permeate the daily experience of most Brazilians. Brazil is known for its vibrant black culture, from which the main symbols of its nationality are drawn: spicy food with *dendê* oil, frenetic musical rhythms led by drums, and black bodies playing capoeira and dancing in the tropical landscapes of the postcards that promote Brazil's image abroad. However, despite these statistics and celebratory iconography, a powerful and persistent Eurocentrism also pervades Brazilian society, determining and classifying standards of beauty and ugliness.

Negative representations of blackness in Brazil can be traced back to the slavery period. Brazil was the last country in the Western Hemisphere to abolish slavery and the largest purchaser of African slave labor in the world. Somewhere between 3.6 and 5 million African slaves were brought to Brazil between the second half of the sixteenth century and 1850, when the slave trade was officially (but not effectively) abolished.[1] The legacy of slavery may have provided Brazil with its exhilarating black culture, but it has also given rise to striking social and racial inequalities and vicious forms of racism. This certainly does not mean that the legacy of slavery alone is enough to keep prejudice and inequality alive. As argued by several scholars of Brazilian racial relations (Hasenbalg and Valle Silva 1988; 1993, among others) present-day racism, continuously recycled and updated, plays a crucial role in the perpetuation of racial inequalities.

The deterministic ideologies of the Portuguese colonizers, who characterized people by associating them with the features of their land, contributed to the development of the racism that exists in Brazil today. The negative images of blackness that permeate Western popular culture originated during the first encounters between the Europeans and the peoples they subjugated and colonized. The first images of Africans disseminated in Europe depicted them as primitive and monstrous beings and mirrored the images that represented Africa itself as a nebulous land, replete with magic and fetishism, revealing, ultimately, the ignorance of Europeans in the face of unknown peoples and lands. The views of the continent and the representation of its people thus became inextricably linked. The enslavement of Africans, carried out both in exploration and settlement colonies, fed Europe's imagination of Africa and its denizens, leaving marks in the way blacks are represented and imagined to this day. Although the term *blackness* did not yet exist, its meanings originated within that historical context, because it was from this point on that "blacks" began to be seen as a group —albeit not a homogenous one, since Europeans began to classify slaves according to the different ports from which they embarked or the places in Africa where they were captured—endowed with common external and internal characteristics seen as inferior by Europeans.

Later, eighteenth- and nineteenth-century theories of scientific racism maintained that each "race" occupied a different position on the scale of evolution and that bodily characteristics, such as skin color, hair texture, and facial features, corresponded to characteristics of the soul; in other words, bodily appearance determined one's "essence." Black bodies were then associated with evil and darkness, or at least with a state of backwardness. Facial traits such as thick noses and lips were considered *grosseiros*, a term that refers to both "rough" physical appearance and "rude," backward behavior. Arthur de Gobineau, a French diplomat who spent fifteen months in Rio de Janeiro in the late nineteenth century, commented on the appearance and behavior of the local population: "It is an entire population of mulattoes, with vicious blood and vicious spirits, and horrifyingly ugly" (quoted in Raeders 1988, 96).

The idea that blacks were ugly surfaced in most colonies to which Africans were taken as slaves. The dark color of the skin, contrasted with the fairness of white skin, has been associated ever since with dirt and sub-humanness, as if the darkness of one's epidermis were able to reveal the shadows of the soul. In addition to the supposed ugliness of the skin, blacks' kinky hair and broad features were seen as signs of lack of refinement and were associated with aggression, since phenotypes were represented as being connected to inherent characteristics or natural traits. After the end of slavery, racial relations in Brazil became even more conflictive as blacks sought to participate in society as free people, leading many whites to view them as rivals. During slavery, clashes between blacks and whites had generally been confrontations between masters and slaves, categories that clearly indicated the social superiority of whites over blacks. With abolition, however, former slaves began to demand their space in society, and the denial of equality of rights to blacks legitimized racism as a distinguishing argument.[2]

Although over a century has passed since abolition, negative ideas about blackness continue to dominate contemporary Brazilian "common sense" or what Antonio Gramsci had defined, in the *Prison Notebooks* (1992), as the arena of general beliefs that constitute the everyday consciousness of the majority of the population in a given society. While they are certainly influenced by scientific theories and philosophical systems, the ideas that constitute common sense are usually contradictory, incoherent, and fragmentary. Commonsense notions are those which have not been elevated by intellectual effort and are therefore the result of predominantly acritical thought. Although it is the product of history and society, common sense represents itself as the "traditional wisdom" or the "truth of the ages." Because it is manufactured much more by consent than coercion, common sense is an arena where ruling-class interests are more accepted than contested. Gramsci's notion of common sense is useful in understanding the subtleties and resilience of racist ideas, because it calls attention to the structures of popular thought and its practical consequences on the lives of oppressed groups.

The racism that exists today in Brazil is visible in police repression and continuation of the status quo, borne out by research that reveals the statistics on inequality between blacks and whites in terms of jobs, infant mortality rates, access to formal education, and many other spheres that determine quality of life (Castro and Barreto 1988; Guimarães 1995; Hasenbalg and Valle Silva 1988; 1993, among others). But there is also a hidden dimension upon which racism acts, which underlies the spaces of explicit racial discrimination. This sphere—invisible to some but painfully visible to others—is comprised of the symbolic representations that inhabit the collective imaginary of Brazilian common sense, rife with negative stereotypes of Africa and demeaning images of blackness.

Individuals represented in a negative light are forced to deal with the damage of stigmatization, as one notes in the pained words of young black members of the *blocos afro*. Their narratives reveal that stigmas of slavery still persist into the twenty-first century, invoking feelings of bitterness and revolt that make it difficult for individuals to find self-acceptance. In interviews, young members of Ilê Aiyê and Olodum offered several examples, often without prompting, of direct experiences with prejudice and racism. They feel racism in their daily lives, which reinforces the stigma of being black. The negative representations of blackness they most often cited were connected to commonsensical readings of the black body: ugliness, filth, stench, and dishonesty — the idea that blacks are always suspect. They also criticized the absence or alleged incompetence of blacks in the job market, and the absence or misrepresentation of blacks in the media. Because these representations are so powerful, the *blocos afro* seek to enact transformations in the dominant cultural politics.

Over three hundred years of slavery in Brazil was enough time to reinforce and expand negative images of blackness. In addition to being considered ugly and rough, black bodies of the enslaved were associated with filth and stench. Mass production of soap in the nineteenth century established new standards of personal hygiene for the upper classes, becoming, along with rituals of cleanliness, central to the demarcation of bodily boundaries and the policing of social hierarchies. While the new standards of personal hygiene acted as class dividers among whites, they defined levels of humanity among masters and slaves (McClintock 1997, 280).

The alleged smell of the slaves' bodies became an additional excuse for classifying them closer to animals than to humans. In Brazil, the widely used Tupi word *catinga* became the main label used to describe what was felt to be the shared characteristic body odor of blacks, Indians, and animals. Over one century after abolition, this word lives on in today's vocabulary and is still employed, along with other derogatory terms, to classify black bodies. The *Grande enciclopédia portuguesa e brasileira* defines the term as a "strong smell. . . . unpleasant smell from the perspiration of blacks, and in general, any bad smell associated with people's or animals' bodies" (1946, 6:306). Similarly, the terms *catinga-de-negro* and *catinga-de-mulata* designate plants that exude a strong odor; the former considered to be repulsive stench, while the latter has a perfumed smell, thus confirming the Brazilian myth of *mulatas* as natural bearers of a sexualized aroma, as exemplified by Jorge Amado's *Gabriela, cravo e canela* and her characteristic clove (*cravo*) scent.

The need to dissociate blackness from filth and body odor, which continues to this day, was one of the main concerns of the Frente Negra Brasileira during the 1930s. Struggling to create a new and positive image for blacks, FNB leaders maintained that black individuals had to make an effort to look suitable for the job market. Based on the era's ideal of integration, FNB members encouraged their peers to overcome their "tendency" toward alcoholism and indolence, and to adopt a "good appearance" (*boa aparência*), which included wearing *roupa social* — a Brazilian expression for formal attire — and looking tidy and clean. This "proper" look also required very short hair for men and straightened hair for women, giving the impression of neatness. Controlling one's body odor was thus part of a wider attempt to contain supposed tendencies and improve the appearance of the black body in order to promote the social acceptance of a stigmatized group.

Although many decades have since passed, the expression *boa aparência* is still used in Brazil. Although the expression was banned by the Constitution of 1988, it is still widely used in want ads, generally as a euphemism for the preference of hiring light-skinned individuals.[3] For jobs in which blacks are more numerous, such as maids, potential employers cite personal hygiene (*asseio*) as a key criteria for hiring. *Patroas* — the maids' female employers — demand that their housekeepers have a "clean appearance," which usually entails "neat" hair (*cabelos bem cuidados*) and a "deodorized" body. Sometimes even teeth and fingernails are discreetly examined before the candidate is approved. Despite the policing of maids' personal hygiene, it is very common for them to be required to use a different set of plates and silverware, and they are frequently prohibited from using the bathrooms used by the family for which they work. Although they must keep themselves clean and perform housecleaning duties, their bodies are seen as bearers of some type of internal filth, and for this reason they are forbidden from touching the objects which require more hygienic care: those connected to food and excrement.

Racist notions that portray the black body as "naturally dirty" and "foul smelling" have resulted in constant discomfort and vigilance by many black individuals, who struggle daily to keep their bodies clean and perfumed in order to counteract the stereotype that blacks have *catinga*. Reacting to this despicable idea, many black individuals take painstaking care of their hygiene and appearance. This personal policing includes preventing sweat marks from showing, especially around the underarms, by wearing an undershirt to absorb perspiration (despite the discomfort of adding extra layers of clothing in a hot climate). Racism operates in such a perverse manner that it forces its victims to adapt their bodies to standards of cleanliness that are humanly unfeasible, and therefore inhuman.

As explained by Michel Foucault (1995), the discipline to power and the internalization of social rules are carried out through an "economy of punishment" in which the body occupies a central place. As the spectacle of punishment gave way to more veiled forms of punishment, regulation and discipline further penetrated the realm of "abstract consciousness." Foucault coined the term "discipline to power" to explain the power that rules the institutions of modern society, where spaces are closed and kept under total surveillance, and individuals are inserted in a specific place where all their movements are registered. While his focus was on institutions of individual functional control that establish binary divisions (especially normal-abnormal or sane-insane), such as asylums, hospitals, and prisons, Foucault's notion of discipline to power can be applied to the context herein analyzed, since in both situations individuals' awareness that they are continuously being surveilled is a guarantee of order. When individuals are subjected to binary oppositions, they seek to avoid being categorized with the negative pole (for instance, as ugly or smelly), thus employing a "technology of power."

The binary clean-dirty continues to be applied to the classification of white and black individuals. These notions were disseminated in several countries that enslaved Africans, and they remain present to this day, as can be seen, for example, in the advertisements in the United States for "heavy duty" deodorants for blacks. Negative ideas about the smell of black bodies also persist in Brazil, like ghosts from the era of slavery hounding the self-image of young blacks, resulting in constant preoccupation to always be clean, smell good, and look neat. As one young interviewee explained, "Because for us the body . . . we have to be like this, real clean, be nice clean girls, always dressed nicely, smelling good . . . I'm always dressed up."

The words of another young member and band leader of a *bloco afro* reveal the concern that young blacks have for their smell and appearance. He explained that this anxiety increases in the presence of outsiders, strangers to the group, as happens when the band travels on concert tours and needs to stay in hotels or share a dressing room with other artists. Smell appears in his interviews as a "problem that needs to be resolved" and something that even results in punishment if a member of the band does not "take proper care" of him or herself:

Because, as you saw here today, if we're here teaching a class and there's a bunch of students without their outfits — without their uniforms, really — with their sandals all scattered around, everything dirty, it gives a bad impression. So that's why I say, "Folks, try to always be policing yourself about this. If you smell under your arms, if you want to fix that problem, it's easy — I'll tell you how to fix it." Many times we've been embarrassed here in the dressing room, so much so that people can't even take their shoes off. On the bus, when we traveled a short distance, to Aracaju, there were some guys who when they took their shoes off, [the smell] filled the place. These people were let go, see? Because, just like it is on the bus, we might be in a dressing room with other people, like it's happened many times, sharing a dressing room with other people, with other groups. So it's bad, real bad, really really bad. So we tried to talk to these people that have this type of problem, we don't talk to them in front of everyone else, we call them aside — "Listen, man, this is what's happening . . . try to resolve it somehow." But it went in one ear and came out the other, so what did we do? We automatically put someone else in their place, you see?

Vigilant control of smell and appearance is a strategy to overcome repugnance toward the black body, so commonly expressed in the Brazilian common sense. It is a way not only to avoid the association with lack of care but also ultimately to prevent other people from feeling disgusted by one's black body, as stated by one of the young women interviewed: "For me, the worst kind of racism is in the gaze. It's through the gaze that you realize someone is staring at you with disgust." This statement illustrates Foucault's argument about the gaze as a crucial element in the complex network of decentralized forces that regulate even the most personal beliefs and behaviors. "There is no need for arms, physical violence, material constraints. Just a gaze. An inspecting gaze, a gaze which each individual under its weight will end by interiorizing to the point that he is his own overseer, each individual thus exercising this surveillance over, and against himself" (Foucault 1980, 155).

The intensity of racism often convinces those who are discriminated against that the fault lies with them, or at the very least responsibility for the discriminatory acts. An example of this is self-policing of appearance, which is also explained as the need to avoid the suspicion that so frequently plagues blacks. As stated by a young male member of Ilê Aiyê, "I keep telling my brother, 'Man, don't walk around looking like that, all sloppy, in flip-flops, without a T-shirt. Don't dye your hair, don't cover your face with a cap, because blacks are already discriminated against, and if we walk around looking sloppy it's even worse.'"

Once again, we are dealing with a negative representation of blackness that can be found in various places of the diaspora, where the black body is seen as a sign of dishonesty and delinquency. Many countries harbor the idea that blacks are always suspect, including the United States, where racial profiling is all too common. In Brazil, there is a pervasive belief that blacks are *"tipos suspeitos"* (suspicious types). In fact, in response to the frequent statement that in Brazil it is impossible to distinguish blacks and whites due to widespread racial mixing, black activists often respond that any police officer will immediately be able to tell you who is black in Brazil. The stereotype of blacks as suspects connects color and gender, since it is mainly applied to dark-colored males, but it is also intertwined with class distinction, especially with how one dresses.[4]

This image permeates racist Brazilian common sense, leading young blacks to once again attempt to solve the problem themselves by manipulating their bodies to minimize the threat their black appearance represents. This plays out more significantly when young blacks go to stores and supermarkets and are closely watched by security guards, as stated by several of the interviewees: "One of my cousins went to Bompreço [a large chain supermarket] and said that because she was black the security guard was following her entire time. So she gave up on buying anything, and she took the things and put them back in place and left the store. Then as she was leaving the guy came over and searched her, told her to open her purse up, and then he said, 'Ah, they should forbid blacks from coming into this Bompreço; it's so much work for us. I come here to follow blacks around!'" Another commented, "Like once when we traveled to São Paulo, you know, a whole gang of Ilê guys, all *negão*. We went shopping and the security guards all had their radios out, watching us." And in yet another example, an interviewee stated, "I see the racism when we go to the supermarket and there's the manager watching us, thinking that because we're black we're going to take something."

Discrimination against young blacks can occur anywhere, including the streets. One young male member observed, "When we go by women they all hold their purses this way, thinking we're thieves, that we're going to rob them." Young blacks cannot escape such suspicion, even in front of their own houses: "Once a cop stopped me right in front of my house," recalled an interviewee. "I was there talking to my friend, who's white, and a policeman came over and frisked me, checked my entire body, turned my bag inside out, and didn't find anything. Now the guy who was white wasn't even searched. Do you think that's a coincidence?"

The job market is also one of Brazil's most active spaces for racism, as demonstrated by the low visibility of blacks in higher positions, as well as the difficulties that blacks have in securing a job in the first place. A young member of Ilê Aiyê illustrated this by stating, "Now, there's also racism in employment. My dad, when he went to look for a job, the man said he didn't have any more openings. Then right after that a white man came and the man said he had an opening. Then when my dad complained he said there weren't any openings for blacks."

Manipulating appearance thus becomes a necessity, a means to control the threat, the fear, or the repugnance associated with black bodies, avoiding, as one of the interviewees said, the gaze of disgust toward one's own body. The act of scornful staring can have a devastating effect on young people who constantly suffer discrimination; as an expression of reproach it can harm the self-esteem of someone in his or her formative years. Contrary to Elaine Scarry's argument (1999), staring fixedly at someone or something is not necessarily an expression of appreciation or approval. Instead, a stare can reify and turn people of certain phenotypes into objects of repulsion. In contrast to Scarry's idea that the act of staring reveals a wish to create and reproduce the beautiful object of the gaze, staring can frequently be an expression of disgust. Above all, as an act loaded with power, the gaze contributes to the complex process of producing subjectivities.

Commenting on the harm done in the name of beauty to people who do not match mainstream standards, African-American writer Toni Morrison explained how she constructed her character in *The Bluest Eye*. Young Pecola, whom Morrison defined as "the most delicate member of society: a child; the most vulnerable member: a female" (1994, 210), desires, more than anything in life, to have blue eyes, believing that this way she would be loved and respected, even by her own family. The novel addresses, above all, the gaze that reified the black girl as ugly, leading her to reject herself and seek references of beauty outside blackness. Through the tragic story of this small human being, we understand the need for affirmation of black beauty as an indispensable means to react against the internalization of ideas about immutable inferiority which result from the external gaze that simultaneously objectifies and produces subjectivity. As Morrison brilliantly demonstrates, beauty is not just something one possesses, but something one can *do*. In her analysis of the meanings of beauty in *The Bluest Eye*, Sarah Nuttall (2006) states that Morrison writes against a particularly Western fascination with the notion that beauty must always be an occasion to gaze. The hegemonic act of gazing has the power to objectify the (black) subject and determines what is and is not beautiful. For Nutall, Morrison's observations reveal the force, the shock, caused by beauty, and also reveal how definitions of beauty necessarily imply definitions of ugliness.

Negative images historically associated with blackness weigh heavily on black people in a country like Brazil. Despite its founding myth as a racial democracy, in which cultural and racial miscegenation is celebrated as one of the main pillars of national identity, the ideals of whitening still persist. For example, it is still widely believed that one should "improve the race" by marrying people with phenotypes that will allow them to have children with straighter hair, lighter skin, and more angular facial features.[5] There are also other ways of "whitening" the body in Brazil, or at least "taming" its black characteristics. The most common strategy is to alter one's appearance through hair straightening, a habit practiced by large numbers of black women until the 1970s, when fundamental changes in black aesthetics started to occur in Brazil and the rest of the world. The desire to whiten the body, controlling its blackness, is indicative of a need for acceptance in a society dominated by Eurocentric values.

Eurocentrism refers here to the dominant and predominantly invisible supremacy of white standards, as if whiteness were the universal norm, the standard from which otherness is measured and defined. Eurocentric versions of beauty predominate in Brazil, and consequently determine the spaces expected to be occupied by blacks and whites in Brazilian society. Magazines, soap operas, commercials, and even the educational system perpetuate distinct representations of whites and blacks and continue to reproduce the negative stereotypes about the latter. The media and advertising are the main means of disseminating the dominant standards, which insist on white beauty, preferably with light-colored eyes. This preference is confirmed by the choices of hosts for children's morning shows and leading actors in soap operas. Blacks are still predominantly represented on Brazilian television as slaves, domestic servants, or villains. Ever since the mid-1990s, this situation has slowly begun to change. In 1995, Rede Globo broadcast the prime-time soap opera *A próxima vítima* (The Next Victim), which starred a middle-class black family. But if we consider the proportion of black actors in soap operas in comparison with their proportion in the Brazilian population, the number is still tiny. Moreover, most soap operas that do have a significant number of black actors are still those centered on the history of slavery. This was the case of *Força do desejo* (The Force of

Desire), aired in the six o'clock slot during the period of my fieldwork. Most of the black youth I interviewed expressed indignation over the treatment given to the slave characters, as well as to the continued representation of blacks as slaves:

> "I don't like watching the six o'clock soap opera, because whites are beating up the blacks, whipping them. It should be the same, all the same, there shouldn't be any slavery, because slavery is over. Because people were born to be free."

> "I get nervous with that six o'clock soap opera. I don't like to see blacks suffering."

Young interviewees also complained about the small number of blacks in advertisements. "They only hire whites for the ads. Ads for shampoo, ads for nail polish, ads for food. They only hire whites. Are whites the only ones who eat? [The only ones] who comb their hair? Who wash their hair? Are whites the only ones who like to smell good? So I think there should be ads to increase the self-esteem of blacks, with a black point of view."

As with the process taking place with TV shows, the presence of black actors and models has also increased in advertising over the past decade. The faces and bodies of black men, women, and children have become more visible in billboard, TV, and magazine ads. Not only are blacks now seen advertising hygiene products, but recently they have also begun promoting commodities associated with modernity such as cell phones and iPods. Yet the black actors and models employed in this new trend of Brazilian advertising are carefully selected from among the young, athletic, and beautiful, and are frequently made to look exotic. Most of the men in these ads have neat dreadlocks or carefully groomed Afros, and the women's skin is often covered with glossy, metallic makeup, possibly to make them look futuristic. Nizan Guanaes, one of Brazil's top advertising executives, explains that blacks are now employed in the advertisement of expensive and ultra-sophisticated products because their image is associated with attitude, style, and transgressiveness. His statement confirms the common-sense notion that black bodies are exotic and endowed with superhuman traits that consequently distance them from normality: "Currently, it's all about having attitude. Black models today are much more linked to sophistication, *chic*-ness, fanciness. Notice that the presence of blacks in advertisements for mobile phones is very strong, [and that is] because they're associated with attitude and transgression. It's easier to see an ad of a black person drinking whisky, or on an airplane, than selling a regular brand product. Blacks today are seen more as sophisticated [individuals] than as members of a regular family" (Guanaes 2006).

In addition to the fact that the increasing presence of blacks in media and publicity has required further exoticization of black bodies, black models and actors are still predominantly competing with the hegemony of whiteness, as expressed in the overvaluing of blonde supermodels such as Gisele Bundchen and Adriane Galisteu. Within the dominant standard of beauty, there is a hierarchy that places blond hair and blue eyes at the top as rare and highly valued traits. The hosts of the most widely watched children's programs—Xuxa, Angélica, and Eliana—are blondes with angular facial features. These women not only establish new fashion trends through the clothing, makeup, and cosmetics they market—they also set the standards of female beauty in a country with a black and *mestiço* majority. They are beauty icons for an audience of mostly black and *mestiço* children and teenagers, and they have an especially negative effect on girls, who unsuccessfully pine for impossible beauty standards. Probably as a way to avoid the accusation that her program does not feature black artists, Xuxa's producers created a secondary, yet very visible, role for a young black dancer named Adriana Bombom. As her name suggests—*bombom*, in Portuguese, means chocolate candy—Bombom is presented on the program as something to be devoured. Wrapped in tiny, racy outfits, the young black woman is put on display to sensually shake her hips while Xuxa takes advantage of the dancer's blackness to announce her own line of ethnic products and cosmetics. Ironically, these products are displayed primarily during a segment of the show called "moment of transformation," during which young girls receive makeovers from a team of makeup artists and hair stylists aiming to make them "beautiful." Not surprisingly, this process of transforming the ugly into the beautiful, or rather, an ugly female into a beautiful female, generally requires relaxing or straightening the curly or kinky hair of black and *mestiça* girls.

However, like blackness itself, beauty is neither inherent nor objective. Contrary to what scholars such as Elaine Scarry (1999) argue, beauty does not exist autonomously as a metaphysical entity that emanates from objects, places, or people. Instead, beauty values are projected by the observer and imbedded within classificatory systems that determine what is good or bad, ugly or beautiful. Just like other values, beauty—and its counterpart, ugliness—only exists within cultural systems and their correspondent production of meanings. Beauty is relational and is not independent from

culture. Thus, aesthetic perfection only exists through the cultural definition of what is beautiful, which is done in connection with the production
and reproduction of power. If beauty dignifies, promotes, and elevates that
which is considered beautiful, then it necessarily excludes, humiliates, and
subjugates that which is considered ugly. Although she briefly recognizes
that beauty is produced within culture, Scarry uses the term as if no debate
existed about its definition, and she exempts it from the processes that
impose hegemonic ideals of beauty.

Not only are dominant beauty standards in Brazil Eurocentric, but so
too is education, which could be a realm for questioning the status quo of
power relations. Instead, school curricula and textbooks have favored the
model imposed by colonization. An explicit example of this is the celebration of the exoticism of blacks and Indians in preprogrammed festivities,
when they rarely appear as part of everyday representations of life or history. All of this perpetuates the privilege of light-skinned people in a country that claims to be multiracial, pluricultural, and democratic (Siqueira
1996). In very contradictory terms, the standard of white beauty is hegemonic in Brazil, even within the realm of Carnaval, considered today the
"reign of black culture," and therefore of the black bodies believed to be the
repositories of this culture. Racism acts in paradoxical ways in the Carnaval
of Salvador, Brazil's "African capital," regarded as the blackest part of Brazil.
Despite its predominantly black population and the exhilarating black musical rhythms that prevail in Bahia's street festivities, intense racial discrimination still occurs, and its defenders use aesthetic grounds to justify their
actions. The *blocos* that participate in Salvador's Carnaval are divided basically into two categories: *blocos de trio*, which use sound stages mounted on
trucks and which are mostly comprised of middle-class and wealthy white
members, and *blocos afro*. However, *blocos afro* currently also have their own
mobile stages, and the most affordable *blocos de trio* feature mainly black
people. Due to the interconnection between "race" and class, the racial
composition of *blocos de trio*, just like everything else in Brazil, depends on
the amount charged for membership dues.

Arguing that they seek only *gente bonita* (beautiful people) as members,
the directors of the snobbish *blocos de trio* discriminate against and exclude
those they describe as "ugly people." In order to join these groups, candidates must fill out an application and attach a personal color photograph,
along with proof of residence. Based on this, directors can select members
on the basis of appearance (which primarily means skin color) and address,
since they also discriminate against those who live in the *periferias* (the

poorest neighborhoods), thus committing "racial, aesthetic, and geographical discrimination," according to the report of a Parliamentary Inquiry Commission established in 1999 by a Green Party councilman to investigate racism in Bahia's Carnaval. Geographical discrimination refers to *blocos* that bar the participation of people who reside in impoverished, and therefore stigmatized, neighborhoods. Aesthetic discrimination means the attempts by *blocos* to only allow "beautiful people" into the group, excluding those considered ugly — that is, those who do not fit the dominant standards of beauty, such as male and female blacks, overweight women, and, frequently, individuals that have "broad facial features," those who are "white but not quite": that is, *mestiços* who enjoy "light-skin privilege" in certain areas of Brazilian society but who are nonetheless viewed as "ugly" because they have "negroid" features.[6]

Reinventing Blackness and Its Beauty

Attempts to ban the participation of blacks in Bahia's Carnaval have a long history that can be traced back to the late nineteenth century. The first black groups to parade in the streets of Bahia during Carnaval suffered brutal police repression and were strongly criticized by the press, on the grounds that they were threatening "civilized" European standards through an Africanization of Bahia. Repression toward groups such as Pandegos d'Africa, Embaixada Africana, and all forms of Afro-Brazilian cultural expression was justified on the basis of their "ugly" and "savage" appearance; they were deemed inappropriate for a Carnaval that was supposed to be refined and elegant, like the ones in Paris and Venice.

As a response to the racial aesthetic discrimination that has historically permeated Bahia's Carnaval, in 1974 a group of blacks who had been denied membership in one of the Carnaval groups founded their own *bloco*, one in which only people with very dark skin would be allowed to participate. Founded under the influence of the Black Is Beautiful movement, which had recently reached Bahia, Salvador's first *bloco afro* marked a profound renovation in the aesthetics of the city and its inhabitants. As argued by Gilroy (1993a), the adaptation of styles, objects, rhythms, and symbols that circulate in the black Atlantic is facilitated by the common and shared experiences of slavery and of similar forms of racism and oppression. Thus, elements of black politics and aesthetics constantly travel from one black community to another, becoming detached from their local origins and reelaborated in the new places where they anchor.

Several other *blocos afro* were founded in the 1970s, following in the footsteps of Ilê Aiyê, which enriched the process of re-Africanizing Bahia's Carnaval and disseminated a wide variety of elements of the new Afro-aesthetics that was then beginning to be created. Braids, dreadlocks, colorful clothing, shell jewelry, *contas* (bead necklaces dedicated to one's *orixá*), and *palha da costa* (raffia) became widespread in Salvador. This production of Afro-aesthetic elements is connected to a wider international context in which black cultures in the Americas have been seeking and producing symbols related to Africa, thus disseminating a diasporic production of Africanness. The production of this imaginary Africa has been extremely beneficial in conferring pride and dignity to blacks in several parts of the world, as well as for the positive transformation of black physical features previously represented as negative.

This transformation has required the creation of new representations of blackness in order to resignify and represent black people in a new light. This need explains why *blocos afro*, like so many other black organizations, seek elements from African history — both those predating slavery in the Americas and those tied to the pro-independence struggles in African colonies — to integrate them with the current awareness of and about blacks. One of the texts written by Ilê Aiyê in 1982 reads, "The long list of African countries that achieved their independence, some of them through revolutionary means, such as Guinea-Bissau, Cape Verde, Angola, Mozambique, Zimbabwe, and Ghana, introduced to Brazilian blacks, especially in Salvador, a different image of black Africans and therefore of Black Mama Africa, making it clear to [these] entities that to be black did not mean to be passive, careless, or underdeveloped, despite media distortions, and that the experience of the African struggle could be reproduced here, since we were the majority of the population" (Ilê Aiyê 1982, 36).

The cultural production of the *blocos afro* has helped perpetuate an increasingly black image not only of Bahia but also of the individuals seduced by the Afro-centered messages and identity narratives produced by the *blocos*. Allied with discourse — and completely permeated by it — is the practice of the *blocos afro*, exemplified through social action projects in their local neighborhoods. Using a powerful arsenal of music, rhythms, accessories, and hairstyles, older *bloco* members invest in children and adolescents, hoping that younger generations will have access to what older ones could not completely reach: entry into dominant society, into the job and consumer markets, into the world of politics, and finally, the achievement of citizenship. From the start, the discourse produced by the *blocos afro* transcended the limits of black organizations, incorporating other individuals who also stand to benefit from these narratives to construct their own identities.

The black identity developed by the *blocos afro* through their narratives of Africanness and representations of blackness is wholly allied with their strategies of social promotion, revealing the inherent connection between discourse and practice, and between culture and politics. Situated in the context of postmodernity, *blocos afro* are based primarily on cultural identity, from which stems solidarity founded on the meaning of ethnic particularity. In this context the body occupies a central role, justifying the importance of the meaning of clothes, hairstyles, and accessories considered Afro. Analyses of the peculiarities of Brazilian racism, and more specifically of Bahian racism, are fundamental for understanding the context in which *blocos afro* operate: that is, the reality that has generated them and with which they interact on a daily basis. As argued by Agier (1992), Bahian racism combines forms of exclusion and segregation with instances of clientelism and integration. Racism is one of the many elements of everyday life for the *blocos afro*, but it is also a factor with which black Brazilians must deal constantly. Based on Afro-descendant ethnic affirmation and an intense effort to elevate self-esteem, the *blocos afro* employ strategies of social action aimed at constructing black citizens.

Since their emergence, black associations in Salvador have functioned as political and resistance organizations, even when they were predominantly religious or recreational in nature. By the eighteenth century, black Catholic sisterhoods and brotherhoods in Bahia and many other parts of Brazil operated mutual aid programs, whose activities ranged from the purchase of slaves' freedom to providing social services to poor blacks. However, the dominant classes in Bahia always tried to disparage the political aspects of these organizations by typecasting them as folkloric (Fry et al. 1988). The first black Carnaval groups, which emerged at the end of the nineteenth century, such as Pândegos d'África, endured an aggressive campaign from the local media, followed by heavy police repression. People were warned about the danger of the Africanization of Bahia during Carnaval, but the groups reacted and continued parading on the streets during the festivities. On the other hand, *batuques* — dance styles performed by different African ethnic groups, accompanied by percussive instruments — were criticized by most of society but defended by some political figures as a question of public security. The colonial administration, represented by the Count of Arcos, believed that *batuques* were capable of overcoming the conflicts that originally fragmented blacks who arrived from different African nations. "That is how *batuques* — vehicles of expression and preservation of ethnicity — were considered a form of guaranteeing the submission of black slaves and more effective control over them" (257). *Batuques* were the most direct expression of ethnic identity, whose preservation was of interest, in different ways, to both masters and slaves.

In the 1940s, *afoxés*, Carnaval groups characterized by their expression of Yoruba dance, music, and liturgy, brought the rhythms and symbols of Candomblé to the street, causing further outrage among the white classes in Bahia. Among the *afoxés* was Filhos de Gandhy (Sons of Gandhi), founded in 1949 by stevedores inspired by Mahatma Gandhi's antiracist and pacifist message. The group went on to become the most famous of Bahia's *afoxés*. Bahian society had always reacted against the various forms of black associations, beginning with the original *quilombos*, *pândegos* (black Carnaval associations of the late 1800s and early 1900s), and *afoxés*, and continuing with newer organizations with a more explicitly political agenda. Reactions from dominant society have varied from surprise and rejection to scorn, but they have also frequently been expressed through more successful attempts to co-opt these entities.

Since the 1970s, there has been a significant increase in Afro-Bahian organizations, which have become increasingly institutionalized and more visible in local life.[7] In the case of the *blocos afro*, institutionalization was followed by change, or rather, an expansion of their objectives. In addition to acting in the realm of Carnaval and entertainment, they also began to develop strategies for social outreach, and their ethnic discourse, initially expressed mainly during Carnaval, expanded to also include social strategies to promote the black community's quality of life. Such change began at the end of the 1980s. Up until the beginning of that decade the *blocos* were still confining themselves to the space and time of Carnaval, as seen in this statement given at the time by Vovô, president of Ilê Aiyê: "The guys from Movimento Negro told us we were outdated, that we didn't know anything, that we were a bunch of stupid blacks who only knew how to do Carnaval. But do they really think that we're going to stop doing this Carnaval thing? That's our biggest message. It's the festivities, the spectacle. They get together and don't do anything, and we, through Ilê Aiyê and Carnaval, without making any speeches, we've already been able to change a lot of things around here" (Risério 1981, 85).

Today the discourse is quite different, for the *blocos afro* have realized that it is possible to go beyond the entertainment realm and take action outside festivities, developing social strategies geared specifically toward the black community, using culture as a "weapon for black struggle." The *blocos afro* surpassed their initial informal and familiar form to become cultural enterprises and associations. Some have even received the title of Municipal Public Service Association from the mayor's office — Olodum was awarded the honor in 1984, followed by Ilê Aiyê in 1989. "The efficacy of this type of political existence can be seen in land and real estate transactions (plots and headquarters). The same happens in the financial realm, when we see groups such as the Council of Black Entities of Bahia receiving praise from the state of Bahia" (Agier 1992, 108).

Since the 1980s, Ilê Aiyê and Olodum have been developing social action strategies geared toward promoting blacks in Bahia. Among the projects developed by Ilê Aiyê in the Curuzu-Liberdade neighborhood are the Mãe Hilda School and the *bloco*'s Educational Outreach Project. The school is located in the Ilê Axé Jitolu candomblé *terreiro* and provides instruction in grades 1–3.[8] Mãe Hilda is the biological mother of Ilê Aiyê's president, Antônio Carlos dos Santos (Vovô), and she is considered the group's spiritual mentor. According to one Ilê Aiyê director, Maria de Lourdes Siqueira (1996), the children and adolescents' exposure to the *mãe-de-santo* ensures an "Afro-Brazilian cultural dimension through educational practice," because the *ialorixá* tells legends and stories, teaches songs, and incorporates the existence of *orixás* in one's personal life. This helps create a new worldview for these students, as well as a new self-image.

The Pedagogical Outreach Project is an afterschool program that includes Band'Erê, a musical group comprised of members between the ages of 8 and 16 who attend classes on music, dance, singing, and citizenship. The band's objectives are "to systematize an educational practice founded on Afro-Brazilian cultural values expressed through music and dance; to establish an integral educational process based on musicality; to consolidate Band'Erê as a space for students from the neighborhoods of Curuzu/Liberdade and surrounding communities to build citizenship."[9] The project was created in 1995, with the purpose of "fostering the reclaiming of African culture and its influences in Brazil, within the perspective of a pluricultural society, through racial identity, the development of critical thinking, and self-esteem of black children and adolescents."[10]

For Siqueira, Ilê Aiyê's Pedagogical Project prioritizes African cultural heritage from a unique standpoint with the following characteristics: (a) Salvador's population is predominantly of African origin; (b) its "reality is marked by [its] colonial slave past, updated through the dynamics of the capitalist system of production, under different forms, from the most subtle to the most obvious" (Siqueira 1996, 159); (c) black children attend schools that do not correspond to the reality of their social imaginary; and (d) Ilê's educational approach trains junior percussionists, developing their ethnic consciousness and preparing them for citizenship. "The goal of Ilê Aiyê's approach is to build cultural and ethnic identity among poor children and adolescents of African descent from the Mãe Hilda School and Band'Erê, extending their actions to municipal and state schools in the neighborhood of Curuzu, in Liberdade" (Siqueira 1996, 159). The project's methodology is to develop practices that increase the self-esteem of black children and prepare them for citizenship in a pluricultural context, through Afro-Brazilian culture, which the group reconstructs and expands in its cultural practices, such as black forms of singing, dancing, dressing, and making music.

Olodum's social strategy goals have some points in common with Ilê Aiyê's, such as the development of "social, cultural, and pedagogical activities to enhance the living conditions of the black population and of the children in Maciel-Pelourinho and other neighborhoods of Salvador" and of "educational activities that emphasize the practice of human rights and defense of the interests of the Afro-Brazilian population."[11] Among Olodum's more socially oriented activities are the Olodum Creative School, the Olodum Publishing House, the Olodum Theater Troupe, and the Carnaval Factory (which manufactures "boutique clothing, Carnaval costumes, accessories, and knickknacks, such as key chains and buttons" [Dantas 1994, 110]). Scholars of black culture in Bahia debate whether the latter program is actually motivated by social concerns or if it just generates profit through low wages. Marcelo Dantas sees the Carnaval Factory in a positive light, arguing that it provides income for some three hundred poor blacks. Lívio Sansone, on the other hand, considers it to be an exploitative enterprise: "Olodum really did put together a so-called Carnaval Factory, a sweatshop that takes fabric from Bolivia, dyes it, and transforms it into Afro-fashion objects" (2000b, 11).

In contrast, there seems to be a greater consensus that Olodum's Creative School is a positive enterprise, and it can be considered the main example of the group's community work. Its goal is to foster the development of children, adolescents, and adults and turn them into "conscious citizens who are ready to play a dignified role in society."[12] In the beginning, it was run as a extracurricular education project, but from 1994 to 1998 it functioned as a full-blown elementary school, with capacity for 150 students from kindergarten through fourth grade, with its own headquarters purchased by the Olodum Cultural Group. Since 1998, the school has gone back to offering extracurricular education, offering classes in information technology, Afro dance, theater, and percussion. These classes include lessons in citizenship and ethics, addressing themes such as racism, blackness, sexuality, and self-esteem. Students must be between the ages of 10 and 18 and must be attending a regular school that does not conflict with the schedule of the Creative School.[13] Unlike Ilê Aiyê, which focuses more on meeting the needs of the young people of Curuzu-Liberdade, Olodum's social outreach programs extend to youngsters in several Salvador neighborhoods, perhaps because its headquarters are located in the central part of the city.

One young Olodum member, who has been connected to the group for over ten years and who is currently a band leader, remarked, "At the Creative School I learned the true stories about blacks. At the other schools [public schools] I went to, I hadn't even heard of Zumbi. I didn't know the value of black people." One of the group's young dancers, who also attends the Creative School, stated, "The Creative School is everything to me. Olodum is my second home. Here, I learned everything about being black. Even my hair—I started braiding it after I came to the Creative School. Here I can say that I actually became blacker . . . and happier too." The young *bloco* members not only acquire the pedagogy of blackness touted by *bloco* leaders but also acknowledge the role of these organizations as pioneers in establishing Afro-aesthetics in Bahia, as stated by one of Ilê Aiyê's young dancers: "Ilê Aiyê initiated all of this, this revolution in Salvador, of blacks waking up to their own value. This self-esteem thing, of not undervaluing people who wear braids in their hair, people with black skin, who have suffered numerous humiliations, who suffer to this day."

In contrast to what was happening before, when black people were trying to whiten themselves as a reaction to racism, the *blocos* encourage the strategy of blackening the body in order to gain self-esteem and dignity. The many hairstyles and forms of manipulating one's hair represent a central element in this new Afro-aesthetics produced in Brazil, which in Bahia looks to the *blocos afro* as its main reference point. Black activists and cultural producers employ the term *Afro-aesthetics* to describe a wide range of elements created to produce beauty, in particular a very specific kind of black beauty based on an ideal of Africanness. I consider Afro-aesthetics as both constituted by Africanness and constitutive of it, and engendered within the continuous process of imagining and reinventing Africa.

The prefix *Afro* has become increasingly important among blacks in Brazil. It is employed as an adjective to describe objects believed to be loaded with Africanness. Thus one can speak of *"roupa afro"* (Afro clothes), *"maquiagem afro"* (Afro make-up), *"cabelo afro"* (Afro hairstyles in general), *"permanente afro"* (Afro perms), *"artesanato afro"* (Afro handcrafts), and *"bijuteria afro"* (Afro jewelry); more recently, it is possible to speak even of Afro nails — artificial plastic nails that become "Afro" simply because they are very colorful and display geometrical patterns that seem African. Thus, everything that seems African or that is imagined to be used in Africa ends up legitimately conferring Africanness in Brazil. As we saw in the previous chapter, the Africanness of the objects considered Afro in Brazil is conferred on the basis of impression and intuition, regardless of where or how these objects were produced. What matters is the meaning of Africanness attributed to these objects. The term *Afro* is therefore used to determine those things that, despite being created outside the African continent, are meant to refer to Africa, or to what Africa is believed to be. If Africanness is defined on the grounds of impression, the same can be said of how Africa is imagined and recreated in the elements that comprise its "African" beauty.

Thus, synthetic weaves and dreadlocks and fabrics imported from India and Bali may seem very African, or Afro, and can therefore be used as symbols of Africanness, comprising, together with locally produced hair and body ornaments, the elements that form and inform Brazil's Afro-aesthetic. Among all the objects that comprise this aesthetic, the most popular are hairstyling products. In addition to artificial extensions that can be woven into natural hair, a substantial number of creams carrying the word "Afro" on their labels are sold in Brazilian stores. These Afro products entered the Brazilian market initially through the importation of U.S.-made products, yet while they arrived through global commercial channels, their success and popularity are nevertheless local. Beginning in the 1990s, the number of shampoos, conditioners, humidifiers, moisturizers, and even more aggressive chemical treatments labeled "Afro" has increased at an extraordinary pace.[14] And most of these hair products are now made in Brazil.

A curious fact about this Afro labeling trend is that the so-called Afro hairstyle that represented the main symbol of the nascent Afro-aesthetics of the 1960s in the United States was named differently in Brazil, where it is called *cabelo black power* (or *bleque pau*, in the Portuguese pronunciation), certainly a homage to that historical moment. The lyrics of the first Ilê Aiyê song to become well-known in Brazil read, "*Somos criolos doidos, somos bem legal. Temos cabelo duro, somos bleque pau*" (We're crazy blacks, we're really great. We've got kinky hair, we're black power).[15] Arguing that history can be intentionally inscribed in hair, Mariane Ferme describes how in Sierra Leone's Mende culture, braiding is associated with historical moments. "Hair weaving was more responsive to changes in style and technology (synthetic extensions, chemical products, and other hair-straightening gadgets, and decorative additions such as beads) than the other forms of weaving. It inscribed the history of the moment on women's bodies, as styles took on the name of events or popular icons on the national or even global scene" (2001, 58).

In Bahia, women's bodies have also been the main site of production and performance of the new Afro-oriented black identity. This process has been carried out through two specific, albeit intersecting, techniques: the "technologies of the self" (Foucault 1988) through which women have taken on embodiments of blackness, and the management of the appearance and "tendencies" of black women's bodies undertaken by male leaders of the *blocos afro*. An important example of the effects of the process of blackening on the development of black female subjectivity is the overwhelmingly female response to *Revista Raça*, the first black magazine ever launched in Brazil. *Revista Raça* has been an important advertising forum for Afro products. The magazine also carries frequent features on Afro hairstyling, such as the column *Cabelo Bom* (Good Hair). While it targets the black population in general, *Revista Raça* is predominantly read by young black females. Commenting on the great number of female readers, Roberto Melo, one of the directors of Editora Símbolo, publisher of *Revista Raça*, remarked that the magazine received hundreds of phone calls and letters from black women thanking them for publishing a magazine that helped them improve their self-esteem: "Female readers called us, in tears, to share moving stories. One of them wrote to us and said: I am thirty years old, and I spent my entire life, my entire childhood hitting the pillow, falling asleep, and dreaming that I was white, that I had just caught too much sun, but that I would wake up white. I spent my entire life, my entire adolescence trying to choke down this problem, and I had this stuck in my throat until now, when I bought the magazine. Now that I have bought the magazine I can say that I am proud to be black" (Kofes 1996, 248).[16]

To a lesser extent, some women have also been creators of Afro symbols of blackness. The clothing brand Didara, created by Afro-Bahian artist Goya Lopes in 1986, is possibly the most successful enterprise in Salvador's new Afro clothing niche. The fabrics' colors are vibrant and bold, and mostly inspired by Afro-Brazilian themes, such as Candomblé symbols.

Stylized drawings of cowry shells and *orixá* artifacts (for example, the mirrors of Oxum and Yemanjá, the sword of Ogum, and the bow and arrow of Oxóssi) abound in Didara's multicolored T-shirts, shoes, hats, bags, dresses, and long dashiki-style robes. Among the main consumers of these Afro objects are local musicians and performers, as well as African-American tourists. Both the store located at the airport of Salvador, as well as the one in Pelourinho, have become stopovers on the itinerary of roots tourists. Lopes's designs also adorn lobby banners in some of Bahia's most expensive hotels, such as those in Costa do Sauípe, and a mosaic created for Pestana Bahia hotel swimming pool. Interestingly, Lopes also designs uniforms for hotel employees, contributing to Bahia's aura of Africanness celebrated by the tourism industry. Commenting on her designs, the artist declared that her work's colors and themes are "tropical" and not just African, and that her work "indicates that the folks in Bahia want to return to their *ancestralidade*, yet keeping an eye on what is contemporary."[17]

When African-American tourists consume these Afro objects, it serves to further situate Bahia within the black Atlantic's web of circulation and communication. As a process influenced by the exchange of objects, symbols, and ideas, Afro-aesthetics in Brazil has been constantly re-created. While it is simultaneously influenced by the interpretation of symbols originating in Jamaica, the United States, and the African continent, Afro-aesthetics in Brazil, albeit to a lesser degree, also feeds the production of black beauty in the diaspora, as illustrated by African-American tourists who consume the Afro jewelry and Africanized clothing easily found in Pelourinho and the bayside market of Mercado Modelo. As I mentioned above, it does not matter whether these Afro clothes are tunics made by artisans from the northeastern state of Ceará or designs invented by Bahian seamstresses inspired by an African aesthetic.

The movement of people contributes to the movement of objects and ideas. When African American tourists arrive in Brazil seeking to enhance their blackness through the Africanness of Brazilian blacks (mainly those from Bahia), they are also exposing their own forms of Africanness to local people. Thus, African-American roots tourism also informs the creation of Afro-aesthetics in Brazil, representing a much updated reference source for the exchange and production of black objects. On the one hand, African American tourists provide a walking "shop window" onto the international black fashion world, and on the other hand, they purchase locally produced Afro-aesthetic objects and use them as part of their own blackening processes.

As merchandise that carries blackness, Afro objects in general and Afro hairstyles in particular are also consumed by white tourists, although one could also argue that the meanings attributed to these objects, as well as to blackness itself, are distinct from those conferred by black tourists or even by black cultural producers. An example of such a distinction is that white tourists use words such as *tribal*, *exotic*, and *different* to define the black look that many of them adopt during their vacation in Bahia. An article in the Brazilian magazine *Revista Veja* entitled "Everyone Is Afro" described the tendency of (white) tourists to braid their hair "Afro style" when visiting Bahia: "Mariana Triches, a 16-year-old from Santa Catarina [in southern Brazil], braided her long blonde hair in a French braid. 'I love the exotic look of black people,' she says. Dutchwoman Marielle Koop, 23 years old, adorned her hair with colorful beads, but she is not sure of the result. 'This hairdo seems to go better with black skin,' she admits."[18] The phenomenon of white tourists — usually from Europe and the United States — braiding their hair while on vacation is increasing, and not only in places with large black populations. There seems to be a correlation between tourists adopting black hairstyles and enjoying moments of playfulness, when they relax and feel distanced from the seriousness of life back home. The classification of life into the opposing binaries of ordinary/extraordinary and work/leisure must be analyzed in connection to the representations of whiteness and blackness disseminated by the tourism industry.[19]

Although initiated by activists and cultural producers concerned with generating racial consciousness, Afro-aesthetics in Brazil surpassed the boundaries of the black social movement, becoming a major reference of beauty for many nonmilitant blacks. One must avoid generalizations, however, and refrain from claiming that all blacks in Brazil use Afro-aesthetic elements to manipulate their appearance. The adoption of Afro-aesthetics varies according to factors such as gender, age, geographical location, and political engagement with the black social movement. Elderly black people, for the most part, feel more comfortable dressing conservatively, abiding by their own standards of what is beautiful and neat. On the other hand, people whose youth was marked by the Black Is Beautiful movement have more-Africanized beauty references. The youngest generation, heir to the ideals of Afro-aesthetics, yet strongly influenced by the movements of reggae and hip-hop, tend to combine dreadlocks and braids with baggy bottoms with low waistlines.

In terms of geographical location, blacks in Bahia are generally more likely to embrace Afro-aesthetics than, for example, those in São Paulo.

Recent governmental efforts have led to the establishment of a black official image for the state of Bahia, certainly contributing to a wider dissemination and perhaps acceptance of Afro-aesthetics in Salvador compared to other Brazilian capitals. Although this was done more for the sake of tourism and electoral purposes than to actually combat racism, the resulting association of Bahianness with blackness has favored the propagation of Afro-aesthetics. In contrast, São Paulo's public image is not as suitable for expanding black aesthetics, since it is commonly associated with work and seriousness, images that are frequently and not unintentionally counterposed with representations of a black and playful Bahia, which blends leisure, pleasure, and indolence.

Nevertheless, even in Bahia there are different levels of acceptance with regard to Afro-aesthetics, depending on the formality of the context. It is acceptable to wear braids or dreadlocks and colorful jewelry in the more informal workplaces of NGOs, for example, and for those who work in tourism or black cultural production, Afro-aesthetics is not only accepted but encouraged. Yet for those who work in banks, schools, government offices, and private companies, the norms of "good appearance" require a more conservative look, making dreadlocks, braids, colorful clothing, and big earrings seem out of place. The appropriateness of Afro-aesthetics is determined by its connection with exoticism and leisure, within a hierarchy that places work and seriousness at the top. Determining the place for Afro-aesthetics is, above all, determining the place of blackness in Brazilian society.

Perhaps the most important factor for the adoption of Afro-aesthetics is black political activism and social engagement. Afro-aesthetics plays a fundamental role in establishing diacritical symbols needed to reinforce racial or ethnic identities. In this sense, in addition to creating beauty references, Afro-aesthetics is also a realm for protesting racism and displaying black consciousness. The techniques for blackening the body's appearance, essence, and tendencies in Brazil are central to the process of becoming black. The creation of Afro-aesthetics in Bahia and in Brazil, as well as in other communities within the black Atlantic, is a crucial component of the movement through which blacks have taken control of the production of blackness.

From Stigma to Esteem

The pejorative ideas that have associated blackness with ugliness, dishonesty, and undesirable work, among other negative images, continue to be produced and disseminated, defining positive standards that are incompatible for those who have dark skin in the so-called racial democracy of Brazil. Recent research has demonstrated the harm these racist standards have on the self-image of blacks. As the work of Ronilda Ribeiro shows, the unfeasibility of achieving an impossible white standard of beauty affects more than one's self-esteem; it has negative social effects as well. "The obligations of defining an impossible ideal for the reality of one's own body and one's personal and ethnic history, leads to an unfavorable self-image and lowered self-esteem. . . . If this relationship is conflictive, rigid, and stereotyped, it will tend to build a distorted self-image that will seek refuge from its physical reality and stimulate mechanisms of negation and compensation incompatible with projects of personal and social fulfillment" (1996, 171).

There are many social action strategies geared toward eliminating racism. Some of the most important ones are the deconstruction of racist vocabulary and images, seminars and courses, educational materials, academic efforts, and the creation of alternative schools (Cunha Jr. 1996).[20] Olodum and Ilê Aiyê have developed all of these strategies with the intention of forming what they call "black citizens." Thus, the construction of cultural identity has become a strategy for reclaiming one's rights. Moreover, one must note that all the strategies above require the production of new representations of blackness. As Stuart Hall (1997a) has argued, representations are always relational and carry images and messages about those that are being represented, framing feelings, attitudes, and emotions, and mobilizing fears and anxieties. Representations are both concepts and practices that function as fundamental elements for constructing the cultural identities on which social movements are based. This means that in order to enter the public sphere and transform commonsense beliefs — whether to reclaim rights or combat racism — it is necessary to produce new representations or to resignify old ones.

The history of Afro-Brazilian culture has thus been reclaimed and inserted in a global context of expansion and plurality of African cultures, with the intention of projecting new images of blacks in society. This cultural and political process undoubtedly owes much to black organizations in Bahia as the producers of new representations of blackness. To Vovô, president and one of the founders of Ilê Aiyê, "the emergence of *blocos afro* and the reemergence of *afoxés* in the beginning of the 1970s greatly impacted racial relations in Bahia. They resulted in the creation of several black civil organizations . . . , but especially in a qualitative change in the self-image of many people in Bahia" (quoted in Fry et al. 1988, 233).

The need to create new images for blacks was a main concern for most black organizations in Brazil throughout the twentieth century. The beginning of this chapter outlined the efforts by the Frente Negra Brasileira in the 1930s to dissociate blacks from the negative images associated with indolence, filth, and alcoholism, which they felt ultimately hindered their entry into the labor market. When the ideal of integration was dominant within the Brazilian black movement, this concern was reflected in a conservative dress code intended to allow blacks to fit in. On the other hand, in the 1970s, the self-images produced by black organizations were following the dominant trend of affirming difference, which explains the emphatic use of diacritical Afro signs. To create new representations, black militants started searching in the emerging African nations for the images of blackness they desired, even though there was some difficulty in determining which African cultures should be exalted.

For Maria Angélica Maués (1991), the dress code that black militants adopted was meant to emphasize the contrast with whiteness. Ordinary black citizens, however, did not adopt this same motive and often did not relate to these colorful images or elaborate braids and dreadlocks. As I see it, this estrangement is probably greater among nonmilitant blacks in São Paulo or in the southern states of Brazil. Yet in Salvador, the image of blackness that emerged within militant groups spread to many spheres of the city, mainly disseminated by cultural entities, especially *blocos afro*. This has allowed Afro-aesthetics to become a fashion statement for young blacks, whether they are militants or not. Thus braids, caps, accessories, and many other Afro objects circulate as merchandise that render people who already have blackness inscribed in their color even blacker than before.

Christopher Dunn notes that the new Afro-aesthetics developed by the *blocos afro* gained popularity outside of Carnaval in Salvador. Contesting Da Matta's (1981) notion of Carnaval as a site of ritual inversion of roles, Dunn (1992, 12) notes that this concept cannot be applied to the context of the *blocos afro*, for it does not answer the important question of how to interpret Afro-Brazilians who masquerade as Africans in Bahia. There is, indeed, much in common between Carnaval costumes and everyday forms of dress for many Afro-Bahians. Instead of a clearly demarcated distinction between everyday wear and the sparkling Carnaval costumes, as DaMatta had argued, there is a continuum of Africanness between the two, even if the degrees of lavishness are different for each context.

Even though it might seem superficial, this changing image is not limited to an external transformation of individuals. Adoption of the new black aesthetics is related to a process of increasing the self-esteem of people who until recently were ashamed of their skin color and hair texture. While identifying oneself as black is a process that frequently produces stereotypes, it also involves a transformation that can be beneficial for individuals, as long as it functions as a means to seeing oneself in the world in a new light, and not as an endpoint in and of itself.

Brazilian blacks adopted the black power movement counter-discourse that used the body as a locus of protest, and despite the fact that black power is no longer in fashion, afros, braids, and dreadlocks are still frequently seen in big cities, in connection with the wide availability of synthetic hair — an important element of affirming blackness, regardless of its artificiality. However, despite the many battles and victories earned through body politics, the standards of beauty that reign in Brazil are still extremely Eurocentric and exclusionist.

A statement given by Ilê Aiyê singer Graça Onasilê, who wears long, beautiful dreadlocks, reveals the suffering endured by blacks as a result of such exclusionist beauty standards:

> When I was young, I used to live in an alley, a street with seven houses, and there was like a main gate, so I would go to the main gate to look out on the street, to watch the movement, to watch the cars, and even to watch the daughters of the white people who were strolling about, crossing streets, shaking their hair, which was different from mine. They had beautiful hair and pretty dolls, white dolls with green or blue eyes. They were different dolls, and it seems like this type of doll only existed for them. They made a point of going by like that, parading by, shaking their hair and all, but I always thought I'd never be able to have a doll like that, and even less so to be able to shake my hair. My hair was bad. That's how it was seen — *cabelo duro* ["hard hair" — that is, tough or coarse]! Many times I lost all my hair; I'd put on so much product to straighten it that my scalp would be damaged. I wanted to at least look like them, to have a good appearance.

Labeling black, kinky hair as "bad hair" — as opposed to whites' "good hair" — is another negative image of blacks that can be found in other countries that experienced slavery. For example, in Jamaica the Rastafari challenged "Babylon," the capitalist system based on slavery, racism, inequality, and poverty, by creating long dreadlocks; in the United States, afros emerged as a similar sign of defiance against the system, a voluminous hairdo as rebellious as the people sporting them. No wonder the expressions "bad hair" and "good hair" can be found in several parts of the diaspora, as well as on the African continent. In an article about hair politics in South Africa, Zimitri Erasmus (2000) explains that in colored communities (people with an intermediate racial type, neither black nor white), the notion of "good hair" refers to naturally or artificially straight hair. Thus it is possible to transform "bad hair" into "good hair," either through straightening irons or chemical products. In Brazil, the opposite occurs: straightening one's hair does not make it "good hair," but instead proves that the hair is "bad" or *duro* precisely because it needs to be straightened artificially.

The appearance of dreadlocks in Jamaica is one of the most famous examples of the creation of a new aesthetic reference meant to reverse the negative meanings attributed to kinky hair. Rastafarians confronted the dominant system by cultivating long and "dreadful" locks, challenging at once the idea that men's hair and bad hair should be cut short, and expressing that what is ugly for the Babylon system is beautiful within the Rastafarian philosophy. In Brazil, dreadlocks became a fundamental component of Afro-aesthetics. Together with other Jamaican symbols, such as the national colors and Bob Marley's face stamped on a great number of T-shirts, dreadlocks became a symbol of a globalized Africanness. Regardless of the fact that they did not originate from the African continent, these Jamaican signs of blackness are perceived to be loaded with Africanness, therefore confirming the transatlantic composition of objects created to imagine and feel Africa.

The black power movement in the United States also used hairstyling as a powerful symbol of rebelliousness when it introduced so-called afros. Worn by men and women alike, this hairstyle created a whole new aesthetics of black beauty that expanded beyond the country and traveled through the routes of the black Atlantic, arriving on new shores. In Brazil, these aesthetic elements intermixed in the late 1960s and early 1970s with a local trend among black activists and cultural producers to seek, in the emergent African nations, elements that would represent pride and dignity for Afro-descendents. The difficulty in determining which African nations or ethnicities should serve as cultural references for the creation of a new Afro-aesthetics in the diaspora dissolved into creative bouts of selecting, blending, and inventing elements that could produce beauty.

According to sociologist Erving Goffman (1963), society categorizes people and establishes traits for members of each category, then labels these traits as natural. The relationship between traits (generally physical) and stereotypes generates stigmas. There are several types of stigmas (physical abominations, vices, or deviant behavior, among others), but what is important for us here are the stigmas believed to be transmitted through lineage — such as ethnic, racial, and national — that likewise "contaminate" one's descendents. Society's attitudes toward stigmatized people prove they are seen as not entirely human. "By definition, of course, we believe the person with a stigma is not quite human. On this assumption, we exercise varieties of discrimination, which we effectively, if often unthinkingly, reduce his life chances. We construct a stigma-theory, an ideology to explain his inferiority" (1963, 5).

The affirmation of difference creates a fertile field for stigmatizing and for viewing the other — those who are seen as deviating from the standard — as impure. Paradoxically, this also helps make difference powerful and strangely attractive, precisely because it represents a taboo or threat to the cultural order. This power explains why black groups adopted the affirmation of difference to produce positive self-representations, within a process that began in the 1970s and which deeply marked the strategies of black organizations in several parts of the world, as we will see in more details in the next chapter. Despite the persistence of negative images of blackness in the collective Brazilian imaginary, antiracism organizations have fought representations that stigmatize Afro-descendants by producing new representations to feed their narratives.

The new black narratives represent a stance in the face of a collective imaginary that has always stigmatized blacks, confining them to pejorative stereotypes. Such narratives challenge the things that are said about blacks and create an alternative history to be told in the public domain. The process of substituting negative representations for positive ones has often required a reversal of the meanings attributed to blackness. The most emblematic example of this reversal lies within the field of aesthetics and beauty. Blacks' skin color, hair texture, and facial traits, previously considered ugly or a source of shame, have become beauty symbols and a source of pride. In Bahia, the *blocos afro* have been the main source of production and dissemination of the new and positive representations of blacks.[21] Young members' statements reflect the groups' efforts to increase self-esteem. After being exposed to the group's teachings for several years, one of the band leaders of Band'Aiyê stated, "Well, Ilê taught me how to be a citizen, to have self-esteem. That beforehand, I wasn't thinking anything, but here at Ilê, after some classes, after some lectures I went to . . . some things here taught me to think well, to think about myself and my black people. Because here, if it weren't for Ilê, many people would be lost, because they wouldn't have found their own identity. Ilê teaches many people how to say 'I'm a *negão.*'" One of the young Olodum conductors offers a similar reflection on the role of the *blocos afro* in building black self-esteem: "Before I started at Olodum, I got into a lot of trouble, I really couldn't care less. Then — and this actually makes me emotional when I talk about it — I became a member of Olodum, and my life changed. Ever since I started playing instruments and learning about the real history of blacks, my life only changed for the better. I am very grateful to Olodum for this."

Statements by young members of both groups reveal that the adoption of Afro-aesthetics has had a significant role in the way they see themselves, acting as a source of beauty and increased self-esteem:

"I like my hair because I always comb it and it looks good. I make braids, I make Rastafari in my hair. Then I like it."

"Do I think I'm pretty?! Oh yeah! I think I'm lucky. My color alone! I don't overrate it, but I know it has a lot of weight. I think it's fantastic. The fact that I'm the color that I am, and with the whole trajectory of my ancestors — this influences and enriches me. And my self-esteem goes even further. And I feel good about being who I am, for having the hair I have. I think this is very beautiful."

"I started braiding my hair after I entered Olodum's Creative School. I think braided hair is really the thing for blacks; it's really the thing for Pelourinho."

"Black women give themselves a boost by braiding their hair. It's much better than taking your hair, that God gave you, and applying a straightener that has nothing to do with blacks."

Commenting on the synthetic weaves used frequently by black women in Salvador, a young female member of Olodum stated, "It's not completely Rastafari, you know, but it's sort of Rastafari. When I walk down the street, people call me Rastafari. And I love it!"[22]

On the subject of Ilê Aiyê's efforts to increase self-esteem among children and adolescents, Jônatas Conceição da Silva, the coordinator of the group's Pedagogical Outreach Project, said, "The project aims primarily at this: First, to strengthen our educational structures, and second, to continue pushing the public educational system to see if teachers and even students themselves can learn a little more about African cultural tradition and can have access to new knowledge." Along the same lines, one of Ilê

Aiyê's composers, Juracy Silva, a high school philosophy teacher, explained the importance of creating new values and images for young black people raised in a predominantly Eurocentric environment:

So, in reality, up until a certain point, we blacks, including myself, we were not black, we were just black in terms of our skin color. See, I was raised since I was a little boy in the Greco-Roman [tradition]. We are Greeks from our toes all the way to our last strand of hair. So what happens? My upbringing, up until a certain point, was a white upbringing. Why? I, like most people, didn't see African culture anywhere or officially at school. The only culture that we saw, up until that point, was the model of white culture. So as a hominal [*sic*], as a construction — because if you look at it, man is a projection, a projection of what is constructed over time — as a construction, in reality, our construction up to a certain point is the construction of the model of white culture. At a certain point, we wake up through other people, or realize, or have a "eureka" moment, and then realize it's possible to construct life in a plural manner, and that this plurality, in this case, in my case, was borne from African culture. So then we started to notice that we, in addition to having this Eurocentric upbringing, that our origins, that our ancestry, is back there, in Africa. So from this moment on, in 1988, I started to discover this and then it really became so; I can say it's irreversible: I started to construct myself as black.

With this ideal in mind, Silva composed the song "Self-esteem, Dream of Liberation," in which he states that it is not necessary to say that black is beautiful, since that would be redundant:

Self-esteem: dream of liberation
Adoring your image black like that
Your image is your mirror, it is beautiful, adore it
"Black is beautiful" is redundant
"Black is beautiful" is exclusion
The label beautiful is redundant here
It's an exception, it's a wrong way street
Be the passion of your image
The lively twinkle of your being
Reflecting this image
In the African portrait of Ilê Aiyê
Adore your black image, go on

Your image is your mirror, it is beautiful
Afro Ilê is a big mirror
A big mirror for me
I love you, Ilê, as much as I love to live"[23]

While the *blocos afro* should definitely be credited for the positive impact of their cultural production on the new self-image of blacks in Bahia, this process has also been marked by control and surveillance strategies deemed necessary to guarantee a homogenous form of blackness. The internal fragmentations of identity groups have become the target of greater internal surveillance. For the most part, men have taken on the duty of managing the bodily appearance, essence, and tendencies of the members of the *blocos*. Commenting on the change imparted by the *blocos afro* with regard to images of blacks in Salvador, Osvalrísio do Espírito Santo, one of Ilê Aiyê's directors, stated,

> We started our citizenship work. For me this is the most important type of work — until we started the educational phase, that was it. Changing people, increasing self-esteem. First, telling women that they should be themselves, to dress like they wanted to, however they wanted, to even use African models, to stop straightening their hair. We caused huge losses, because many people were making a living from straightening hair, and now people don't do that anymore. Nowadays women can do whatever they want. Before, women were forced to straighten their hair; today they can straighten it if they want to, they can use a chemical straightener if they want to, shave their head if they want to. Because in the past a black woman with a shaved head would have to walk around with a turban because people would say she was being initiated into Candomblé, a religion which to this day suffers from discrimination. So even people who were in Candomblé didn't admit it, because they were seen as inferior, as belonging to an inferior religion. Nowadays, everything is changing. Women can wear their hair just like Ronaldinho and they're beautiful, and no one asks if they are going into Candomblé.[24] So all of that is the fruit of our labor of increasing awareness, self-esteem. There's no formula as to how this was done; we planned on doing it. We started practicing it in our community and all work has to be done within a community.

Although the statement above stresses women's right to choose, it is clear that they can choose from only a specific set of hairstyles deemed suitably black. Furthermore, the statement reveals an anxiety over women's bodies, while there is no mention of how men's bodies should be supervised. This is not to say that men's supposed appearance, essence, and tendencies are exempt from management, but they are certainly a much lesser target of policing. Despite affirming that there is no formula for how blackness should be correctly embodied, Espírito Santo clearly indicates that there is, indeed, a plan to be followed or, as Foucault (1988) would put it, a pedagogy to be internalized, especially as it pertains to the embodiment of a female form of blackness. Stressing that oppressed groups are not exempt from reproducing internal forms of domination, Seyla Benhabib (2002) asserts that men have predominantly defined, controlled, and policed the identity boundaries of the women, children, and youth of most societies.

In addition to responding to the surveillance of others, human beings also act upon their own bodies and souls with the intention of transforming themselves in the pursuit of happiness or perfection. Michel Foucault (1988, 16–18) coined the phrase "technologies of the self" to explain how individuals act—on their own or with the help of others—on their own bodies and souls by internalizing rules of conduct, behavior, self-control, and ways of being. The choices individuals make are intimately connected to what they learn to be "true" and "correct." In turn, truth is defined through "truth games," which are related to techniques that individuals use to understand and construct their selves. Acting upon our selves is as much about choice as it is about interdiction. Black individuals who have achieved "consciousness" view hair straightening with discomfort, as we saw in the statements of *bloco* members.

The idea that the black body must be recaptured from previous hegemonic representations imposed by others so that it can be transformed by blacks themselves can be compared to the 1970s second wave of feminism, when the female body was to be recovered from the male-dominated, scientifically oriented medical gaze. Notions of women's inferiority, passiveness, and status as objects would be transformed only when women took control of their bodies and the representations of their bodies (Thornham 2000). This "authentic delight in the body" (Barkty 1982, 138, quoted in Thornham 2000, 161), sprinkled with a dose of narcissism, has been advocated by feminists and black activists alike and has been considered crucial to the process of consciousness raising. This recapturing requires the existence of a "natural female body," or, respectively, of a "natural black body" which needs to be worked on if one is to achieve liberation. The evident risk is that it once again reduces women and blacks to their "natural bodies" as the foundation for authentic womanhood and blackness. Yet, we must remember that there is no authentic body which is prior to or disconnected from history. The body is produced within and by history. This contradiction between the need for culture as a means to transform the body as representation, and the belief that there is an a priori natural body to be found, seems to be rooted deeply in processes of reconstruction of identities. However, more than recognizing parallels between black and female oppression, it is necessary to analyze how gendered and racial dominations intersect (Carby 1982). Notions of "race" and blackness have always been constructed together with the production of gender and sexuality.

To defeat racism and create equality requires us to challenge Eurocentrism and overcome the undignified forms in which blackness has been represented. Yet it is quite striking that the fight against racism has been frequently disconnected from an awareness of the intrinsic relationship between "race" and gender. The *blocos'* antiracist discourse, played out in their social strategies and projects, has either left out or overlooked an analysis of gender. Not only do the *blocos* make few references to how racism affects men and women differently, but they also fail to question their own sexist practices. In this context, the female black body is still the preferred locus for performing the pedagogy of blackness. Ilê Aiyê's annual black beauty pageant, Black Beauty Evening (Noite da Beleza Negra), clearly illustrates this process. The pageant is one of the most important activities carried out by Ilê Aiyê to increase the self-esteem of black women. It debuted in 1980 and was heavily influenced by the American Black Is Beautiful movement of the previous decade.

Black Beauty Evening selects the *bloco*'s Carnaval queen. Contestants don outfits of African inspiration (fabric with geometric designs and colorful patterns) and wear hairdos also inspired by Mama Africa as they walk down the runway to the beat of drums. Participants must have black skin — the darker the better. In the beginning, Black Beauty Evening was held at the old Fantoches da Euterpe club, located in downtown Salvador. By the late 1980s, the festival had gained prestige and was moved to some of the city's more stylish locations, such as the Convention Center, sports clubs situated in Barra, and Aeroclube, a Miami-style seaside shopping mall that functions as a rendezvous for the elite of Salvador.

Black Beauty Evening is a key event for Ilê Aiyê. Carried out every January, it elects the next "Goddess of Ebony": that is, the young woman who shall reign during an entire year, representing Ilê Aiyê at all the *bloco*'s presentations with her blackness, beauty, grace, and *ginga* (bodily rhythm, also called *gingado*), starting with Carnaval. At the conclusion of several preliminary stages, approximately 14 finalists dance in front of an enthusiastic audience and a focused jury. An emcee exalts the "qualities of black women," employing a discourse that mixes protests against the reality of poverty and struggle of most black women and praise for their natural traits as sensual warrior women, gifted with the best *ginga* in Brazil.[25] In several of their songs, the group providing musical accompaniment exalts the "inherent sensuality" of black women: "Your body can move and sway, braided black woman, you drive me crazy. I want to see your black body at Ilê Aiyê."[26]

Ilê Aiyê's beauty pageant is intended to increase black women's self-esteem and dissociate their image from the myth of the sexy *mulata*, the kind who is seen as always willing to wait on white men at their tables and beds. What is noticeable about the candidates is the deliberate absence of sexual appeal; at no moment are their bodies erotically exhibited or exploited. Contrary to other female beauty pageants, in which there is always a swimsuit segment, during Black Beauty Evening young women compete against each other in African-style outfits, displaying elaborate hairdos and an array of colorful accessories, but never explicitly exposing their bodies. Their dances are a far cry from the hip-swaying women in samba groups from Rio de Janeiro, who are obnoxiously called "*mulatas* for export." Contestants' body movements are based on Candomblé steps, mixed with recreated African tribal dances. According to Aliomar Almeida, one of the directors and vice president of Ilê Aiyê, "Here we instituted a black beauty contest precisely to show off what blacks have. Beauty is not only found in an hourglass figure. So we wanted to show women's black beauty through traditional outfits, dance, *gingado*, motion, [and the] original black features: thick lips, meaty lips, noses that aren't so thin—that's the beauty of black people."

Analyzing the phenomenon of the "inculturated" Mass (Missa Afro) created by progressive Catholic priests with the goal of celebrating the participation of Afro-Brazilians in the church and elevating the self-esteem of black women in Brazil, John Burdick identifies a similar situation of control and surveillance over women's bodies. He contends that, despite its good intentions, the Missa Afro extends and deepens the definition of the female body as a site of male pleasure, spectacle, and desire. Akin to the Black Beauty Evening, the Missa Afro challenges the hyper-valuing of whiteness while preserving the notion that women's bodies are the source for the discovery of women's value. "The logic of ethnic politics is the logic of women's bodies serving as vehicles for drawing black men back from white women, and for reproducing and strengthening the black 'race,' through fertility and the family" (1998, 21). Similar to the work carried out by the *blocos afro*, one of the main objectives of the activity of the Missa Afro developed by Pastoral Negra is "to teach blacks about themselves, about their own history, about their own values and the values they have for themselves" (57), as expressed by one of its lay leaders.

Despite the fact that Ilê Aiyê's beauty pageant does not eroticize its contestants' bodies, it still demands that women's bodies continue to be the repositories of the principles of ethnic obedience, obligation, and duty. As Gilroy (2000, 83) explains, minority groups have increased their production of ethnic absolutisms by grounding their "camp mentalities" on the lore of blood, bodies, and fantasies of absolute cultural identity.[27] Their response to the threat of internal fragmentation requires that women's bodies be offered up to the reproduction of ethnic purity. It is no wonder that in Ilê Aiyê's beauty contest, "the darker the better." The practice of choosing the darkest candidate was not invented by Ilê Aiyê. In the 1940s, the Black Experimental Theater held beauty pageants in which "the directors of these competitons would choose the darkest women in the black community, in an effort to counteract the brainwashing of Brazil's white aesthetic" (Davis 1999, 197). Women's bodies, both in Ilê Aiyê's and in TEN's beauty pageants, are not as sexualized as the bodies of the stereotypical *mulatas*, but they nevertheless continue to be objects onto which men — in this case, especially the group's leaders — project images and impose their ideologies. After all, why should beauty be a female trait?

The black beauty pageants developed by several of Bahia's *blocos afro*, the Missa Afro, the glossy pages of *Revista Raça*, and the countless Afro products marketed to enhance the beauty of black women are part of a wider struggle to replace stigma with esteem. Yet these strategies sustain problematic constructions of black womanhood centered on the female body as a site of male pleasure. They also all circulate sweeping notions of African culture and promote black women's bodies as repositories of this culture. Akin to the creators of the *blocos*' beauty pageants, those who conceived the Missa Afro contend that black women's bodies are natural containers of *axé* (magic energy central to Candomblé beliefs), which should overflow through their dance and *ginga* (Burdick 1998, 90–91). As carriers of a generic black culture, and subjected to the surveillance of the black male gaze, the value of black women's bodies is to be found as much in its appearance (beauty) as in its natural tendencies to dance and radiate *ginga*.

The Constraints of Inventing Blackness

A transnational black aesthetics emerged in response to a dominant white standard of beauty, feeding the production of counter-discourses of blackness by black groups in the diaspora. This became a political stance for confronting collective imaginaries that had confined blacks in stereotypes and for creating new narratives to be told in the public sphere. The production of Afro-aesthetics in Brazil, therefore, arose within a wider movement of black self-affirmation in many other parts of the world. Adopting a new Afro-referenced look plays an important role in the process of producing beauty and dignity. Although the changes in self-image may seem superficial, their meaning extends beyond the mere external transformation of an individual's appearance, as they have the power to recover self-respect for people who learned to feel ashamed of their bodies. To become black, therefore, is a means of elevating self-esteem and restoring dignity. But it also confirms that blackness itself is produced, rather than inherent.

In the 1980s blacks significantly increased their production of representations of blackness. The question of representation has become, more than ever, a realm for struggle and protest, giving birth to what can be called a "politics of representation" (Hall 1997a). Despite the fact that the politics of representation have served to increase affirmation of blackness and the self-esteem of young blacks in several parts of the world, they have also helped reinforce old stereotypes and create new stereotypes about blacks. The biggest problem in the production of stereotypes is that they reduce people to a small set of characteristics understood as fixed and as part of the essence of those who are represented. Stereotypes place an exaggerated focus on a few characteristics of a given group, while at the same time reducing this group to these characteristics, which are overexaggerated so as to be easily recognized and static, as if they were incapable of transformation. For Hall, "Stereotyping reduces, essentializes, naturalizes, and fixes difference" (1997a, 258).

The production of stereotypes also reveals the context of profound inequalities of power in which the represented people are inserted, and it can be understood as what Foucault (1980) called the "power/knowledge" game, since it classifies subjects according to the norms and constructs of discursive and hegemonic power, which operates through culture, production of knowledge, and bodily discipline. The circulation of stereotypes, even the supposedly positive ones or those created out of black identity narratives, ends up confirming a position of inferiority, since whites remain as the neutral standard that does not need stereotyping. "The problem with the positive/negative strategy is that adding positive images to the largely negative repertoire of the dominant regime of representation increases the diversity of the ways in which 'being black' is represented, but it does not necessarily displace the negative. Since the binaries remain in place, meaning continues to be framed by them. The strategy challenges the binaries, but it does not undermine them" (Hall 1997a, 274).

I certainly do not intend to deny the importance of the work carried out by black organizations to elevate self-esteem. I believe that self-esteem and self-image exert significant influence on the spheres of economic, social, and political power and should therefore be considered fundamental elements of social transformation.[28] I also believe that to this day, social sciences have not given due value to the issue of self-esteem, which has been analyzed almost exclusively as an object of psychology, probably because it is still considered something individual and few sociologists or anthropologists have realized its social impact (Ribeiro 1996; 1999a; 1999b). The same happens with the study of beauty in the Brazilian social sciences. Insufficient attention has been paid to studying it in relation to power, especially within the production of a specifically black kind of beauty created to reverse the dominant negative images of blackness. By creating new forms of beauty, Afro-aesthetics has contested mainstream values and prevailing Eurocentric standards, confirming that beauty itself is constantly being created and transformed through the production of new representations. In that sense, the study of beauty should consider how it works — both internally, in the self-esteem of individuals, and externally, in terms of producing new representations and concepts.

However, one must consider how the terms *self-esteem* and *beauty* have been used, and for what purposes. In Brazil, both terms have become easy slogans for commercial purposes and electoral campaigns.[29] If the meaning of self-esteem is confined to the surmounting stigmas within isolated groups in a fragmented humanity, the term will continue to be co-opted by the market as an easy slogan or become just a therapeutic solution, limited to individuals or segregated groups. The banalization of the term, as well as its appropriation by the government, the media, and the market, have transformed its meanings and reduced its political power, since they even determine what is necessary for someone to be able to increase their self-esteem, defined generally by the capitalistic ideals of possessing material goods, status, and beauty.[30]

Just as it adopted the defense of difference, the Brazilian Right also incorporated an appealing and sympathetic theme of self-esteem into its discourses. This reveals an attempt to resolve conflicts within a liberal order that aims at convincing the excluded that they participate in the division of power. Wendy Brown (1995) clarifies this when she states that the formation of subjects and categories (blacks, women, and homosexuals, among others) in liberal societies demands an artificial development of self-esteem, because it is inserted within the orders of regulation, exploitation, and domination. "It registers the possibility of generating one's capacities, one's self-esteem, one's life course, without capitulating to constraints by particular regimes of power. But in so doing, contemporary discourses of empowerment too often signal an oddly adaptive and harmonious relationship with domination insofar as they locate an individual's sense of worth and capacity in the register of individual feelings. . . . Indeed, the possibility that one can feel empowered without being so forms an important element of legitimacy for the antidemocratic dimensions of liberalism" (Brown 1995, 22–23).

And in light of this, one must ask: to what extent can increased self-esteem — within an order of regulation, exploitation, and domination — transform the ruling power if it uses promotional strategies that reinforce stereotypes? Increased self-esteem can only enact transformation if it values the connection between the individual and society, the individual and history, the individual and the world. The promotion of black beauty and increased self-esteem can be radically liberating for the individual if they are capable of transforming the collective sphere, both by transgressing racist standards imposed as universal and by liberating the black body from new ethnic tasks or racial impositions.

As long as they are informed by raciology, the strategies employed by oppressed groups to elevate the self-esteem of children and youth will contribute to the goal of enhancing identity boundaries rather than overcoming racial barriers. As a result, identity projects continue to set groups apart from one another, further distancing them from the prospect of an inclusive understanding of humanity. Instead of simply elevating self-esteem of one or another group, or contenting ourselves with temporary comforts or therapeutic solutions, we can seek to recover the human dignity that has been so violated throughout the enduring history of colonialism and racism. By revisiting this pain, humiliation, and loss of dignity we can help create a planetary humanism, an idea powerful enough to make solidarities based on cultural — and especially racial — particularities seem insignificant (Gilroy 2000).

Certainly, there have been fundamental changes in the ways blackness has been understood and felt. The struggles of black movements and organizations all over the world have led to significant gains and have turned negative images into positive ones. The production of new representations of blackness has played a significant role in this reversal, stimulating feelings and attitudes and mobilizing fears and anxieties (Hall 1997a). Afro-aesthetics has thus been one of the major realms for the production of new representations of blackness, reversing the injurious meanings previously attributed to skin color, hair texture, and facial features into signifiers of beauty and pride. Nevertheless, despite their good intentions, such attempts to reverse the meanings of blackness have not been able to surpass the boundaries imposed by binary oppositions (Hall 1997b). These oppositions are still a cruel and reductive way of representing blacks and establishing meanings. "They seem to be represented through sharply opposed, polarized, binary extremes — good/bad, civilized/primitive, ugly/excessively attractive, repelling because different/compelling because strange and exotic. *And they are often required to be both things at the same time!*" (Hall 1997b, 229, emphasis in original).

Based on an idealized and exotic ideal of Africa, Afro-aesthetics runs the risk of reproducing the exoticism often attributed to blackness. We must keep in mind that the concept of blackness — or the supposedly objective and subjective characteristics attributed to blacks — was initially a product of slavery and colonization. In its embryonic stage, this blackness was conceived as exotic, in all of its various meanings: mysterious, curiously interesting, but at the same time bizarre, strange, alien, and abnormal (Hall 1997b). However, narratives produced by black cultural movements to reverse the pejorative meanings of blackness frequently help reinforce the exoticism associated with blackness and Africanness. One way they do this is by expecting that all blacks will identify themselves with the ideals of not only beauty, but especially of blackness, disseminated by Afro-aesthetics, in such a way as to fit into the new positive categories established to define blacks. These categories generally include the stereotypes connected to physical abilities that propagate the notion that blacks are naturally predisposed toward sports, dance, and music. Such ideas are frustrating for those who lack these gifts and are simultaneously dismissive of the hard work others have invested in the development of these abilities, by not acknowledging the effort and training they put into them.

These new ideals of blackness also demand that black individuals correspond to Afro-aesthetics, requiring them to adopt it in their lives, "dressing as blacks" and wearing black hairstyles, offering definitions of right and wrong and functioning as forms of self-regulation. By asserting, for example, that straightening one's hair implies the desire to whiten oneself and therefore a lack of racial consciousness, Afro-aesthetics can become an obligation instead of the liberating project it was intended to be, leaving little freedom for those who desire non-prescribed forms of blackness. Moreover, if Afro-aesthetics can function as an obligation for those of dark skin, it can also be a prohibition for those of light skin. At the very least it may seem unsuitable, since many believe that braids, dreadlocks, and colorful clothes do not "match" whites or light-skinned *mestiços*. Consequently, Afro-aesthetics ends up producing its own normativity. Meanwhile, the project of developing antiracist education, as proposed, for example, by the *blocos afro* through their strategies for social action, is challenged by the requirement that people behave according to what is supposedly inscribed within their bodies.

Just like the old racial theories of the nineteenth century, which represented the body as the undeniable proof of difference, transforming it into the discursive locus through which much racialized thought was produced and circulated, Afro-aesthetics also uses the body to reconstruct blackness and essentialize contrast, thus confirming the notion of an insurmountable difference forever dividing blacks and whites.

As expressed in the interviews with *bloco afro* members, the imposition of a racial pedagogy is much greater for women and youth. Many black women in Brazil, especially those with ties to black groups or organizations, feel policed if they decide to straighten their hair once in a while, and they are frequently accused of denying their natural blackness or of wishing to whiten themselves. Commenting on the policing of hair straightening in South Africa and the United States, Zimitri Erasmus contends that by counterposing "natural/authentically black" hair with "artificial" or "whitened" hair, we are again limiting black bodies to binary oppositions. "One cannot deny that hair-straightening as a practice has been shaped by colonial racist notions of beauty. However, the notion that straightening one's hair is a mark of aspiring toward whiteness and that we should thus abandon it misses the complexity of this [important] black cultural practice. It also represents a simplistic and false binary: black women who straighten

their hair are reactionary / black women who do not are progressive"
(2000, 385).

Moreover, all hair is managed to a certain extent, even styles that have a more "natural" appearance. Dreadlocks, considered in Brazil to be the most "natural" black hairstyle, require many hours of meticulous labor twisting the locks with beeswax or other natural substances. In addition, there are various styles of dreadlocks now, and some are so "neat" that they need to be constantly retouched either in hair salons or with special products that are "less natural" than the symbolic and aromatic beeswax. If, on the one hand, these sophisticated dreadlocks displease the more orthodox Rastafarians, on the other hand they prove that rules can be broken, creating infinitely creative forms of blackness. Afros, another emblematic example of natural black hair, also require a lot of work and dedication. The time spent first detangling and then pulling hair upwards with a metal comb to give it a perfectly round shape confirms how much this "natural" look is a result of constant effort and care. The use of specific products, such as hairspray, and certain tricks, such as trimming the hair every two weeks to preserve its round shape, are other artifices to maintain the "naturalness" of the Afro look.

Social practices enacted on the body play a fundamental role in the perpetuation of identities and the preservation of traditions, no matter how invented these may be. It is therefore necessary to analyze not only inscribed traditions, but most of all traditions that have been literally embodied in the process of the formation of a collective identity (Connerton 1989). The process of constructing identities using codes of behavior based on bodily appearance entails specific forms of individual and collective regulation. Adopting an Afro-aesthetics in Brazil means more than just confronting the supremacy of white standards of beauty. It is also a way of reinforcing a contrastive and oppositional racial identity in a society that celebrates miscegenation. Adorning the body with elements of Afro-aesthetics is a way of becoming blacker, by emphasizing the blackness believed to be innate to the body. But as we have discussed above, blackness is not innate. If we recall the central role played by colonization and slavery in inventing "races" and molding what we today label *blackness*, the horrors implied by this process may lead us to do more than turn blackness into a positive sign. We can seek to reclaim the condition of humanity that has been fragmented and suppressed among those whom history has defined as black.

Rather than striving to reinscribe Africa on the body, it is probably more liberating to follow a wandering path through the multiple channels of communication and interaction of the black diaspora. As we widen our horizons, ethnic absolutisms — constructed out of uniform definitions of blackness and shaped by unicentered notions of Africanness — become unappealing. The compelling epigraph that opens this chapter might inspire us to opt for boundless and open-ended routes through which the African diaspora can work as a seed in the body. In this way, we could conceive of the Afro-aesthetics created in Brazil as one among many fruits or flowers emerging from that seed. We could then discover how scattered seeds spread around the fertile grounds of the imagination obey no predetermined pattern, flourishing into infinite colors, smells, and forms.

CHAPTER FOUR

Africa in the Soul

When identity refers to an indelible mark or code somehow written into the bodies of its carriers, otherness can only be a threat. *Identity is latent destiny.* Seen or unseen, on the surface of the body or buried deep in its cells, identity forever sets one group apart from others who lack the particular, chosen traits that become the basis of typology and comparative evaluation. No longer a site for the affirmation of subjectivity and autonomy, identity mutates. Its motion reveals a deep desire for mechanical solidarity, seriality, and hypersimilarity. The scope for individual agency dwindles and then disappears. People become bearers of the differences that the rhetoric of absolute identity invents and then invites them to celebrate. Rather than communicating and making choices, individuals are seen as obedient, silent passengers moving across a flattened moral landscape toward the fixed destinies to which their essential identities, their genes, and the closed cultures they create have consigned them once and for all.

— Paul Gilroy, *Against Race*

In the struggle against the racist forms through which black peoples have been defined, the body has been used to produce new and dignified representations of blackness. The manipulation of appearance with the goal of "blackening" the body and the adoption of diacritic symbols that reinforce the connection with Mama Africa have been important components in the process of constructing black identities. While I previously emphasized the meanings attributed to the "external," or to appearance, in this chapter I examine the meanings given to the "internal," or the supposed essence of the black body. The myth of Mama Africa encompasses the idea that for a black appearance there is a corresponding black essence, and that there are characteristics considered to naturally belong to black people, such as rhythm and aptitude for music and dance. I argue that by taking nature — defined here as the combination of appearance and essence — as blacks' main form of identification, and by disseminating the notion that "black tendencies" are transmitted by blood, the importance of culture for understanding the construction of black identity is undermined. Thus, even though it is culturally constructed, racial identity is seen as something natural and inherited — something that cannot be taken away, just like the very phenotypic factors used in its construction. In this sense, the powerful notion that it is necessary to "become black," so crucial to antiracist social movements, is threatened by the contradictory belief that one needs to reclaim tendencies that are innate to the body. Grounded on the idea of "race," body-centric identities employ techniques of subjectification to police the artificial boundaries built around cultures.

Blood and Boogie

Following the logic of Simone de Beauvoir's claim that "one is not born, but rather becomes a woman" (1993 [1953]), there is a general consensus within the current Brazilian black movement that individuals "become black" in the sense that they go through a process of awakening to and thus assuming their blackness. When interviewed, many members of *blocos afro* in Salvador indicated the close connection between joining the groups and beginning to see themselves as blacks. Even the youngest members revealed an awareness of this connection, and many stated that they only discovered themselves to be black when they joined Ilê Aiyê or Olodum. A young member of Olodum stated, "Before studying here [with Olodum] I considered myself to be white; now that I'm studying here, now I know I'm black." Similar statements were made by Ilê Aiyê youths:

"I came here [to Ilê Aiyê] because I liked it, because I thought it was a beautiful race. I came here to learn what race I belong to. For me, Ilê brought many things; it taught me what my race is like, because I didn't know what I was like — oh no! People would say, 'You're *morena*, you're not black.' After I started with Ilê I came to learn that my race is black."

"I'm not going to lie; I was like that. If someone called me black, I didn't like it. I'd tell them I was *morena*, or whatever, that I didn't like it. After I joined this school, I started to think and learn about many things. Today I make it a point to know, to learn things that I didn't like before. I'm very grateful to Mother Hilda, Vovô, and my teacher, because she taught me many things."

If in the discourse of the young *bloco* members the relationship between joining the *bloco* and becoming black is explicit, interviews with producers of this discourse reveal the extent to which it is intentional and necessary to "develop a black racial awareness" by "working the minds" of those who consider themselves to be *morenos* or *mulatos*, so that they will become black.[1] When discussing the selection process by which Ilê Aiyê decides who is sufficiently black to participate in the *bloco*'s parade, Osvalrísio, one of the directors, remarked,

I define as black all of the people who have some link with African ancestry, whatever that link may be. Now, there are those Afro-descendants with lighter skin, and their minds tell them what they are. . . . Here at Ilê Aiyê, after some years, about seven years, we started to adopt the policy that when people come to register at the *bloco* headquarters, when we interview them, we ask, "Why do you want to participate [with the *bloco* in the Carnaval parade]?" And when the person would say, "I want to participate because I'm black, my father's black, my grandmother was black, my hair's like this but my grandfather was black and so forth," there were never any problems. Now, when even people with darker skin come to us asking, "Can I participate with my color?" then that person is going to be worked on first so he knows what color he really is.

Like gender identity, blackness is not innate: it has to be acquired. It is a project which entails the acquisition of skills. The premises put forward by

Judith Butler in explaining the experience of "becoming a woman" can be applied to the process of "becoming black," since both are processes of constructing the self: "Gender must be understood as a modality of taking on or realizing possibilities, a process of interpreting the body, giving it cultural form. . . . To be a woman is to become a woman . . . an active process of appropriating, interpreting, and reinterpreting received cultural possibilities" (1998, 31). In a similar vein, Afro-Brazilian psychoanalyst Neusa Santos Souza, author of *Tornar-se Negro* [To Become Black], explains, "To be black . . . is to become aware of the ideological process that, through a mythical discourse about one's self, generates a structure of unawareness that imprisons the individual in an alien yet recognizable image. To be black means to claim this awareness and create a new one that reasserts respect for differences and dignity free of any type of exploitation. Thus, to be black is not an a priori condition. It is something you become. To be black is to become black" (1983, 77). An interview with Graça Onasilê, an Ilê Aiyê singer, sheds much light on the role of black culture in the process of becoming black, which she describes as a rebirth. She started following Candomblé shortly after she joined Ilê Aiyê and cites these two entities as fundamental to her process of becoming black:

> When I joined the *bloco*, they were talking about Senegal. I learned the dialects, the culture, and everything about Senegal. And in my first year with Ilê Aiyê, I traveled to Palmares, then I participated in the recording of the album. I traveled to Rio, then I was chosen to represent Bahia in Nice, France, and things just started happening. And since '88, Graça really was born with a race, with a people, with an identity, and with a very big mission. So I will never forget this: That Ilê Aiyê provided and provides me with a family and my people. That my [biological] family also did not have any knowledge. It is only through Graça and Ilê Aiyê that today my family is also black. So much so that this second family I adopted, my *mãe-de-santo*, who supported and supports me morally, spiritually, physically, tenderly, I think this mother, after God, is above all else—even above my work, because she was able to take care of me at the moment when I most needed it and gave me another life, a plentiful one, with respect—a spiritual life. I didn't want to have anything to do with this; I thought it was all nonsense. Taking a leaf, rubbing a leaf in water and bathing in the juices of that leaf, that it'd have some effect—I thought this was nonsense. Spending money to buy a candle, light it, watch it burn—I thought that was nonsense. To worship a [*pause*] to kneel in

front of a person who was there dancing — all of this was nonsense to me. I usually say in interviews that before joining Ilê Aiyê, I didn't have an identity; I had worked since I was a child with the community, but I had never heard anyone talk about prejudice at all. Not racial! Least of all racial. Everybody was the same!

The powerful concept of rebirth to express the process of rediscovering one's blackness in a new and positive light has also been employed in other parts of the African diaspora. Commenting on black characters in her novel *Praisesong for the Widow*, who were forced to disdain black culture in order to ascend socially, bell hooks explains that their self-esteem could only be recovered through a process of "reawakening" to their culture. To reclaim love for oneself it is necessary to "be born again," which entails relearning the past, assuming one's ancestry, and "helping other black folks to decolonize their minds" (1992, 19).

If a racist culture originally invented blackness as dreadful, only a renewed set of cultural representations can transform the meanings of blackness. Accordingly, every interviewee emphasized the importance of culture — whether understood as a set of symbols or as a way of life — to the experience of resignifying blackness, revealing that "becoming black" is a process steeped in dynamism and reflexivity. However, this description was, more often than not, intertwined with static notions of blackness, revealing the belief in a supposed African essence of black people. When members of the *blocos* were asked about what constitutes blackness or being black, most interviewees — both discourse producers and discourse interlocutors — stated that among the main characteristics, the natural abilities to dance and produce music were the inarguable and unquestionable determinants of blackness.

Kwame Anthony Appiah explains that the essentialism present in ethnic identities is the result of racialism: that is, the view that "there are heritable characteristics, possessed by members of our species, which allow us to divide them into a small set of races, in such a way that all the members of these races share certain traits and tendencies with each other that they do not share with members of any other race. These traits and tendencies characteristic of a race constitute, on the racialist view, a sort of racial essence" (1992, 13). The basic difference between racism and racialism is that the former uses the notion of "race" to harm certain human beings, while the latter is generally a component of discourses for forming and affirming identities of disadvantaged social groups. The doctrine of racialism also argues that each race's essential hereditary characteristics are responsible for more than visible morphologic characteristics (color, hair, features), determining predispositions and tendencies as well.

Black's supposed natural characteristics were the first factors used for determining the limits that separate blacks from whites, and in fact so-called racial attributes were the main artifices used for legitimizing the domination and subjugation of black groups in many parts of the world during the centuries of enslavement of Africans. However, if natural characteristics were used to justify the notion of black inferiority, they are also the ones which are now infused with new meanings and used by black movements to construct their ethnic identities. As a defensive reaction against a practice that subjugated and underestimated blacks in the many societies where they were introduced as slaves, black organizations have confirmed the biological grounds of "race" that feed their identity narratives. Thus, the combination of supposedly black appearance, essence, and tendencies act as a source for the reconstruction of blackness.

Commenting on the differences in the dance and musical abilities among lighter and darker young *bloco* members, Aliomar Almeida, one of Ilê Aiyê's directors, stated, "In terms of playing drums, usually black boys do better, because white boys in the beginning are a little . . . until they start to assimilate the discourse, until they perceive that they're also involved, sometimes it takes time. But we have some much lighter boys who thought they were white and who did very well, and [are now] good musicians. Not the female dancers [though]; we don't really invest a lot in lighter dancers, only in the black ones." Following the same logic of associating appearance with tendencies, most of the young people in the *blocos* stated that blacks had more *gingado* (rhythm, swing) and that they had more talent for dance and music—or at least for those types of dance and music considered "black," as was expressed by several youths:

"The lighter girls have a hard time learning the steps."

"Now for dancing you have to have *gingado*; if your body's stiff you're not going anywhere."

"It's easier for black women to learn the steps. Since that other one is white, it's a bit harder for her—a bit complicated, because black people already have a bit more inspiration."

"Percussion is for black people. Piano and guitar are more for white people."

"I think that blacks don't have the feet for ballet. Well, dancing is dancing, but I don't think it seems right for a black to do it, I don't know if that's because of upbringing, you know. I'll watch a ballet, but if it's a black ballet, I don't know."

This firm belief that black people have inherent abilities that whites lack and are less prevalent among lighter-skinned individuals is coupled with the notion that there are innate black male talents (e.g., playing drums) and innate black female talents (e.g., dancing). If young *mulato* men do not play the drums as well as darker ones, at least they can be "worked on" to achieve improvement. Black girls and adolescents, on the other hand, have the natural ability to dance, but there seems to be no chance of progress for those girls who are not "dark enough." Entrenched in a natural world, only black male talents can be (at least to a certain extent) learned or developed, while talents considered female are either present or absent from birth, revealing the widespread belief that women are closer to nature. Incapable of transcendence, black girls are thus destined to immanence; they are passive, static, and self-immersed, merely enacting the abilities to which they were conditioned by men. The notion that "the blacker the girl, the more she can dance" is consistent with Ilê Aiyê's preference for dark-skinned female dancers who are placed in very visible positions during the *bloco*'s performances.

In addition to being circumscribed by gender, these "natural aptitudes" are believed to be transmitted by blood, as expressed in the following statements from Ilê Aiyê discourse producers. Alioma Almeida stated, "But [even] if they were raised in different environments, it's obvious that a black man or a black woman is going to have a lot more *ginga* [swing], because it's in the blood, you see? . . . Now, for example, I have a niece who's the daughter of one of my brothers, she's a year and three months old — music plays on the radio and the girl starts to sway. . . . The thing about this type of dancing is already in the rhythm. I mean, it's in the blood." Graca Onasilê commented, "It has to be in the blood, you know, because talent can be discovered, but a gift is something you're born with." Osvalrísio do Espirito Santo, another discourse producer, recalled, "During Carnaval [one time] our theme was 'An African Nation Called Bahia,' and we portrayed blacks from Bahia, the religion, the *orixás*, things from Bahia. This runs in the blood. Ilê Aiyê didn't create this — oh no. This runs in black people's blood."

Even when blood as container of culture is recognized to be a metaphor, and not a literal statement, the essentialist understanding of blackness is not abandoned. In the following interview with Osvalrísio do Espirito Santo, one of Ilê Aiyê's directors, the difference between blacks and whites is compared to the distinctions between a dog and a sheep:

> Because there are certain things that we say are in the blood. It's not that they're in the blood, but it's just the way you are, the way you walk. It's like trying to get a dog to walk just like a cat. They're raised together, so the habits might be similar, but they're not the same. . . . I went to a farm one day, and when the guy opened the gates so I could get in he was on a horse, and four dogs and a sheep were accompanying him. The dogs were barking and jumping up and down and the sheep was jumping up and down—it wasn't barking but it was jumping around just like the dogs. Because the sheep was raised with the dogs. The dogs were already grown, and the sheep was what—probably eight months to a year old—and it was imitating the way the dogs came out jumping up and down—the jumping, but not the barking. So that might be what's happening; white girls might have the desire, they might be doing something similar, but it's not the same. So in terms of performance in dance school, black girls perform Afro dance better.

The belief that blacks' natural tendencies are transmitted by blood is widespread in Brazilian common sense, and is especially prominent during Carnaval. Every year, Rede Globo actresses who are invited to participate in the samba school parades make the same types of observations. One model announced to a television reporter, "We have to learn in a few days what black women are born knowing how to do. For blacks and *mulatas*, samba is in the blood. They have a *gingado* that's uniquely theirs."[2] Certain black samba-school dancers have confirmed this notion of natural tendencies: "We black women perform better because we have more endurance and because we have more fire in our bellies"; "It's rarer for a white woman to have swing, but they also put on quite a show"; "We're the queens of *gingado* and the muses of Carnaval. The entire country should recognize this."[3]

In Brazil, the myth that black blood is "stronger" has become widespread because blacks have been historically represented as being closer to nature. It is believed that blacks are naturally stronger and physically hardier than whites. This racist representation is a legacy from slavery, when blacks performed tasks that required great physical strength: that is, tasks that should have been assigned to draft animals. "The popular idea persists that blacks 'have stronger blood' and that they extract from the forces of the species' heritage and from their inner strength a longevity that life denies to the white man: 'light skin, thin blood'" (Brandão 1989, 17). The myth about the strength of black blood is also transposed to another liquid produced by the human body: black women's breast milk. Throughout slavery, the masters' white babies were breastfed by black wet nurses, not only to allow more leisure time for their biological mothers but also because it was believed that black women's milk was "strong" and that it would better nourish those who drank it. The idea of blacks' superior physical endurance and hardiness is also confirmed in the proverb "*negro quando pinta, três vezes trinta*" (roughly, "when blacks dye their hair, they're three times thirty"), referring to the belief that black people's hair turns white at a later stage in life. This is another example of the dehumanization of blackness, since it implies that blacks don't grow old and are therefore always fit for work. According to Carlos Rodrigues Brandão (1989), this is a "compensatory view" of blacks, as if nature were externally correcting, through appearance, black people's faults, which lie internally in their supposed essence.

The value conferred upon blood as the transmitter of tendencies and characteristics of a certain group has been a central factor in the imagination of many groups throughout the history of humankind. Paul Connerton (1989) illustrates the importance given to genealogy and blood in the ceremonies in which the body plays a central role. European nobility, for example, believed that some qualities—such as behavior, table manners, and the use of silverware—were exclusive to those with "blue blood." Thus, an ethereal and yet distinctive characteristic is attributed to a bodily element. Similarly, the discourse about "black tendencies" presupposes that qualities linked to dance and music belong exclusively—or at least mostly—to those with "black blood." Blood assumes the value of a sign, capable of connecting people with their ancestors, as if this automatically meant that they shared the same culture (Connerton 1989).

The belief in the transmission of culture through blood is present in the black identity narratives in Salvador, and this notion has been widely disseminated in the *blocos afro*. With the intent of increasing self-esteem and reversing negative images of blackness, including what is said about the body itself, new representations are projected for the self and for others within a perspective initiated long ago in Brazil's black movement. Although this campaign is well intended, the effort to value blackness ends up creating new myths and reinforcing old ones, restricting the group's positive characteristics to natural ones based on "race." The adolescents who benefit from the *blocos'* social actions perpetuate the notion of a "black race" taught to them by their teachers, believing that when they learn to dance or to play a percussion instrument they are simply developing their innate potential as black people. Aptitudes for dance and music, as well as supposed inherent sensuality, are considered natural attributes of black individuals, transmitted from one generation to the next by the blood of those who have a similar phenotype.

The belief that the youth's dance and musical talents are natural tendencies of black people ends up repeating the same logic defended by racial theories of the nineteenth century, which considered that among whites, culture stood in opposition to nature, and among blacks it coincided with nature. In addition, these naturalizations solidify stereotypes of blacks, ultimately resulting in the opposite effect from what was initially proposed—in other words, imprisoning those whom one had wished to set free. The statement below of a discourse producer from one of Salvador's *blocos afro* illustrates this point. This person criticized black female instructors for straightening their hair: "The instructors here go through training, continuing education; I mean, they're constantly being trained and being worked on in order to perfect themselves. But it still isn't the ideal, we're really aware of that. . . . So much so that some instructors relax their hair . . . And blacks shouldn't have straight hair, they should use braids, Afro hair."

The management of appearance should be analyzed along with the supervision of the tendencies of the black body. As role models for the young members of the *blocos afro*, the instructors' look must be "impeccably black," so that they not only teach music and dance but also act as a point of reference in the process of becoming black. The definition and enforcement of the rules of blackness occurs mainly within the sphere of men's actions. But this is certainly not exclusive to blackness. Analyzing religious minorities in the Western world, Seyla Benhabib argues that gender asymmetries have functioned as a major means of reproduction of internal forms of oppression. "Women and their bodies are the symbolic-cultural site upon which human societies inscribe their moral order. In virtue of their capacity for sexual reproduction, women mediate between nature and culture, between the animal species to which we all belong and the symbolic order that make us into cultural beings" (Benhabib 2002, 84).

The *blocos afro*, just like most black organizations in Brazil today, create identity counter-narratives and alternative representations and values as a means of challenging representations of blacks and writing their own history to be told in the public domain. However, as black organizations increasingly become the subjects of discourse, developing their own narratives of blackness, racial stereotypes and gender asymmetries do not necessarily disappear; sometimes they are replaced by others, and sometimes they are strengthened in the exaltation of talents considered natural to black women and men.

Thus, people are persuaded into an "appropriate" form of identity and need to be taught how to become black, both internally and externally. They must be trained so that their bodies automatically reproduce what is allegedly in their cells, such as the habits of dancing, playing instruments, dressing in a preestablished "black way," "recovering" and "re-remembering" the potential of the melanin present in their bodies. In this way, individuals who are born dark (*preto*) become black (*negro*), but they do not free themselves from the essentialist beliefs that posit the existence of tendencies hidden behind the color of their skin. Undeniably, the body and bodily practices play a fundamental role in preserving traditions and perpetuating group identity and memory, regardless of the fact that these are, to a greater or lesser degree, invented. Yet when tradition is understood as a set of rigid rules that must be repeatedly applied while ignoring historical conditions, it ceases to be a sign of ethnicity and paves the way for conservative manifestations of political culture and social regulation.

It is thus important to consider how traditions become embodied in the process of forming a group's social memory. For Connerton (1989), this means that it is necessary to give priority to group performance, because through it one can observe "bodily automatisms," or what he terms "habit-memory," which is the human capacity for reproducing a specific performance. In his view, this type of memory has been ignored by analysts of memory and identity when it should be foregrounded, since habit-memory is an essential ingredient in the preservation of group codes and rules. A habit is transmitted from one generation to the next by repetition, with older individuals encouraging younger ones to carry out repetitive bodily movements; the belief is that these movements naturally crop up, as if the members of a given group were born knowing how to perform certain movements or as if these behaviors were part of their genetic heritage.

In Western societies, people are constructed as entities, and the body functions as a delimitation of an individual biography. Thus, subjectivities, whether related to gender, "race," or other bodily references, are realized in conjunction with "regimes of the body." Taking Foucault's theory of the technologies of the self as a starting point, Nikolas Rose questions some of the current certainties about "the kinds of people we take ourselves to be." Rose underscores the importance of conducting historical studies in order to understand the genealogy of the self, which would lead to a destabilization of what we consider natural and inevitable in our self-constitutions. A critical history disturbs and fragments its object of study, revealing the fragility of what we consider solid, while allowing us to think "against the present, in the sense of exploring the horizon and its conditions of possibility" (1996, 41). To learn to be what we are and to become what we have become demands a great deal of uniformity, normativity, and regulation.

Foucault (1988, 18) explains that, operating together with the technologies of production, systems of signs, and power, technologies of the self require specific modes of training and the acquisition of specific skills and attitudes. To take care of the self requires that one not just take care of the body but also take care of the soul. In turn, the care of the self as soul is care of the activity. The soul is defined by contemplation of the divine element, or, I would argue, of what is unattainable. "In this divine contemplation, the soul will be able to discover rules to serve as a basis for just behavior and political action" (25). Being occupied with oneself entails political activities and involves "a network of obligations and services to the soul" (27).

Hence, to become black, a process that seeks empowerment for the oppressed, can become a tool for internalizing authority and discipline through self-regulation. The more body-centered an identity, the more it is compliant to techniques of subjection, and consequently to means of regulation and obedience.[4] Automatically connecting nature and culture, the myth of Mama Africa not only establishes that black bodies must enact black tendencies but also that black cultural expressions should be performed exclusively by black bodies. This logic is informed by the belief in "races" as groupings of distinct types of human beings that transmit their essential qualities from one generation to the next. Simultaneously, this notion also serves the purpose of ethnicizing black identities — which, as I have argued, is among the goals of the *blocos afro*. Reclaiming black culture for black bodies has been a means of intensifying opposition and strengthening the boundaries between the black and white "races."

Black Culture for the "Black Race"

To become black not only requires that those who have a black appearance recover their black tendencies, corresponding thus to the cultural practices considered to be black, but also postulates that black culture itself must be reclaimed for black individuals. This demand has occurred in a context in which Brazil's so-called national symbols were formed based on elements originally associated with black culture. Samba, for example — persecuted and prohibited until the late 1920s precisely because of its association with blackness — was transformed into Brazil's most celebrated national symbol. And if in foreigners' eyes it confirms Brazil's African heritage, in the Brazilian imaginary — and thus fulfilling the function of national symbols — samba represents mixture, the element that transcends different classes and races.[5]

The current Brazilian black movement has tried to reconstruct an ethnic identity by reclaiming an Africanness that it argues has been diluted after centuries of miscegenation.[6] According to the black movement, the mixture of peoples and cultures is responsible for the country's appropriation of symbols previously considered to be exclusively black. For this reason, the movement believes it is necessary to reclaim the icons of Africanness in Brazil, in order to return to blacks what is supposedly theirs by origin. Scholar and activist Kabengele Munanga believes that black organizations need to emphasize the reconstruction of racial and cultural identity "as a mobilizing platform on the road to gaining full citizenship" (1996a, 189).

In order for this to happen, in the opinion of Munanga and activist Sueli Carneiro (2000), just to cite a few, it would be necessary to "break with miscegenation" and construct a black ethnic identity dissociated from the idea of a mixed Brazilian nation. Munanga thus conceives of Brazilian *mestiçagem* as inherently negative and an obstacle to achieving citizenship for blacks. "In the cultural realm, Brazilian ideology is characterized by its strong cultural syncretism, that is, its historical inclination to accept, without much resistance, the cultural influences of all ethnic groups. . . . Both biological and cultural miscegenation helped weaken the feeling of formation of private identities and the protest power of the excluded" (1996a, 190). The proposal to shape a black identity clashes, in his view, with cultural miscegenation, because the playing field for identities is not clearly delimited. "How can one tend to his garden if it is not separated from others' gardens? Currently in Brazil the fences and boundaries between identities fluctuate, images and gods brush shoulders, assimilate each other and unite; for this reason, there is a certain difficulty in constructing racial and/or 'pure' cultural identity, one that does not mix with the identity of others" (189).

Munanga implicitly resorts to the epistemology of the word *culture* — from the Latin *cultura*, meaning the act of cultivating a farm or garden — to argue against contact, syncretism, and miscegenation, and in favor of building fences and boundaries around each group's supposedly pure culture. More than merely bothered by his "aborescent scheme" (Deleuze and Guattari 1987) of roots, soil, and garden, I am dumbfounded by an academic notion of culture that requires the construction of fences in order to protect those who supposedly own that culture. This is the same logic of "camp mentality" (Gilroy 2000) that operated as the basis for Nazi thought, in which "impure subjects"—Jews, Gypsies, and homosexuals—would contaminate Hitler's Aryan citizens. The fences and walls of concentration camps were then considered the best solution to avoid biological or cultural mixture. Fences are once again presented as the answer to bar the entrance of "aliens" into U.S. American soil—"illegals" who insist on crossing the border with Mexico, bringing with them foreign phenotypes, food, and the threatening Spanish language that should be halted at all costs to avoid polluting the U.S. nation, and its supposedly hegemonic "Anglo culture." This logic explains why immigrants are constantly portrayed by sectors of the U.S. media as those whom the nation should "weed out" of their land.

The discussion about "bounded" cultures continues to take place in both militant and academic realms in Brazil, focused mostly on the question of the reappropriation of Afro-Brazilian symbols by black organizations. In contrast to the United States, where a clear distinction appears to exist between what is ethnic and national, in Brazil, cultural elements of African origin that were shunned and repressed in the public eye, such as Candomblé and samba, later became symbols of nationality and Brazilian-ness.[7] Peter Fry (1977) provides an example of this in the culinary realm: *feijoada* in Brazil came to be considered a national dish, while in the United States a very similar dish is part of the black ethnic cuisine termed *soul food*.[8] The origin of the dishes is similar in both countries: slaves used pork leftovers that were thrown away by their masters. The difference is that in Brazil, *feijoada* was transformed into a national symbol, while in the United States it remained a symbol of blackness. Just like *feijoada*, other black cultural items were assimilated and appropriated as national symbols, emblazoned on tourism brochures, and used to represent Brazil abroad. Fry had claimed that "The original producers of this cultural item were, to a certain extent, dismissed from their leadership role and relegated to the position of additional extras" (1977, 46). Fry has recently reconsidered this idea in his latest book, *A persistência da raça* (The Persistence of Race). In the chapter entitled "Feijoada and Soul Food, 25 Years Later," he admits a certain embarrassment with regard to his previous position, which he now sees as a "naïve interpretation" of Brazilian racism. He recognizes that his earlier analysis required an absolute division of Brazilian society into two distinct actors: on the one hand, powerful exploitative whites, and on the other, weak exploited blacks, thus overlooking any possibility of agency, negotiation, or interpenetration between these groups. Instead of a reductive and functionalist interpretation where culture is taken to be the epiphenomenon of social structure, Fry now advocates looking at culture as "establishing specific modes of colonization" (2005, 160) and, I would add, specific forms of racism.

Conceiving of black culture as a set of elements that have been hijacked to decorate the stage of Brazilian nationality, black organizations in Brazil have been trying to disentangle specific cultural expressions from the miscegenated images of Brazilian culture by reclaiming them as "black." They thus try to bring to the fore elements such as Candomblé, samba, and capoeira, in an effort to (re)construct an Afro-referenced black identity. However, identity narratives are not constructed solely according to the will of movement leaders and academics. The specific demarcations that grant meanings to narratives cannot be determined in such a compulsory manner. Michael Hanchard (1996) criticizes this attitude of the Brazilian black movement, stating that it has led to a fetishization of black cultural practices, which in his view is a limited political means for enacting positive transformations in the lives of blacks and fostering social advancement. In his understanding, examples of such fetishization are the idealized construction of the African past, the attempt to reclaim black cultural symbols, and the nearly exclusive use of cultural practices—music, dance, religion, apparel—to express dissatisfaction, solidarity, and resistance.

For anthropologist Rita Segato, the problem is not that the leaders of Brazilian black movements have overvalued Afro-Brazilian cultural elements but that, on the contrary, they have not given enough value to these symbols. While Hanchard argues that black culture has been transformed by these leaders into an emblematic trend that opposing groups wrestle over in a struggle to gain exclusive control, for Segato the question is not simply of reappropriating Afro-Brazilian symbols or imbuing them with new meanings, thus politicizing them, but instead "listening to what is encoded within them and discovering the political strategy inscribed in them. . . . Symbols do not constitute an ornamental, epiphenomenal secretion; rather, they convey values, choices, and a metaphorically expressed philosophy that all too often contradicts, in its own terms, state hegemony" (1998, 133).

Since the 1970s, Brazilian black organizations have been working within a perspective of reclaiming what they consider to be their black or African culture. This belief resonates in other parts of the African diaspora, where black culture has been considered the voice of the black social movement, providing important moments and contexts of recognition among its members and retaining great powers of aggregation. However, black culture is not bound to a set of cultural expressions. Culture is integrated within a social movement, but it does not comprise its totality. It is therefore necessary to analyze the political position of the black social movement in order to understand what type of collective political agency emerges from racial subjectivity.

For Munanga, however, reclaiming black culture is indeed necessary, for it recaptures "one's negated and forged historical past, one's awareness of a positive participation in the construction of Brazil, of one's belittled skin color, etc.; in other words, the recovery of one's blackness, in all its biological, cultural, and ontological complexity" (1999, 101). This statement explicitly reveals the importance assigned to biology in the process of recovering blackness and constructing oneself as black. Munanga's late-twentieth-century antiracist statement has a lot in common with the racist thought of nineteenth-century French diplomat and philosopher Joseph Arthur de Gobineau, including the belief that racial mixture promotes the degeneration of a group's culture and value: "In applying the word *degenerate* to a people, it must and does signify that these people no longer have the intrinsic value they possessed at an earlier time because they no longer have the same blood in their veins . . . definitively speaking, they will die, and their civilization will die with them" (Gobineau 1983 [1853–55], 34–35, quoted in M. Wright 2004, 40).

During the period of colonization and slavery, the black body was conceived as an object, both for economic exploitation and for sexual desire, but always as an object of political dominance. Affirming that racial marks were incorporated onto the skin, black movements from several regions of the diaspora began to consider the black body as the locus of identity and the arena for battles and protests. Even though this has allowed for accomplishments in the realm of aesthetics and self-esteem, it has also helped reinforce the belief in natural attributes and the consequent stance of defining blackness based on biological characteristics. This logic postulates that phenotypical factors be considered the bearers of cultural truths and the determinants of blackness.

If biology has played an important role in defining blackness in several parts of the diaspora, in Ilê Aiyê it is the first factor used to determine who is or is not black. According to the group's president, "what defines someone as being black is still skin color. So that you can also require it, you know? It's skin." For other group directors, biology is important because of racism itself and because it was socially imposed. As Aliomar Almeida states, "To me, a black person is someone who has dark skin, I mean, I'm telling you this not in scientific terms, but in terms of what society imposed."

The belief in the power of biology in conferring blackness and determining who is or is not black consequently leads to the groups' political stance of forming their identities by linking biology, culture, and politics. Ilê Aiyê's internal policy of barring the participation of nonblacks is reflected in the group's external policy, which states that it supports black politicians, regardless of their party affiliation or whether they claim to be on the Right or the Left. One *bloco* director explained this relationship by stating, "If a black politician, of whatever party, wants to use Ilê facilities to come present his agenda, his platform, the microphone's open. Regardless of party, we support any black politician! We're here to encourage the black man, we aren't here to encourage Party X, Y, or Z." Another director observed, "Ilê always positioned itself as a black entity. Now what we want to make real clear here is that there is no such thing as blacks have to be leftists, belong to Party X, belong to PT [Workers' Party], belong to PC do B [Brazilian Communist Party]. I think you have to belong to any party. We don't rule in any party, not in any party on the left or on the right; blacks don't have power in any of them. You can look at the city council, at the state legislature, you don't see any *negão* ruling a party, so I don't have any reason to be loyal to a single party."[9] Yet another director commented, "Look, the politics of Ilê Aiyê are politics geared toward the development of the black community. We aren't party politicians; our party is the black man. Any and all black candidates to public office have Ilê Aiyê's support. Now we aren't radicals, like they tried to pin on blacks in Bahia, [saying] that all blacks have to be leftists. Ilê Aiyê is not leftist; Ilê Aiyê is not rightist. Ilê Aiyê fights for the interests of the black community."

Michael Hanchard employs the concept of "faint" and "strong resemblances," which occur when members of a given group recognize their similarities in phenotype, experience, and subjectivity, potentially propelling them toward political action. Commenting on a Brazilian black activist who frequently declares in both lectures and informal conversations that "I'm neither Left nor Right: I am black," Hanchard (1994, 80) states that this type of posture reveals "faint resemblances," which in his opinion do not have any political direction and are therefore insufficient to enact changes in the broader spectrum of power. Hanchard also argues that no current social movement acts outside the existing political context and that even those who opt for "race-first activism" must necessarily define their political and ideological affiliations.

When asked whether it is more important to support a black politician, regardless of his/her agenda, or a politician committed to fighting racism and defending the black cause, regardless of skin color, the answers provided by Ilê Aiyê directors were consistent with what had been said before. Osvalrísio, for example, stated, "It's kind of complicated, but I'd still rather invest in the black person and try to prepare him. Because for us it's a matter of models, of self-esteem . . . because this thing about a white man committed to blacks . . . that's kind of complicated. Committed up to what point, right? . . . As much as he might be, he's white, so he can't feel deep down what we do; there's a point after which he can't represent us."

Speaking about a black candidate belonging to a party on the right and supported by the *bloco*, Aliomar said, "People kept saying, 'But he belongs to the government party.' At that point, for us, it didn't matter who he was, what mattered was that he was black and he was there; he was someone we had to capitalize on." All of the discourse producers in Ilê Aiyê stated that if they could vote in São Paulo they would have voted for Celso Pitta, a black mayoral candidate with no history of engagement with black activism. Supported by right-wing politician Paulo Maluf, Pitta—a wealthy businessman with no previous participation in partisan politics—was labeled by the press as a *candidato sabonete*, a soap candidate whose candidacy was marketed and commoditized like a household product.

Defining identity in absolute terms and presenting definitions of blackness on the basis of biology and phenotype pins identity politics onto biopolitics. Expanding the concept coined by Michel Foucault (1978), for whom biopolitics meant the power of the state to manipulate, manage, and regulate human bodies,[10] Gilroy (2000) shows that biopolitics is not carried out only by the state but also by social groups, through the construction of their identities. Biopolitics is the predisposition to define people and to forge identification and solidarity patterns based on the body, reinforcing the power of political anatomy and epidermalization. This tendency finds especially fertile ground for perpetuation in contexts in which the points of origin, real or imagined, seem increasingly distant, creating concerns about the limits and boundaries of sameness and leading individuals and groups to seek safety and legitimization in embodied differences.

Anchoring itself on the body, biopolitics obviously selects certain specific bodies to be upheld as exemplary. In the case of black biopolitics in the United States, for instance, exemplary bodies belong mainly to strong and muscular athletes, such as Michael Jordan and Venus and Serena Williams. If we examine black Bahia's biopolitics, exemplary bodies are those capable of producing Afro music, Afro dance, capoeira, and other black arts, spontaneously and instantaneously. The biggest problem is not that biopolitics contributes to the aestheticization of politics, but the fact that it works to create political connections based on the body, further positing "race" as a determining element in the division of humanity (Gilroy 2000). Instead of supporting and trying to elect politicians committed to fighting racism and all forms of discrimination, or instead of supporting a candidate for ideological and political reasons, discourse producers position identity in a manner so as to privilege what is most external: the skin.

One can certainly address the importance of the racial subjectivity of politicians who are black and therefore experience racism in their everyday lives, and how this factor is central to their commitment of the antiracist cause. However, there are several examples of black Brazilian politicians who are not committed to fighting racism and who often do not even acknowledge that it exists in Brazil. In affirming this, I am not referring to those individuals who, due to class affiliation and wealth, do not identify themselves as blacks even when their color or phenotype would possibly classify them as such. Whether dark or light-skinned, politicians engaged in the antiracist struggle in Brazil have been historically situated on the left. Political ideology has been a far greater predictor of engagement against racism than the politicians' color or physical features.

Flávio Pierucci warns that the increasing use of the body as an element for defining politics has been a basic ingredient for forging popular conservatism. The value of belonging to "natural" groups (family, "race," and region, among others) is granted through bodily markers. The centrality of the body is present in the populist Right's discourse of intolerance as much as it is in the discourse of historically oppressed groups who are constructing oppositional identities. Ethnic and racial movements are thus "moments in which the body strongly erupts onto the political scene, in which group and even individual body peculiarities are placed, next to other sense-related dimensions of the body, at the center of collective action, aiming to either recognize or deny rights to individuals who share undesirable or deprived situations" (1999, 98).

The centrality of the body in ethnic discourses is justified by the fact that specific groups have been discriminated against precisely because of the negative connotation attributed to their physical markers. Thus, it is necessary to resignify the body by endowing it with positive meanings. The production of new representations allows a discriminated group to construct a consensus capable of, in specific situations, providing elements for its members to recognize themselves the same, and defining those who are located outside the group as different. An example of the use of the body to define difference and sameness is Ilê Aiyê's selection process. Founded as a response to the racism pervading Bahia's carnaval, Ilê Aiyê reversed the game practiced by Salvador's traditional *blocos*, which surreptitiously banned — and still ban — the participation of black people. Reacting to this exclusionary act, from its inception Ilê Aiyê has explicitly prohibited the participation of nonblacks in the group. Because it is such a complex issue, this attitude has elicited numerous discussions in defense or disagreement of the group. Those who defend its stance base their arguments on the right to difference, fearing that if the *bloco* were to open its doors to nonblacks it would "lose its identity." Another strong argument employed to defend Ilê Aiyê's right to remain selective is that the group is comprised of discriminated individuals — black, poor, and victims of racism. This type of argument is based on the idea that identity, while it is situational and contrastive, is also polarized. Racialism is considered a legitimate response to the discomfort and suffering caused by racism.

Several so-called *blocos de trio*, charged with committing "racial, aesthetic, and geographic racism," were investigated by a Parliamentary Inquiry on Racism spearheaded by Salvador's legislature and Bahia's state prosecutor's office.[11] Questioned by the press as to why Ilê Aiyê was not under investigation as well, since the *bloco* publicly bars nonblacks from participation, members of the inquiry justified themselves by invoking a UN convention that allows entities representing discriminated groups to behave in this manner (Bandeira 1999). What they failed to mention is that the convention recommends that such actions occur only during the group's organizing phase and that the stance of racial exclusion be temporary, to be practiced only during the entity's first founding years. However, according to the discourse of the *bloco* itself, Ilê Aiyê has already "come of age" and in 1999, the year when the inquiry was established, the group was completing its 25th anniversary.[12]

With its stance of not accepting those whom the *bloco* determines to be nonblacks, Ilê Aiyê has continuously dealt with the inconsistency between its discourse and practice. Racism, the group discourse's main target, is fought by means of a racialist practice. Critiquing the unquestioned use of the body by oppressed groups, Eugeen Roosens states that there is a commonality between the discourse of classic racists and the discourse of its opponents, mainly among movements that call for ethnic pride or that reinforce a common genealogical origin. "Both genealogy and racism operate using the body and its specificities in quite a literal way as an undeniable reality. . . . Genealogical self-representation also provides feelings of integrity which should be defended against outside polluting aggressors" (1994, 99). The focus on differences explains the racialization process that has been increasingly gaining ground in ethnic discourses.

Ever since the 1970s, the Brazilian black movement has been striving to construct an explicitly oppositional identity. In order to challenge the myth of racial democracy, activists have attempted to adopt a bipolarized racial classification that places blacks in opposition to whites and excludes the possibility of chromatic variation between the two extremes. Believed by many activists and academics in Brazil to be an essential part of the U.S. "model of racial relations," the quest for such a binary racial classification has been an attempt to fight the celebration of Brazilian *mestiçagem*, which is seen as hiding racial conflicts under the guise of fantastical harmonious race relations between lighter and darker *mestiços*.

While in the United States the one-drop rule has separated whites from blacks, in Brazil the opposite is true: there is a predominance of intermediary terms. The oft-cited Pesquisa Nacional por Amostra de Domicílios/ Instituto Brasileiro de Geografia e Estatística survey carried out in 1976 (Nelson do Valle Silva and Carlos Hasenbalg 1988) demonstrates this clearly: 134 different color labels were provided by Brazilians asked to self-identify their color. The demand by the Brazilian black movement to adopt a binary racial classification, inspired by what is believed to exist in the United States, carries important political consequences along with it. A major controversy exists among scholars who study race in Brazil with regard to the adoption or rejection of binary systems of classification. Some scholars, such as Antônio Sérgio Guimarães (1995) and Michael Hanchard (1994), argue that Brazil should mirror itself on the U.S. "model," since color is also a main racial category in this country.[13] Other researchers position themselves against the adoption of what they also view as "the U.S. race model" (Fry 1995/96; Segato 1998). Writing about the bipolarity demanded by the black movement, Peter Fry explains that it is an imposed idea that goes against what he defines as Brazil's "multiple mode of classification." This multiple mode allows individuals to be classified in distinct ways, depending on the situation, which represents, for Fry, a "de-racialization" of individual identity. The term *moreno*, for example, can be applied to a vast array of appearances, from white individuals with dark hair all the way to those with very dark skin. This type of classification is based on people's physical appearance and not on their ancestry, confirming Oracy Nogueira's theory (1985) that in Brazil, phenotype is more important than origin when it comes to classifying individuals racially.

Even within most Brazilian black organizations, the consensus for defining who is black is an evaluation based on appearance, and especially color. Despite the fact that the black movement claims *mulatos* among its ranks, it demands that they have dark skin, contrary to what occurs in the United States, where light-skinned, mixed-race individuals are considered black and where the very expression *light-skinned blacks* does not sound like an oxymoron. Aliomar Almeida, one of Ilê Aiyê's directors, commented on these different ways of defining who is black: "We're very surprised when people come here, groups from the United States, African Americans, who come here for the *bloco*'s rehearsals; and we are bewildered by these people, practically light-skinned, with curly hair like this, saying they're black and that they want to parade [with Ilê Aiyê], and we're put in a difficult situation because for us these people are white!"

It is understandable that the black movement in Brazil does not see light-skinned *mulatos* and *mestiços* as blacks; after all, these individuals suffer significantly less discrimination than those who are dark-skinned. However, such forms of classification confirm the argument defended in this book: that it is primarily racism that determines an individual's "race." The black movement's intent in breaking with Brazil's multiple classification system is to underscore the danger of the intermediate categories such as *moreno* and *mulato*, believed to dilute black identity, weakening the idea of basic opposition between blacks and whites present in everyday conflicts. Yet Fry maintains that this "U.S. bipolar model," which classifies as black any person with the remotest African ancestry, also implies a racist notion: the idea that one drop of black blood is enough to taint white purity (1995–96).

Several Brazilian black leaders lament the fact that racial roles in Brazil are not as defined as in the United States, where British colonization implemented a drastic separation between blacks and whites. Even the expressions of racism vary between the two countries because of the differences in colonization. In the United States, the definition of ethnic groups is socially systematized, and whoever has the slightest black ancestry is considered black; "genetics have given way to a rigorously dichotomous racial fantasy" (Risério 1995, 103). In other words, African Americans comprise the most biologically heterogeneous group in the United States but are perhaps the most socially homogeneous — at least apparently, since there are great internal inequalities within the group, mainly due to the generally overlooked but nonetheless striking class differences among blacks (see hooks 2000; Gilroy 2000; and Appiah 1992).

Scholars of racial politics in Brazil have positioned themselves on opposite sides of the debate of the so-called U.S. racial model, generating a curious "bipolarization of the bipolarization" where it seems imperative to choose between one of two restricted options: one is either for or against the adoption of the bipolar black-white model in Brazil. In addition to reducing the possibilities of solving racism to just two alternatives, this discussion is problematic also because it shrinks the very complex racial reality of the United States to a simple and static "model." Not only have racial politics in the United States not always been bipolar; they have become increasingly less so, especially with the entrance of the Latino population onto the scene.[14] While U.S. academia has been little influenced by Latin American intellectual discussions on "race" and blackness, the effect of immigration, especially of Latin Americans, on the U.S. conceptualization of "race" is undeniable.[15] Nonetheless, more than the reality of U.S. racial politics, my concern is with how black activists in Brazil envision that reality and how their understanding of what happens in the United States is important in shaping their thoughts and attitudes toward their own racial identities. Thus, black activism in Brazil situates itself between an "African past" and a "U.S. future." Clearly, these notions refer to how Africa and the "U.S. model" have been imagined, conceived of, and thus reinvented within the sphere of black activism and black cultural production in Brazil.

At this moment, when the options and possibilities for crafting and implementing public policies to socially promote blacks in Brazil are being debated, once again the most prominent references are those which come from the United States. Just as they influenced the recently formed ideas on diversity, ethnicity, and "race," U.S. standards are at the center of the discussions of public policies in Brazil, despite the significantly different ways in which blackness and whiteness are defined in both countries. In fact, even U.S. segregation has been cited as a model by those generating ideas within the black movement in Brazil. Kabengele Munanga, for example, states that the promotion of a mobilizing ethnic and political awareness among the Brazilian black population is only possible through a self-definition based on African heritage, which for him includes history, culture, religion, race, and a clear distinction between whites and blacks. For Munanga, "this identity stems from one's color, in other words, from the reclaiming of one's blackness, physically and culturally" (1999, 14).

Thus, those who have fought to escape the biologization of their social subordination find themselves once again caught in a trap in which lineage and common origins join color and "race" to define one's identity. Ilê Aiyê, for example, defines itself as an entity in which there are only "true blacks." A televised interview with Vovô illustrates this point: "I think Ilê Aiyê today is the greatest reference for blacks in Bahia and perhaps in Brazil. I think we are the *only truly black entity* here in Bahia."[16] "Race" is thus understood as the authentic grounds upon which black identity is constructed. The cultural process of "becoming black" has often slipped into a search for a black essence, where one must simply awaken the dormant blackness of the body and the soul.

Black Race/Black Soul

Expressions such as "soul music" or "it's a black thing; you wouldn't understand," and the ideas that black people have more rhythm, or that black culture "is in the blood," can be found in several parts of the African diaspora. To one degree or another, they all share the common belief in an African essence innate to black people wherever they are located. Aiming to go further than the binary studies of black culture that have been predominantly either essentialist or antiessentialist, my analysis of the alleged African essence of black people is guided by an "anti-antiessentialist" perspective (Gilroy 1993a). In other words, while I certainly do not support the notion that there is such a thing as black essence I find it important to recognize the existence of a black particularity, or better yet, of several versions of it. Studies of black cultures should acknowledge and value black "structures of feeling" (Williams 1961) — the characteristics related to the process of being, feeling, and becoming a subject — as constitutive of black identities. On the other hand, we should not lose sight of the fact that black subjectivities are, unquestionably, socially and historically constructed. What does it mean, then, to create and constantly renew the belief in an African essence? I argue that there is an intimate connection between asserting an African essence — or black soul — and the need to reaffirm the humanness of those whose personhood has been for so long doubted or denied during the lingering history of enslavement and its aftermath. Central to the history of slavery and the Western production of blackness is the concept of "race" and its dehumanizing effects.

The concept of race has held different meanings, but it has always been related, to some extent, to lineage and connection between people who have a common origin. The fact that they share the same ancestry would confer such people with shared qualities that were considered naturalized, interweaving characteristics viewed today as distinct and dissociated, such as physical and cultural traits. An example of this are Native Americans, whom Linnaeus, in his classification of the *Homo* subdivisions, categorized as simultaneously "copper colored, choleric, and erect" (Wade 1997, 7). Since the eighteenth century, when the concept of race began to be defined in academic terms, ideas about human differences were strongly structured by the fundamental notion of European superiority.

Beginning around the time of the "discovery" of the so-called New World, Europeans began to judge whether the groups that inhabited the recently discovered lands possessed a moral sense. They were then classified according to their "natural qualities." It was in this context that the most suitable groups for slavery were defined. Later on, the concept of race as a type was developed, and it was this definition which permeated the entire nineteenth century, crystallizing the notion that races are groupings of distinct types of human beings, whose innate qualities are transmitted from one generation to the next (Banton 1987). The racial types were then classified hierarchically through anthropometric studies, developed mainly by medical doctors under the guise of anthropology. Linguists, historians, and biologists were also competing to structure the knowledge on races.

What became known as scientific racism, however, was only established in the second half of the nineteenth century, when slavery had been abolished in most Latin American countries. But this timing is not a mere coincidence, for it became ever more necessary at this point to confirm the inferiority of nonwhite "races" in order to ensure the continuation of dominance over them. Proof of this is the fact that during slavery in Brazil, the condition of being a slave was more important than one's physical appearance. After abolition, physical appearance, more than African ancestry, began to be used to define individual status, as shown by Mariza Corrêa (1982). Hall (1997a) makes a similar point about reactions in the Americas against the discourse of abolitionists who, in their effort to prove the humanity of blacks, jumbled the hegemonic cultural boundaries which had for so long distinguished blacks and whites. The racist response was the strengthening, among the general population, of stereotypes of blacks as animal-like and the intensification of scientific racism among academics.

Scientific racism only lost force in the mid–twentieth century, after the repercussion of the horrors committed by the Nazi regime in the 1940s, creating a consensus among scientists that it was biologically impossible to speak of human "races." Considering the difficulties of using the term *race*, especially after World War II, scientists began to use the term *ethnicity*, derived from an old term coined by the ancient Greeks to designate people or nation: *ethnos*. Ethnicity began to replace race mainly because the latter was now loaded with the stigma of racism and tended to naturalize what began to be recognized as socially constructed categories. Using the terms *ethnicity* or *ethnic group* in some way filtered out the contamination contained in the word *race*, as if it were possible to focus more on their social construction, since this would emphasize cultural differences rather than natural ones. However, we have seen that in the daily coexistence between different ethnic groups, *ethnicity* is also fraught with problems, as witnessed by the bloody "ethnic conflicts" between Serbs and Croats or Hutus and Tutsis — the first two groups belonging apparently to a "white race," and the latter two to a "black race."

Despite the fact that social scientists describe race and ethnicity as distinct, they also recognize that the terms have common characteristics, since both are partial, unstable, contextual, situational, and fragmentary. It is necessary to note, however, that the two terms have very different histories, which endow them with distinct meanings. The term *black*, for example, is a racial concept, for historical reasons, carrying within it the history of slavery, resistance against domination, and the encounter between colonizers and colonized. The ways in which whites and blacks are currently defined worldwide are also connected to this history, confirming Gilroy's statement that "black and white are bonded together by the mechanisms of 'race' that estrange them from each other and amputate their common humanity" (2000, 15). Different contemporary forms of racism are also connected in various ways to the history of colonial encounters.

Within the Brazilian black movement, the concept of race has been gaining value since 1970, often explicitly countering the term ethnicity, which according to some scholars represents a strategy by "white academia" to weaken the force of a struggle taking place on the battlegrounds of race. Sociologist Antônio Sérgio Guimarães (1995) agrees with the black movement's stance and defends the use of "race," positing that "ethnicity" is a euphemism, a way to cover up prejudice and discrimination based on individual color or phenotype. For Guimarães, highly educated Brazilians are afraid to use the term "race," a term much more frequently employed in everyday language and in social movements, whose activists feel discriminated against because of their color and physical complexion. In his view, if people are singled out for their "race," then it is this term that should be used in the political field. It is therefore unnecessary to find a biological reality on which to base the use of this concept in sociology. People who suffer the effects of racism do not have any other choice but to reconstruct the notions of this same ideology.[17]

Guimarães also argues that blacks in Brazil should seek their reidentification in ethnic and cultural terms and thus use racialism to position themselves as a segregated group. "It seems that only a self-defensive racialist discourse can recover the feelings of dignity, pride, and self-confidence. . . . Ethnic reemergence is almost always supported by the mirror ideas of a *land* to reclaim . . . and a *culture* to redeem and repurify, through contact with an imaginary Africa, an Africa brought and maintained as a memory" (1999, 58).[18] Despite basing his arguments on Appiah's definitions of racialism, extrinsic racism, and intrinsic racism, Guimarães does so in a contradictory manner. He does not make it clear that he is not following Appiah's line of thinking, especially since the latter is a scholar known for pointing out the problems of racialism. For Appiah (1992), although racialism is not necessarily a dangerous doctrine, it has nevertheless been used as a precursor to racist regimes that have been the basis of great human suffering and the source of innumerous moral errors.

Following this line of thought, like Gilroy and Hall, Appiah writes "race" in quotation marks, and explicitly states that the "false ideas" of "race," "tribe," and "nation" stem from the concomitant evils of racism and wars between peoples. "'Race' disables us because it proposes, as a basis for common action, the illusion that black (and white and yellow) people are fundamentally allied by nature and, thus, without effort; it leaves us unprepared, therefore, to handle the 'intraracial' conflicts that arise from the very different situations of black (and white and yellow) people in different parts of the economy and of the world" (1992, 176). African and black unity and identities therefore need more secure bases than the notion of "race."[19] Racialism is not the solution for racism, precisely because it favors the same biological bases of "race" employed by racism.

In addition to Appiah, there are several other scholars who position themselves against the use and strengthening of the notion of "race." Stuart Hall (1996a; 1996c), for instance, argues that the term should gradually lose force, both in academia and in social movements. He contends that the more we acknowledge the roles of culture and politics in the construction of the category *black*, the more we must recognize that this category cannot be based on physical characteristics set by "race" or nature. Inevitably, this will weaken the meaning of race as a term. "Race" and "black" are expressions that, according to Hall, should never be used without being connected to other variables, such as class, gender, and age. Whenever these categories are used in isolation, as if they were self-sufficient, we are inversely endorsing the very same principle of racism that we are trying to fight.

In Brazil, despite strong pressure from the black movement and academia's penchant for adopting politically correct trends, some scholars explicitly oppose — or at least question — the perpetuation of the notion of "race." Lilia Schwarcz (1996) points out the danger of using this term by demonstrating that it demands a biological definition, which means a regression toward the evolutionary criteria that constructed race as a stable and defining element of physical, cultural, and moral tendencies. It is even more problematic, she argues, when the return to race occurs through criteria that privilege phenotype. Joel Rufino dos Santos, a black activist and scholar, notes that opponents of racism in Brazil, beginning with black movements, still employ the term race with its nineteenth-century connotation. "They are antiracist racialists. They speak for the black race, and in response to the negative attributes that prejudice heaps upon blacks, they counteract with their positive attributes" (Santos, 1996, 219).

As argued by Appiah (1992), those who deny the biological reality of "races" are often treated by nationalists as if they were proposing the destruction of ethnicities and nations, or, at the very least, as if they were ignoring the existence of racial subjectivities. Of course, when we analyze social identities, we must recognize that not all elements of human life can be explained through reason. Identities beget feelings, values, and moral forces that cannot be reduced to rational explanations or material reasons. Thus, my criticism of certain aspects of identities — essentialist beliefs, crystallized stereotypes, and the perpetuation of the notion of "race" — is not presented merely to prove that these are inventions, illusions, or even falsities, but rather to scrutinize how these truths were constructed and to understand their effects in the constitution of reality. By criticizing the importance given to the terms *race, essence, tendencies, authenticity*, and *originality*, I am attempting to examine their political meanings and conse-

quences, especially in the lives of those who have been hurt by such "truths."
As Appiah states,

> To raise the issue of whether these truths are truths to be uttered is to be
> forced, however, to face squarely the real political question, the question,
> itself, as old as political philosophy, of when we should endorse the en-
> nobling lie. In the real world of practical politics, of everyday alliances and
> popular mobilizations, a rejection of races and nations in theory can be
> part of a program for coherent political practice, only if we can show
> more than that the black race—or the Shona tribe or any of the other
> modes of self-invention that Africa has inherited—fit the common pat-
> tern of relying on less than the literal truth. We would need to show not
> that race and national history are falsehoods but they are useless false-
> hoods at best—or at worst—dangerous ones: that another set of stories
> will build us identities through which we can make more productive
> alliances. (1992, 175)

In my view, those who defend the use of the term race have the same primary goal as those who propose eradicating the term—fighting racism in all
of its forms. The biggest distinction is the strategy for achieving this goal.
Those who defend the use of "race" reiterate the arguments of Jean Paul
Sartre, who in the 1940s stated that blacks should accept the existence of
"race," because otherwise it would not be possible to fight against that which
does not exist. However, it was Sartre himself (1948) who said that blackness is the root of its own destruction, that it is a transition and not a conclusion, a means but not an end. Its end is human triumph in a raceless society.

In criticizing the use of "race," one must not ignore the weight that color
or phenotype exerts on the life and well-being of individuals socially classified as black. Even though they are historically elaborated social constructs
and not something essentially linked to individuals, color or "race" are
employed as instruments to perpetuate privileges and as determinants of
the social spaces that people with different phenotypes can occupy. Without a doubt, people are still classified according to the old-fashioned definitions of "races." However, one must also remember that identities—
whether they be racial, ethnic, or gender based—are constructed in the
context of late capitalism, in which liberalism and discipline, coupled with
bureaucracy, impinge on the most subjective conditions of identities. For
this very reason, we need to envision the possibility of constructing identities that are not based on the same terms that emerged out of colonialism
and that circulated as a means to legitimize subordination and power.

Therefore, to defend the continued use of "race" confers it with legitimacy. It is ill advised, and even dangerous, to do so in light of all the suffering caused throughout history in the name of "race." Instead, the best strategy to fight racism and all the wrongdoings committed in the name of "race" is to strive to imagine our existence beyond this idea. The defense of racialism perpetuates ethnic absolutisms and feelings of pride that can approximate or become expressions of hatred toward those who do not partake in our "sameness." It is widely believed that victims of racism are exempt from becoming racists, or that only whites can be racists. This pegs whites as potential racists and blacks as automatic victims. But in the midst of all this, "race" continues to be a determining factor of the essences of human beings. Frantz Fanon (1991 [1952]) considered epidermalized power to be a violation of the human body in its symmetric and subjective capacity for humanity. "Fanon's notion supplies an interesting footnote to the whole history of racial sciences and the exclusive notions of color-coded humanity that they specified. How many skin colors are there? How exactly, scientifically, is skin shade supposed to correspond to the variety of 'races?'" (Gilroy 2000, 47).

We must recognize that not only are variations in phenotype and bodily appearance used to construct "race," but that in so doing, only certain bodily traits can be used, since some physical characteristics relate to other identities, such as those connected with gender, age, and sexual orientation. The bodily markers that form a so-called racial phenotype are exclusive and specific and derive mainly from a combination of skin color, hair texture, and facial traits. This illustrates the extent to which the concept of race is linked to European history and thoughts on differences and therefore cannot be a concept that describes an objective reality. Only certain phenotypical characteristics can be used for racial categorization, and these traits are not chosen in a neutral fashion, independent of social context. "This means that races, racial categories, and racial ideologies are not simply those that elaborated social constructions on the basis of phenotypical variation—or ideas about innate difference—but those that do so using the particular aspects of phenotypical variation that were worked into vital signifiers of difference during European colonial encounters with others" (Wade 1997, 15).

The ethnic absolutisms present in the construction of black identities have helped create the illusion that, despite deep social divisions stemming from class and gender differences, "race" continues to be the main cause for such divisions. "Race" is, on the one hand, considered the basis for what is divisive; nevertheless, it is also considered responsible for what is unifying. Thus, emphasis is placed on the belief in an absolute and indivisible black subjectivity that remains intact and resistant in the face of factors such as class, gender, age, or sexual orientation. Once again, the body and its representations are considered responsible for connecting blacks, regardless of the profound differences related to individuals' conditions of wealth, health, or sexuality. As Gilroy argues (2000), the body is thus considered the cipher of absolute difference and sameness.

The discourse that defends the use of "race," justifying the term by arguing that blacks were victimized in the name of "race" and should therefore be liberated under this sign, makes it impossible to imagine an alternative form of modernity. For Mbembe, racialized thinking creates a notion of the African as a castrated subject, as if he were a mere instrument manipulated by the other. This view prevents the formulation of radical utopian thinking because it imposes, upon the construction of black identities, a logic of suspicion and denial toward those who do not partake in black "sameness," leading to "the mad dream of a world without Others" (2000, 8).

Arguing that it is worth overcoming the logic of race, Gilroy explains that the first task is to convince the racially oppressed that this process should not be feared and that there will be more gains than losses. If, on the one hand, those who have historically benefited from racial hierarchies do not want to relinquish their privileges, we must also deal with the fact that those who are oppressed and subordinated in the name of race frequently find safety and comfort within the same repertoire of power that produced their suffering. It is, in fact, difficult for the racially oppressed to let go of the logic of race because, inversely, black-produced representations have functioned as a source of pride, pleasure, and joy. The statements of the black youth of the *blocos afro* illustrate the nurturing power of the belief in race. Below, a young black female dancer of Ilê Aiyê declares the safety and comfort she encountered as she "became black" in the *bloco*:

> Nowadays, whether it's a little bit or a lot, whatever I know I have Ilê to thank for. I didn't know what it is to be black. In the beginning, people would call me *negona* and I didn't like it; [but] after I started to stop to think about it, I started to think that I really was black, and today I am very proud to be black. I didn't like to be called black; nowadays I like it — I want people to call me black. After I joined Ilê and after they started to

tell me things, to explain to me what it means to be black, I stopped and thought, "Yeah, it's very good to be black." It was only later that I came to see that I am black and that I have to defend my race.

Racially oppressed groups usually consider ending the logic of race a threat to their integrity, alterity, and to the very essence of their identities. Overcoming raciological thinking is frequently interpreted as a betrayal of one's origins and a menace to the bonds believed to emerge automatically from shared phenotypes or cultures. Thus, in the attempts to create new black identities, the old belief in "races" and their fixed destinies still has a great deal of force. For black ethnic discourse, thinking beyond race is more often than not understood as whitening. Either one embraces one's undeniable and inevitable black race or one loses a predestined identity. This is made clear in the statement of Sueli Carneiro, one of Brazil's most important black activists, as she defends the use of the term *Afro-descendant* in the process through which *pretos* and *pardos* become black:

> It is important to reclaim this identity in a country that refuses to embrace us, that invites us to betray our origin as a precondition for achieving social mobility! In order for blacks to be able to escape the place in which society has placed them, they must carry out certain rituals; this path has prerequisites and the main one is for you to renounce your identity, renounce your community, in other words, you need to whiten yourself. . . . The expression [Afro-descendant] reclaims blackness for this entire legion of people who are trying to distance themselves from their black identity but who have blackness deeply inscribed in their bodies and culture. (quoted in Carneiro 2000, 25)

As Gilroy contends, all of us who are linked to histories of suffering and victimization — either through blood relations or affinity — have an added responsibility of not betraying our capacity to imagine democracy and justice in an undivided and nonsectarian manner. To rise above the premise of "race," new identities must envision a future beyond blackness and whiteness, and bury the primitive status that tied blacks to subhumanity and prehistory. For such, the body can no longer be conceived as a repository of racial truth that preestablishes and automatically connects the meanings of appearance, essence, and tendencies. Critiquing preestablished forms of blackness, Frantz Fanon had warned against the idea that "the black man is supposed to be a good nigger." To demand that blacks correspond to archetypes is the same as to entrap and subject them to an essence and an appearance whose meanings they often do not control. In order to fight this, it is necessary to move beyond investing in a single and normative form of education for blacks. It is necessary to "teach the black man to not be a slave of his archetypes" (1991 [1952], 35).

For a long time, very strict notions of blackness were imposed on blacks from both inside and outside the movement. Postmodern critiques of essentialism challenge the idea of a static identity and are thus useful for black movements concerned with reformulating worn-out notions of identity, for they can open up new possibilities for the construction of the self and for new types of collective agency. Agency — as the organizational capacity of individuals, communities, and movements to interfere in the ruling order and transform the "regimes of truth" — can be aimed at promoting a political culture that dares to go beyond the notions of blackness and whiteness. In this perspective, black resistance is rooted in a process of decolonization opposed to the obligation of continuously reinscribing the supposed essential elements of black identity.

Yet although it is important to avoid falling into the trap of essentialism, the opposite is equally perilous: that is, thinking that since black particularity is constructed socially and historically, any move toward the unification of contemporary black cultures would be wrong. Black particularity should be recognized and valued in any analysis, because it is defined by cultural practices and political agendas that connect otherwise dispersed blacks. Thus, attempts to locate cultural practices that unite blacks scattered around the New World should not be considered cheap essentialism. The need to create new representations of blackness is understandable, especially if we consider the depth of prejudice and racism experienced on a daily basis, as we witnessed in the pained statements by young black people presented in the previous chapter.

The intricate processes of constructing identities indicate that there is not one single path to follow or one exclusive formula to be adopted. As proof of this, the same organizations that preach the existence of a black or African essence constantly claim that it is necessary to "become black," that is, to construct one's self socially and in consort with a political stance. The expression "to become black" inevitably implies a process, and the idea that racial identities are socially constructed and not simply naturally inherited. Analyzing racial politics in post-Apartheid South Africa, Vron Ware (2001, 6) explains that the expression "What makes you black?" opens up the possibility of discussion and questioning around the contents of blackness, for the very reason that the word *make*, despite carrying connotations of obligation and authenticity, also complicates these notions and demonstrates that what counts in forming racial identities depends, most of all, on political choices. Nevertheless, the process of becoming black has more often than not required a great amount of naturalization that culminates in the establishment of fixed patterns of blackness.

In the process of resignifying blackness and restoring dignity, Africa is reinscribed not only onto the surface of the body, as discussed in the previous chapter, but also reenacted in the inner being of black individuals, or in the soul, thus establishing an ideal combination of appearance, essence, and tendencies. Although it represents the more ethereal or metaphysical elements of blackness—that is, the essence and tendencies—the "soul" is, ultimately, and according to this logic, another facet of the black body. The soul is therefore entrapped in the order of raciology. "Race" is considered by many—even by those who recognize it as social construct—to be "objectively visible" through skin color, facial features, and hair texture, among other bodily factors. However, the power of "race" to produce divisions among human beings is only possible due to the role of the cultural representations that shape racial particularities and subjectivities. We should not forget that what seems to be the undeniable reality of physical difference only makes sense within a shared cognitive map through which we learn to read bodies.

Bodily differences do not exist prior to reasoning; they do not belong to an a priori natural order that is subsequently culturally interpreted. Culture is not a secondary layer that uncovers a natural or objective world. It is the only means through which any world, any thing, can make sense to us. Women only exist through what Simone de Beauvoir called the "myth of woman," the eternal, unchanging, "feminine essence" conceived of by men, and which attributes to women the natural and static traits of irrationality and sensitivity. Likewise, *black* and *white* owe their existence to the maintenance of the myth of "race." Conformity to, and regulation of, a set of abstractions judged "properly feminine" or "adequately black" lie at the core of both myths.

The next chapter shall take us to the end of our journey to Bahia and Africa through the black Atlantic routes. As is often the case when we travel, the last days are dedicated to purchasing souvenirs—mementos we take home from our visit. Even though they stem from the abstraction of feeling and memory, mementos are also quite concrete, since they are comprised of objects whose color, size, shape, and smell connect us to the place we visited. As discussed throughout this book, culture cannot be reduced to objects, but it needs them in order to reproduce and circulate. The relationship between culture as a way of life and culture as objectified and commodified representations, specifically in the process of constructing Bahianness and blackness, shall be the subject examined before bidding farewell.

Milking Mama Africa

This business of black mammies breastfeeding you
Has filled your bottle to the brim
Go nurse somewhere else!
— Riachão, "Cada macaco no seu galho"

Akin to other members of the African diaspora, Afro-Brazilians have used black cultural production as a way to interpret the world and articulate their own place within it. Blacks have used religion, music, dance, and aesthetics to organize their lives, resist oppression, and reinvent identities. At the same time, narratives of the Brazilian nation have employed many black cultural expressions, as can be seen in the imagery from Candomblé and capoeira that decorates tourist brochures and postcards, the bossa nova musical style that found a worldwide audience, and the national dish of *feijoada*, savored by members of all races and classes and even familiar to gourmands abroad. If representations of Brazilianness have drawn heavily from black culture, a similar but much more intensified process has taken place in the invention of Bahianness.

The process of objectification and commoditization of black culture in Bahia has continued apace in recent years, in connection with the development of the notion of Bahianness. I focus on a particular set of Afro-Bahian cultural elements that have been manipulated simultaneously by black groups in the construction of their identities, and by those sectors of Bahia's elite which have invested in the concept of *baianidade* — especially local politicians and agents of the tourism industry. These actors have employed black bodies and their allegedly contagious culture to promote Bahia as the "Land of Happiness." In addition to the iconography of Candomblé, more recently produced symbols of *negritude* (blackness) and *baianidade* (Bahianness) include *gingado* (the internal "rhythm" believed to run through the veins of blacks/Bahians), musical styles, and Afro-aesthetics — all widely developed within the *blocos afro*. The myth of Mama Africa, created by black groups as a site of resistance, overlaps with, and to a great extent, feeds the totalitarian notion of Bahianness. The commercialization of blackness has allowed sectors of Bahian society to milk the myth of Mama Africa for purposes other than fighting racism and inequality.

Blackness and Bahianness in the "Land of Happiness"

What today is termed Bahianness originated in the 1930s, when celebration of the racial and cultural miscegenation of the Brazilian nation erased the then hegemonic belief that its citizens were a "sad people" and that its national project was unviable and incapable of ever becoming a cohesive unit due to its mixed character.[1] The mixture of "races" and cultures, which beforehand had been equated with the nonviability or at least vulnerability of the formation of the Brazilian people, was resignified in the opposite direction, and was adopted as the nation's myth of origin. Brazil was classified not only as *mestiço* but also deemed devoid of racism as a natural consequence of its *mestiçagem*. Miscegenation thus became the founding condition of the "Brazilian character"; Brazilians were considered essentially joyful, playful, and drawn to matters of the heart. That same decade, the myth of *mestiçagem* was complemented by the notion of Brazilians as cordial people, whose "unpretentious kindliness, hospitality, and generosity — virtues praised so highly by foreigners who visit us . . . — represent, in effect, strong traits of the Brazilian nature" (Buarque de Holanda 1990 [1936], 106).[2]

In this narrative of the Brazilian nation, Bahia was projected as the locus of the highest expression of Brazilianness, especially because its black culture, conceived as a set of symbols, was largely used as one of the pillars of Brazil's "fable of the three races" (Da Matta 1981). Gilberto Freyre played a fundamental role in the dissemination of the notion of Bahia as the "birthplace of Brazil" to the point of stating that "sad is the Brazilian who does not have in him something of the Bahians."[3] Upon his first visit to Bahia in 1926, Freyre wrote the poem "Bahia de Todos os Santos e de Quase Todos os Pecados" (Bay of All Saints and Almost All Sins), which is filled with visual and tactile allusions, and references to the senses of smell and color of a magical Bahia. The aromas of Bahia come from its food, incense, and *mulatas*. The poem depicts the people of Bahia as "black, brown, purple, and *moreno* / the colors of the good Jacarandá trees of Brazil's sugar mills . . . / with no faces the color of cold cuts / no faces the color of cold turkey . . . / Bahia sizzling with hot colors, warm flesh, spicy flavors / I hate your orators, Bahia of all Saints / Your Ruy Barbosas, your Otávio Mangabeiras / But I like your *angu* [cornmeal mush], your *mulatas*" (Freyre 1990, 16).

Besides dissociating Bahianness from whiteness through his rejection of the state's famous political orators, Rui Barbosa and Otávio Mangabeira, and dismissing "bodies the color of cold turkey" and "cold cuts," Freyre exalts the dark colors of Bahia's *mestiço* population. The cultural elements produced by the dark-skinned people of Bahia were also central to Freyre's (and later to Jorge Amado's) narrative of Bahianness. "Typical" Bahian cultural expressions, described as emanating from the very bodies of the human types, are abundant in both authors' work: the flavors of Afro-Bahian cuisine, the magic of Candomblé, the physical skills of capoeira, the sensuality of *mulatas,* and, in the words of Freyre, "all that is the most expressive within the exclusive creative and maternal force that Bahia holds to this day" (Freyre 1990, 27). Freyre was proud of seeking in Bahia "the values of the expressive ethos of the people," instead of those symbols that are "official, bourgeois, conventional, or Rotarian." Ironically, in this inversion proposed by Freyre, popular expressions of African origin, such as the Afro-Bahian cuisine and the *baianas de acarajé* (female food vendors), ended up becoming precisely the official symbols of Bahianness, as can be seen in tourism brochures and state government marketing campaigns.

The black presence occupies a central position in the idealized Bahia of Gilberto Freyre as much as in the subsequent overall construction of Bahianness. Yet the exaltation of blackness in the construction of Bahianness is much more problematic than it may seem at first sight, especially because it wraps a veil of harmony around a reality of conflict and pervasive inequality. While Freyre fathered the idea of harmonious miscegenation, Jorge Amado was fundamental in transforming what had been an obstacle into the very driving force behind the formation of the Brazilian nation. His work is filled with "Bahian types," black and *mestiço* heroines and heroes set in a mystical landscape, complete with *mães de santo*, capoeira performers, feisty *mulatas*, *baianas de acarajé*, and all types of artists. Despite the fact that many of Amado's literary creations portrayed Ilhéus, imagination concerning this Bahian town was also a stage for disseminating a *mestiço* and enchanting Bahianness, confirmed in his later novels set in the streets, alleys, and neighborhoods of an entrancing Salvador, the so-called City of Bahia.

In the 1930s, specific elements of black culture began to be used to compose Bahia's image and to define the characteristics of Bahianness. The Candomblé religion, for example, while still repressed by the police, started to function as a symbol of the celebrated cultural and racial mixture of both Brazil and Bahia, precisely because it contained Africanisms, a quality that previously had justified its repression. Jorge Amado, along with other intellectuals, played an important role in the affirmation and defense of Candomblé, since he not only contributed to the resignification of the religion through his books but also preached against the legal persecution of *terreiros*.[4] In 1961, Amado was invited to occupy the prestigious position of *obá-mangbá* of the Ilê Axé Opô Afonjá *terreiro*.[5] Pierre Verger's foundational work also led to the affirmation and defense of Candomblé. Verger traveled between Bahia and Africa during the 1940s and 1950s to study the similarities between the worship of the *orixás* on both sides of the Atlantic.

Social recognition of Afro-Brazilian religions was the result of intense negotiations between individuals from different classes and "races," as Beatriz Góis Dantas, an anthropologist, aptly argued in her groundbreaking book *Vovó Nagô e Papai Branco*, suggestively subtitled "Uses and Abuses of Africa in Brazil."[6] Instead of a mere mixture of cultures or a consequence of the imposition of the will of whites over blacks, alliances between Candomblé priests and priestesses on one hand, and politicians and anthropologists on the other, were the main reason for the new meanings then given to Candomblé. It is not a coincidence that the social acceptance of Candomblé and the selection of Afro-Brazilian symbols were promoted by scholars from Brazil's Northeast during this specific time period. In the 1930s, particular black cultural elements were chosen to promote a cultural brand of nationalism. By then, the southeastern metropolises of Rio de Janeiro and São Paulo had become the economic, political, and social centers of the nation, having replaced Salvador and Recife. "Culture" then became one of the few sources from which northeastern intellectuals could draw regional elements to be included in this narrative of the nation. For

Dantas (1988), while the glorification of a broad *black* culture was employed in the creation of a national culture, it was the exaltation of *African* culture—or better yet, Africanisms, allegedly preserved in Bahia and to a smaller extent in other northeastern states—that would be utilized to mark regional distinctions. This configuration helped boost Bahia's status as the most African state of Brazil.

Jocélio Teles dos Santos (2005) argues that the black image of Bahia originated in the 1950s as the result of a process through which Bahia shifted from being a symbol of Brazil's melting pot to becoming the most African of Brazilian states. In contrast, I argue that Bahia's increasing aura of blackness is in line with its image as site of harmonious racial relations. In my view, this process began as early as the 1930s under the influence of Gilberto Freyre's work, even though the process of constructing the official discourse of Bahianness did not follow a linear path. Some decades were more important than others in the process of emphasizing the "blackness" on which Bahianness was being grounded. Santos (2005, 66) correctly notes that the 1960s witnessed a significant change in the publicizing of Candomblé in the Bahian press. Compared to the previous decade, newspaper reports on Afro-Brazilian religions in Bahia had by then become predominantly positive, showcasing the elements of tradition, originality, and beauty of Candomblé. This shift takes place in a period when the Brazilian federal government was seeking to establish greater economic links with the African continent. The economic interests were tied with what Santos defines as a rediscovery of African culture, both at home and abroad.

In addition to Candomblé, other icons loaded with Africanness were incorporated into the notion of Bahianness beginning in the 1930s. Among these black symbols were the *baiana de acarajé*—women street vendors who sold deep-fried black-eyed pea fritters of Yoruba origins—and the African dishes or combinations invented by slaves in Brazil and consumed by the lower classes, but which gained fame and moved up the social ladder by being classified as "typical Bahian food." Two striking examples of the social mobility of African-derived dishes in Bahia are the quasi-sacred dinner of Good Friday—composed of *moqueca* (a fish stew cooked in palm oil) accompanied by *vatapá* (a dish made with peanuts, cashews, dried shrimp, and flour, cooked in palm oil) and *caruru* (a dish made with mashed okra cooked in palm oil), which has become a tradition among Bahian families of all colors, classes, and creeds—and the "Caruru de Sete Meninos" (Caruru of the Seven Boys), a dinner-offering to saints Cosmas and Damian usually made following the fulfillment of a wish believed to have been caused by their power.[7] Not only is Candomblé food eaten by hosts and guests and offered to the saints in little bowls, but Candomblé songs are sang in the ceremony, accompanied by hand clapping and sometimes even by some samba dancing. Ironically, this tradition is carried out in Bahia by many Catholics who demonize Candomblé and thus refuse to recognize the syncretic character of this ritual.

Another contradiction of the Bahian celebration of Africanness is that the black contribution to Bahian cuisine is not only the dishes themselves but also the labor of black people, especially black women, who are perceived as naturally and almost magically endowed with the ability to prepare the dishes. Freyre stated, "Bahia has given us some of the empire's most important lawmakers and diplomats, and the tastiest dishes of Brazilian cuisine are prepared nowhere better than in the old houses of Salvador and the Recôncavo" (1990, 9). The flavor of African-derived delicacies, which Freyre celebrated as symbols of Bahia's *mestiçagem*, is enhanced when they are served by the fat black hands of old Bahian women: "Because there are foods that are not the same if made at home instead of bought from the platters [of the *baianas*]. *Arroz doce* [a type of rice pudding], for instance, is almost always tastier if made by the hands of a *negra de tabuleiro* [black female street vendor] than if made at home. And the same can be said of other sweets and delicacies. Fried fish, for example, is only appetizing if made by the *preta de tabuleiro*" (Freyre 1952 [1926]).

With their natural aptitudes for preparing the region's typical dishes, the black and *mulata* females of Jorge Amado's novels guarantee the longevity of one of the major ideals of Freyre's *Manifesto regionalista*: guarding against the "increasing loss of characteristics of regional cuisine" (Freyre 1952 [1926]). These female characters indicate the importance of gender representations for the process of constructing Brazilian nationality. Nations have been imagined based on identities that are racialized and perceived as either masculine or feminine. Grounded on idealized notions of "race" and gender, the narrative of the nation, in turn, reciprocally contributes to strengthening representations of femininity, masculinity, blackness, and whiteness.

Enthusiastic about both Afro-Bahian food and the Afro-Bahian women who magically flavored it, Freyre stimulated the spread of restaurants that sold typically black food. As early as the 1920s, Freyre defended this type of restaurant as an icon of Afro-Brazilian cultural fusion. Criticizing his passionate regionalism, an unknown modernist scholar had mocked Freyre's

Manifesto regionalista by stating that, if one was to follow its guidelines, "one would establish in the city [of Salvador] a restaurant serving 'black foods,' where a *preta da Costa* [a black woman from the coast of Africa] would stand at the front door roasting corn-on-the-cob, or cooking tapioca. Not served by conventional waiters . . . but by *mucamas* [female domestic slaves] wrapped in burgundy shawls and wearing slippers without socks, and offering the clients coconut water inside the coconut itself, tamarind juice, passion-fruit juice with *cachaça* [alcoholic beverage made of sugar cane]" (Freyre 1952 [1926]). Ironically and unintentionally, this caricature of the early twentieth century provides a meticulous description of Salvador's current and most famous restaurants that serve typical Afro-Bahian food, where waitresses are indeed dressed as domestic slaves and serve tropical fruit juices and dishes cooked in palm oil to tourists and Bahians alike.

Gilberto Freyre amalgamated *people* — especially black women — with *place* to narrate a magical notion of Bahia. In the article "Bahia à tarde" (Bahia in the afternoon), which Freyre wrote upon his first visit to Salvador, the city is described as a female. Granted, *"cidade"* (city) is a feminine noun in Portuguese, but Freyre literally depicts Bahia as a woman, and more specifically, a black woman. Alternating between representations of Bahia as an old mammy endowed with a cozy lap and large breasts, and as a young, juicy *mulata*, Freyre employed the epithets *"cidade-mãe"* (mother city), *"cidade ama de leite das cidades do Brasil"* (wet-nurse city for Brazil's other cities), *"cidade gorda"* (plump or fat city), *"de igrejas gordas e matriarcais"* (filled with plump and matriarchal churches). Akin to the young *mulatas* that gave birth to Brazil's *mestiços*, the city of Bahia was also portrayed by Freyre in terms of its maternal role: "a city of mounds jetting out like the wombs of women in the final months of pregnancy, avowing to deliver more cities to Brazil" (Freyre 1926, reprinted in Freyre 1990, 13).[8]

Still merging people and place, Freyre described *baianas de acarajé* — whom he termed *"pretalhonas imensas"* (huge black women) — as flesh-and-blood statues who, together with trees and monuments, compose Bahia's scenery.

And the tableau became . . . an art, a science, a specialty of the *"baianas"* or black women: women who are nearly always spectacularly fat, sitting on a street corner or in the shade of a church, seemed to become, from their sheer corpulence, the street's center or the church's courtyard. Their majesty was sometimes akin to that of monuments — gigantic statues made of flesh. And they weren't just like any other woman. Many grew so old they became eternal, like monuments — the springs, the fountains, the matriarchal trees — selling sweets or cakes to three generations of ravenous boys and even men, in those same courtyards and same street corners. (Freyre 1952 [1926])

The "plump church buildings" inhabit and enliven the Bahian landscape as much as the round bodies of the old mammies and the young *mulatas* in Freyre's celebration of the city. This fusion of the city and its people, represented by the rounded shape of both the churches and the women, is also recurrent in the novels of Jorge Amado. In *Dona Flor and Her Two Husbands* (1966), the male character Vadinho hooks up, during Carnaval, with a literally "monumental" *mulata* whose body Amado compares to one of Salvador's most famous church buildings: "Vadinho . . . stood in front of the *morena* dark-tanned woman, a very big woman, monumental like a church building, like the church of Saint Francis, for she covered herself in a splurge of golden sequins" (quoted in Salah 2000, 97).

Both Freyre's and Amado's oeuvres described the bodies of dark-skinned women as naturally predisposed to provide pleasure. Elsewhere (Pinho 2006a) I have discussed the recurring representations of young sexy *mulatas* and old maternal black women in the work of both authors. I argue that these binary and complementary opposites have helped confirm the notion of Afro-descendant women's innate inclination for servitude. The famous poem written by Freyre to celebrate Bahia reads: "Old black women from Bahia / selling *mingau* [porridge], *angu*, *acarajé* / Old black women with bright red shawls / sagging breasts / mothers of the most beautiful *mulatas* of Brazil / *mulatas* with plump breasts, nipples erect / as if ready to breastfeed all the children of Brazil" (Freyre 1990, 17).

If the old black women are the *mulatas'* mothers, Freyre is assuming — or better yet, proposing — that racial miscegenation occurred. The old women's sagging breasts suggest that a great part of their lives was spent breastfeeding. Left with worn-out bosoms and genitals, the old black women can now offer pleasure only through the flavor produced by their hands. No longer useful in bed, they still know how to please at the table. The plump breasts of the young *mulatas*, on the other hand, point toward an endless source of pleasure, comfort, and entertainment to be provided by their blackness. Conditioning their existence to the contentment of others, these representations of black femininity have functioned as metaphors of Bahia's blackness. The fact that the myth of Mama Africa put forward by the *blocos* is greatly centered on the black body further contributes to the convergence of the apparently oppositional discourses of blackness and *Bahianness*.

Black Bodies and Contagious Culture

The celebrated black image of Bahia certainly owes much to the representations of its population's black bodies. Since early on, foreign travelers were perplexed by the abundance of black people in the city of Salvador, and they commented extensively and in detail about the supposed exotic aspects of the male and female black bodies, such as their strong muscles, luminous skin, sensuality, rhythmic strides and movements, and intensely dark tones — in addition, of course, to their supposed unabashed nudity. In 1714, Amédée Frézier wrote, "Ninety-five percent of the people you see in Cidade Baixa are black women and men, completely nude except for the parts over which prudence calls for coverage, so that this city resembles a new Guinea" (quoted in Verger 1999a, 21). From the beginning, Bahia had a "black face," for it received most of the five million enslaved Africans brought to Brazil during the three and a half centuries of the slave trade. In addition to being called a new Guinea, the city was also nicknamed "Negroland" by poet Robert Southey, who was impressed by the majority black population in 1819 (quoted in Verger 1999a).

In 1859, explorer Avé Lallement wrote, "If one did not know that Bahia is located in Brazil, one could easily imagine it to be an African capital, the residence of a powerful Black prince. . . . Everything looks Black: Blacks on the beach, Blacks in the city, Blacks in the low part, Blacks in the high city. Everything that runs, shouts, works, everything that transports and carries is Black" (quoted in Verger 1999a, 21). Fascinated with this sight of muscular slave bodies, Lallement continues in a voyeuristic tone: "Squeezed up against each other under the clothesline, these jet-black men form the most admirable athletic group ever seen. What most impressed us with regard to muscle development was the great mobility of the joints, which infuses even the heaviest labor with a certain grace. Carrying loads is almost a dance" (quoted in Verger 1999a, 22).

Currently, the vast majority of Bahia's postcards, especially those portraying people, include black bodies performing capoeira, dancing samba, or cooking *acarajés*, not to mention the postcards displaying close-ups of black and *mestiço* women's buttocks in minuscule bikinis. Travel posters and Jorge Amado's novels, translated into 49 languages, transmit to other countries an image of Brazil that is sensual, heartwarming, and exotic.[9] In addition to the sexualized image, the female black body is also represented by the "*baiana de acarajé.*" Their platters filled with *acarajé, abará, vatapá, caruru, cocada,* and *mingau, baianas* are among the symbols that most Africanize Bahia's public image and are inarguably the major icons of Bahianness.[10] Their black bodies, dressed in white "African" outfits and adorned with necklaces, *guias,* and *balangadans,* have long been considered picturesque objects that "blacken" the landscape of the city of Bahia.[11]

In the beginning of the twentieth century, Austrian writer Stefan Zweig stated, "In the enduring picturesque scenery the most picturesque [things] are *baianas*, the fat black women with dark eyes and special outfits. . . . The importance of these *baianas* is not exactly in their outfit; it is the elegance with which they use it, in their stride, in their manners. Sitting at the market or on a doorstep, they arrange their skirt as if it were a royal gown, so as to look like they are sitting inside a flower" (quoted in Verger 1999a, 5). In the fantasy of such foreigners, the people and the city blend together, forming an inseparable whole. Currently, many Bahians themselves seem to have been convinced that there is a continuous cycle fusing the curves of their bodies to the winding streets and alleys of Bahia.

The invention of Bahianness, like the process of establishing the characteristics of any people or nation, requires setting up a sense of homogeneity that can eradicate internal differences. However, there are many Bahias within Bahia. In each of them, very different black bodies inhabit the landscape. The enormous favelas where most of Bahia's black population lives are inhabited by fragile and tired black bodies that are considered unattractive, while tourist sites and city landmarks are adorned with lively, healthy black bodies, deemed aesthetically pleasing. The much visited neighborhood of Pelourinho is graced by athletic black male capoeira performers and young black women chosen to literally pose as *baianas* for tourist photographs. Most of these black dancers, performers, and models are hired by the state tourism board (Bahiatursa) or by stores and restaurants that cater to tourists. The sad irony is that, as during the period of slavery, black bodies are once again selected according to their size, shape, and ability to be displayed at the center of the city of Bahia and its public image.

The ubiquity of black bodies is coupled with the notion of their allegedly natural rhythm, the *gingado*. This "essential trait" of the black body, epitomized through the sensual forms of the new dances invented each Carnaval season, has become a symbol of the Bahianness rooted in blackness; the black body's "natural inclination" toward dance and music has been at the heart of Bahianness. At times, especially during Carnaval and street festivals, the black body's *gingado* curiously spreads out to inhabit the bodies of all Bahians, regardless of color. Santos (2005, 89) explains that in the 1970s, in its attempt to promote a mystical and exotic image of Bahia and its people, the state-backed tourism industry invented the notion of a "Bahian way of life" (*"viver baiano"*) characterized by "affection," "magic," and "infectiousness" — all seen as typically black characteristics. I would add that this "infectiousness" of black culture, which had been a source of fear in the past, began to represent a desirable trait that is now seen as being transmitted from blacks to nonblacks, supposedly bestowing upon all *baianos* the natural propensity toward dance and music. As Browning (1998) argues, the "infectious rhythm" of black culture is a metaphor that contradictorily implies both "contagion" — as in the threat of pollution represented by the Africanized Carnaval groups of the early twentieth century — and that which is "irresistible." It is both catching and catchy. The delightful "Bahian way of life" was captured in the official slogan of Bahia chosen by Bahiatursa: *"Bahia: Terra da Felicidade"* (Bahia: Land of Happiness). Cutting across "race" and class, the infectious rhythm of Bahia's blackness fulfils the role of regional / national symbols while it simultaneously reinforces the notion of joyfulness as an inherent characteristic of black people.

Endowed with its supposed natural tendencies, the black body has circulated simultaneously as a sign of resistance to racism and as an object that can be consumed. Afro-Bahian culture, and the black bodies that produce it, are marketed mainly in the spheres of the tourism and music industries. This commercialization is only made possible due to the relationship between cultural producers and Bahia's state government. The use of the black body as a commodity is more evident in the "explicitly black spaces": that is, the spaces in which being black is an advantage: *blocos afro*, capoeira, and Candomblé *terreiros*. "The explicitly [black] spaces operate around activities considered typical of the [black] 'race,' in which blacks have always been able and expected to shine. They are the moments during which a significant percentage of blacks — especially lower-class blacks — feel more comfortable, able to openly express characteristics of their own personality and cultural creations considered out of place elsewhere. In these spaces, blackness is often openly addressed; blacks are in charge and nonblacks must negotiate their participation" (Sansone 1995b, 183).[12]

The moment of Carnaval, for instance, is an explicitly black space which, coupled with the oft-cited inversion of values that takes place during this period, leads whites to imitate blacks through hairstyles and outfits. The *abadás*, the *blocos'* Carnaval costumes, are sought by young white members of the middle class, who braid their hair or wear Rastafari hats with fake dreadlocks only during this celebration. During the 1990s, Olodum's *abadás* became a much-desired commodity for Bahia's middle classes, not only because of the mainstream popularity the *bloco* enjoyed but also because, as a predominantly black but nevertheless inclusive *bloco afro*, it allows for a negotiation of whites' participation in an explicitly black space. Above all, Carnaval is a moment when nonblack Bahians emulate the black *gingado*, or better yet, try to "awaken" the blackness that Bahian bodies supposedly carry.

Realizing the importance of Carnaval — both for its more immediate objective of obtaining votes, as well as for its longer-term goal of shaping a harmonious image of Bahia — in 1981 the state government extended the Carnaval season from three to six days. The justification for this measure is signaled in the following excerpt from a former governor's Web site:

> Bahia's Carnaval is a street celebration, a festival of the people. It is not a spectacle to be observed from a box seat. Everyone strolls through the streets, accompanying their *blocos*, *afoxés* (African *blocos*), which are a spectacle in their own right and impart a religious tone to Carnaval's profane festivities. In the past, Carnaval lasted three days and three nights. Today, it captivates and involves everyone for over a week. *Trios elétricos* first emerged in Bahia, with three people playing primitive guitars on top of a regular car. Today, they are huge, brightly lit trucks with powerful sound systems blasting amazing rhythms. As one poet has stated, "The dead are the only ones to not follow behind a *trio elétrico*." One song says, "Joy is a state called Bahia."[13]

Confirming the tendency initiated in the 1930s, when scholars and politicians from the Northeast were striving to challenge the hegemony of the southeastern urban centers, the above narrative establishes Bahia's regional identity as rooted in the authenticity of people's participation. This explains the implicit yet unmistakable reference to Rio's Carnaval, "a spectacle to be observed from a box seat," as opposed to Bahia's "festival of the people." *Blocos afro* and *afoxés*, represented as belonging to all Bahians, supposedly purify, with their religious overtones, the profane character of Carnaval. Not only is the idea of purification borrowed from Candomblé's emphasis on cleansing, but it also functions as the other side of the same coin of infectiousness. By emphasizing that Carnaval "captivates" and "involves" all Bahians, the quote reiterates, simultaneously, the contagiousness of black culture, the "Bahian way of life," and the natural association between joy, blackness, and Bahianness.

The contagiousness of black culture is also celebrated in the Festival of the Bonfim Church, an annual event where female Candomblé devotees wash the steps of Bahia's most famous church in a ritual of cleansing. As early as 1947, Freyre declared his admiration for the syncretic character of the event and publicly criticized the intransigence of the bishop who prohibited the women from washing the steps of the church as a means of detaching Catholicism from Candomblé. For Freyre, syncretism was not only a matter of fusion of religious traits of different cultures but a means through which Christianity was "sweetly gaining victory" over African cults, "without the need of police or soldiers to carry out this tender process of Christianization" (Freyre 1990, 89). Nowadays, the Bonfim Festival constitutes one of the major stages for the performance of Bahianness, where black cultural expressions — such as the Candomblé cleansing ritual of the washing of the steps and the pre-Carnaval parade of the *blocos afro* and *afoxés* — are supported by conservative politicians who milk the occasion to gain popularity and legitimacy amongst the people. As they circulate among Candomblé devotees, seeking their blessings by being sprinkled with the perfumed waters brought for the cleansing, these politicians demonstrate that the gentle process of domesticating conflicts is vigorous and ongoing.

Paradoxically, the more black culture loans its "contagious" aura for the purpose of promoting Bahianness, the more it is reduced to a fixed or limited set of cultural expressions. The relationship between blackness and Bahianness can thus be defined as a sort of synechdoche, since it elects a small segment of culture to represent culture as a whole and thus confer authenticity upon it. In general, a synecdochic representation of a particular culture makes it appear to be a component of the national cultural heritage, like a contemporary remnant of the roots of miscegenation (Briggs 1996). The following excerpt, from Senator Antônio Carlos Magalhães's Web site, further illustrates the process through which Bahia's official public image handpicks objects from black culture to narrate the myth of Bahianness:

> In Bahia, religious belief is not solely a spectacle or an enactment of beliefs. Mysticism is present at all times and in all places. The young and the old, of all social classes, regularly tie colorful ribbons around their wrists, on their rearview mirrors, and even around work tools. These

ribbons are not merely for decoration; they are symbols of faith in our Lord of Bonfim [Jesus Christ], the saint of Bahians. In Candomblé, the Lord of Bonfim is *Oxalá* [one of the orixás, or Yoruba gods]; white is the color dedicated to him; and Friday is his day. For this reason, on such days, you will see many people in Bahia dressed in white, even those who have no affiliation with Candomblé. A symbol of good luck, the *figa* — a talisman of a fist with its thumb sticking up between the index and middle fingers — is everywhere. Although they may look like decorations, some plants are specifically positioned to protect household residents. Bahians have the habit of crossing themselves when they walk by a church, and roses and perfume are commonly thrown into the ocean as gifts to Iemanjá [one of the Yoruba goddesses whose realm is the ocean]. Even typical dishes served in restaurants — *vatapá, caruru, efó* [a stew of vegetables and shrimp] and so many others — are basically the same as those offered to the *terreiro* deities. Women of African origin sell *acarajé* and *abará* in the streets, which are types of African bread made with beans, providing them with a means to survive as well as a means to fulfill their duties toward the *terreiros*, the religious temples of the *orixás*.[14]

Based on the fact that Bahian food, religion, and habits are undeniably syncretic, the above narrative deliberately emphasizes the contagiousness of the icons and beliefs of Candomblé in mainstream Bahian culture. Not only are the elements originated within black culture represented as available to all, "even those who have no affiliation with Candomblé," but black bodies are at the same time portrayed as the disseminators of this contagious culture, as exemplified by the "women of African origin" — *the baianas de acarajé* — that generously offer all Bahians an entrance into the mystical world of Afro-Brazilian religion. This synecdoche couples "old" black cultural elements, such as those originated in Candomblé and Afro-Bahian cuisine, with "new" symbols of blackness, especially those produced by the *blocos afro*. My emphasis here is less on the market than on the political meanings that these black symbols acquire as they circulate in Bahia's mainstream culture.

Although it first started in the 1930s, the process of constructing Bahia's regional identity continues at full steam. The novelty is that it now incorporates black cultural elements that were recently created or resignified by black activists to establish a diacritical and oppositional Afro-descendent identity. The representations of *blocos afro* in state and tourism advertising, as illustrated in the quotes discussed in this chapter, are emblematic of this process. The hyper-black Afro symbols — black hairstyles and the Afro look consisting of "African" fabric patterns, turbans, and bold colors — have also been incorporated into the process of forging Bahianness, since they have been increasingly employed in the images produced and circulated by the tourism industry and the state. Paradoxically, the black ethnic identity that has been meticulously produced by grassroots organizations with the intention of emphasizing the boundaries that separate blacks from whites and which reclaims "black culture" for the "black race has become ever more absorbed into the discourse of *baianidade*.

Emblematic of this process is the fact that the Bahian media, despite dedicating significant time to publicizing black cultural production, always emphasize the ludic, "cultural" side of black organizations, thus representing them as pieces of the dominant Bahian culture. For example, in the media, Ilê Aiyê is constantly referred to as the most traditional *bloco afro from Bahia* and a practitioner of Bahian culture. Olodum is generally portrayed as the most famous Bahian *bloco afro* in the world. Rarely do media representations refer to the groups' social and political activities; the emphasis is on their musical and artistic nature. The main black organizations of Salvador are treated in the same manner, despite their dissonant ethnic discourse. Their diacritic black symbols are thus dissolved into the notion of a homogenous Bahianness.

Araújo Pinho (1998; 2000) points out that, more so than in previous decades, black culture currently occupies a central position in the representations of Bahian culture, depicted predominantly by folkloric and hence alienating elements. These elements are used not only to define Bahian culture but also to construct black identities, comprising the market of symbolic goods and creating an overlap that further confounds the social and racial situation in Salvador. I concur with Araújo Pinho's notion that Bahianness is a myth spread by the dominant sectors of society, in which gaiety and emotion replace reason. However, we should not lose sight of the fact that myths are not imposed from the top down. They are neither lies nor masks created to deceive the oppressed sectors of society, as if they were formed by gullible individuals devoid of agency. If the celebration of this Bahianness grounded in blackness is an ideological device sold as something natural, it can only gain legitimacy if those who are at the bottom also embrace the myth, even if they employ it for what seems to be their own benefit.

If the notion of a Bahianness grounded in blackness is useful for the economic and political Bahian elites, specific black cultural producers also capitalize a great deal on the myth of *baianidade*, while simultaneously lending it legitimacy and authenticity. In effect, the myth of Bahianness largely overlaps with the myth of Mama Africa, not only because both narratives share the same black symbols and objects, but because they are endorsed by the same social actors: tourist agents and politicians on the one hand, and black activists and cultural producers on the other hand. Rather than operating in opposition to one another, these sectors of Bahian society work much more in tandem than it may seem at first sight.

Criticizing what he terms the assimilation of black cultural production into national culture, Kabengele Munanga states that black Bahian pop music, called *axé music*, while primarily produced by blacks and defined as Afro-Bahian, is sung by all Brazilians without racial distinction. "The world sees it as Brazilian music and therefore an element of Brazilian identity to be integrated within a plural, non-syncretic Brazilian culture. This integration of cultural diversities or pluralities is what characterizes, in my opinion, Brazilian assimilationism. It allows for so-called national culture — stitched together like a quilt made of scraps instead of synthesis — to not hinder cultural production of ethnic minorities, despite repression in the past, but to only inhibit their political expression as an opposition within the national context" (1999, 108).

I differ with Munanga's position, arguing that the transformation of black symbols into Bahian symbols should not be understood merely as assimilationism or cooption of black/ethnic into Bahian, in the same way that Brazilianist social scientists have argued concerning the cooption of ethnic into national. The founding text of this perspective was Peter Fry's (1977) discussion of Brazil's national *feijoada* as compared to African-American ethnic soul food, examined in chapter 4. Certain specific conditions must be considered in the fusion between black and Bahian cultures. We should not see this relationship as an attack on black culture by Bahian culture, modeling ourselves on the logic of Afrocentrism, which contends that the Greeks stole knowledge from Egyptians to claim it as their own. The intricate and complex fusion of black culture and Bahian culture cannot be grasped under such a Manichean and superficial judgment.

First of all, we must understand that the labels *black culture* and *Bahian culture* are, to a great extent, artificial. While elite sectors of Brazilian society have deliberately employed symbols and objects previously identified as black to create a harmonious image of the nation, nonblacks have partaken in the production and consumption of these same cultural expressions from the very beginning. Poor whites were composing and listening to samba long before it became Brazil's national rhythm. Unrestrained and rebellious, black cultures in the diaspora do not obey the delineations imposed by intellectuals and activists. Culture is unbound and cannot be fixed to a limited realm of objects or expressions, nor can it be effectively appropriated by a specific group.

In addition to the complex question of ownership of culture, the agency of cultural producers should also be taken into account. While Munanga's perspective represents black cultural producers as victims of extortion, I prefer to focus on the process of negotiation that takes place in the objectification and commoditization of black culture. This is certainly not the easiest choice, because, by emphasizing black agency, I also bring to light the pragmatic practices of compromise and surrender. The collaboration between black leaders, politicians, and intellectuals in Brazil can be traced back at least to the 1930s, when together they organized the movement to resist and overcome police repression against Candomblé *terreiros*. While extremely important for establishing freedom of religion, as well as social acceptance of Candomblé, this process also instituted a hierarchy that valued the "most traditional" *terreiros* over those considered more "mixed."

The Africanized aesthetics of the allegedly purer forms of Candomblé played a crucial role in attracting the members of the political and intellectual elite who could then manipulate black symbols in order to adorn state-sanctioned public festivals. Dantas (1988) described the process through which the hegemony of the Jeje-Nagô (Yoruba) Candomblé was established in the Northeast. Perceived by scholars and promoted by its devotees as "purer" and "more traditional" (compared to *caboclo* Candomblé, for instance), Yoruba *terreiros* became the archetype of Afro-Brazilian tradition due to the negotiations carried out between priests and priestesses and Bahian authorities. In the preface to Dantas's book, Fry proposes that this same logic can be attributed to the *blocos afro*. Similar to the process that established a hierarchy of Candomblé *terreiros*, politicians and scholars have played a crucial role in defining Ilê Aiyê, the most "African" of them, as the quintessential Bahian *bloco afro* and putting it front and center in the official imagery of Bahia.

The negotiation between local politicians and black cultural producers has been especially noticeable during electoral races. The strategy of mixing

Bahianness and blackness with local politics was quite evident during An-tônio Imbassahy's campaign for reelection as mayor of Salvador. From mid-August to the end of September of 2000, through federally mandated and financed daily radio and television ads, the candidate used the exact same theme song used in that year's official Carnaval commercials, broadcast extensively on TV Bahia, owned by Magalhães's group. With Ivete San-galo's voice in the background singing Timbalada's lyrics: "This city is a beautiful sight / This city is a beautiful sight / Welcome to our headquarters / Saint Salvador was born for you," the ad campaign used images very similar to those used in the Carnaval ads six months earlier, featuring *baianas de acarajé*, capoeira performers, and black dancers swaying along the streets. The reelection campaign also relied on the support of many local musicians and black cultural producers. Carlinhos Brown, Gerônimo, and leaders of Ilê Aiyê and Malê de Balê provided their images and voices, as well as their "blackness," to publicly endorse the candidate. In radio ads, Ilê Aiyê's presi-dent praised the mayor's work in the city's poor suburbs and argued in favor of his reelection. He then urged black community members to identify themselves as blacks in the 2000 national census. Such actions are considered a type of political exchange by the *bloco afro*, because the group's president— and consequently the group itself, and ultimately Bahia's black culture— were used by the political party and at the same time themselves used the party as a channel of racial awareness, since the *bloco*'s president addressed the issue of racial identification on the census.[15]

This exchange between black organizations and local politicians is not restricted to opportunities for propagating racial awareness. The group often allows use of its image—a symbol of blackness and Bahianness—in exchange for material rewards. Ilê Aiyê's president discussed the 2000 elec-tions in an interview: "We are a group of interest to Bahia, we represent Bahia very well, so there must be some reward for that. . . . I think that today there is no longer that romanticized thing where you simply show up and do something. For example, two of our projects were funded by the government, and that doesn't mean that you're committing to the govern-ment, because the project's there, the money's there; if you have a compe-tent project they should approve it. That doesn't mean there's a political affiliation." Christopher Dunn (1992, footnote 15), however, defined *blocos afro*'s patronage relationships with conservative politicians as an obstacle to their process of establishing power. Upon visiting Salvador in 1990, Dunn noticed Ilê Aiyê T-shirts with endorsements for a local white elite politician. When asked about the connection, Vovô responded that the exchange of advertising space for financial support did not mean official endorsement of the candidate.

Such attitudes represent a change with regard to the initial stance of the *blocos afro*, who previously emphasized the need for independence from politicians' control. In the early 1980s, Ilê Aiyê distributed an article that strongly criticized exchange relationships between local politicians and *blocos afro*:

> There are a small number of independent [*blocos*], among them Ilê Aiyê and Malê de Balê, that carry on activities outside the commercial folkloric circuit, and that do not depend on politicians to survive, but they suffer continuous harassment from white organizations and politicians to join them in a relationship of patronage or protection, a very common form of exploitation in Africa and here in Brazil, in Bahia, during the 1930s and 1940s. This patronage or protection happens on two levels: promises of headquarter sites, percussion instruments, materials, open space for rehearsals, and money, in exchange for sponsorships, public appearances for candidates and future candidates . . . ; at the cultural level, sponsorship is at the same time more aggressive and subtle, for it manifests itself through white academic institutions that are home to a few assimilated blacks, whose eloquent antiracist progressive discourse hides the intentions of colonial and racist anthropology that studies the exotic black, the black outside the sociopolitical context. (Ilê Aiyê 1982, 36–37)

Bahia is not the only place where black organizations negotiate their cultural production with local politicians. Myriam Santos describes the mutual exchange of favors between politicians and samba schools in Rio de Janeiro that began in the 1930s. In the beginning there were two types of samba school leaders: those who had power and money to finance parades and those who exerted charismatic influence on the population, the so-called *malandros*. As the parades became more regulated, these leaders were replaced by men backed by the government and the press: that is, leaders who have had the ability to negotiate with politicians. Since then, politicians have actively sought out relationships with samba schools. Santos argues that samba schools thus represent a place of constant negotiation, in which "musicians want to sell their music; black and poor people want their culture to be recognized, along with the right to march down the streets; the school directors want money and prestige; the middle class wants entertainment; [companies] want to sell products; and politicians want to legitimize their leadership" (1999, 75).

Although I agree that there is an intense process of negotiation between *sambistas* and politicians, I believe this process is much more complex than Santos describes. The "currency" offered by each social actor has a very different value, and such exchanges restrict the role of black culture to a mere form of entertainment for the middle class and a source of empowerment for political leaders. Considering the power disparity between the agents, and the greater benefit that politicians derive from this relationship, we should view such exchanges with caution, since they can result in further dominance over those who have fought so long for freedom and autonomy. As Bahia's public image has become blacker, local politicians have increasingly sought to negotiate with producers of culture. However, there is a great difference between the overwhelming power exerted by politicians and the limited power of Candomblé practitioners, members of *blocos afro* and capoeira schools, and *baianas de acarajé*.

In the northeastern state of Maranhão, the relationship between black cultural producers and local politicians follows along the same arrangements of cooption and consent. Carlos Rodrigues da Silva, an anthropologist, describes the participation of politicians in *bois* — performances carried out during the festivities for Saint John in the month of June — explaining that this brings recognition to both politicians and cultural groups. There are also similarities with Bahia regarding the use of local black culture in forming and disseminating a public image of the state of Maranhão: "The State Board of Culture, supported by the political agendas of [political parties] PSDB and PFL, in turn, is geared toward movements of modernity, 'opening Maranhão from the inside out,' such as the proposal of Governor Roseana Sarney, whose family has controlled the main sociocultural and political decisions in Maranhão during the last decades of the twentieth century. This 'openness toward modernity' involves implementation of both socioeconomic projects and cultural manifestations, which range from Jamaican reggae to *axé* bands from Bahia, to *forró* [a dance and musical style from the backlands of the Northeast] groups from Ceará" (Silva 2001, 24).

The use of folkloric elements of local cultures to create an official state image is not limited to Brazil. Charles Briggs (1996) describes the control that Venezuelan state institutions exert over popular culture by financing performances that reflect the interests of governmental bodies. Government representatives determine which groups should be included in the performances, as well as which cultural forms should be selected to be presented to the public and the media. Peter Wade writes about a similar process in Colombia: "A public space financed by the local government had been created for 'blackness,' and the space was created around music. This is a double edged sword. On the one hand, music can have a great public impact and on the other hand, it is being constantly subjected to cooption and trivialization" (2000, viii).

In Bahia, the *blocos afro* are not the only ones who trade their blackness to confer Bahianness on the state's official image. The vast majority of Bahian cultural organizations offer their cultural production as a commodity in exchange for material goods and gifts, which can vary from musical instruments to facilities to serve as headquarters. Olodum, which initially took an oppositional political stance and which openly supported the candidacy of the leftist coalition in the Salvador mayoral elections in 1992, later changed its tune. Up until 1993, the year in which Pelourinho underwent a major revitalization project conducted by the Bahia state government, Olodum had always taken quite a different stance from other local black groups, pronouncing itself openly as a leftist organization and supporting the candidacy of politicians who opposed the old Bahian oligarchies.

However, once Pelourinho was revitalized the group's stance changed — a shift reflected even in the group's lyrics. The song "Olodum, filhos do sol" (Olodum, sons of the sun), written in 1994, exalts the "new Pelourinho" as different and better than the old Pelourinho, represented as a site of crime, prostitution, and decay: "Pelourinho is no longer the same / Look at its face / You're no longer lost / There are lots of good people [here]." The revitalization of Pelourinho was itself very controversial. Among other things, the state government deceived the neighborhood's residents, providing much lower financial compensation than promised. The residents were evicted from their colonial-era homes — which were in terrible shape but were quickly restored and occupied by tourism-related businesses — and relegated to poor and distant neighborhoods in Salvador's periphery. Olodum's image also became employed in the state's official advertisements. The publicity campaign for the supermarket chain Cesta do Povo, for example, featured two of its main singers dressed in green, yellow, and red — originally the colors of Ethiopia and adopted by Rastafarians but which in Bahia are considered to be the colors of Olodum — advertising modestly priced products such as beans, rice, and cooking oil. Cesta do Povo, despite being limited geographically to Bahia, is one of Brazil's largest supermarket chains. The state-sponsored business was founded in 1980 as part of EBAL (Empresa Baiana de Alimentos — Bahian

Food Company), along with a series of other populist measures by then-governor Magalhães. Devoid of luxuries and other overhead costs, Cesta do Povo sells food at below-average prices. The supermarket's first publicity spokesperson was a black singer who enjoyed some popularity in the 1980s, ironically named Chocolate da Bahia.

Two recent events further illustrate the intricate relationship between the official Bahian culture and the black culture produced by grassroots organizations. This connection involves not only cooption, assimilation, and consumption on behalf of the state, but also permission, conformity, and consent on behalf of the cultural producers. The quincentennial celebration of the Portuguese "discovery" of Brazil, in 2000, and the public "reaction" in Bahia to the national campaign to impeach Senator Antônio Carlos Magalhães in 2001, offer evidence of a complex relationship that is not simply one between victims and victimizers.

In the prelude to the quincentennial celebration, in April of 2000, Bahia's state government aggressively repressed grassroots organizations such as black and indigenous groups and the Landless Movement, among others, who were protesting the event in Porto Seguro (the site where the Portuguese first landed, in southern Bahia). At the same time, many black cultural organizations of Salvador participated in the official parade organized by the very same government. The parade route stretched from Campo Grande to Castro Alves Plaza, two of the state capital's politically significant points. One of the parade's icons was Princess Isabel, represented by an actress who spent endless hours on top of an electric float, simulating the historical figure's signing of Brazil's abolition law over and over. Even more confounding was the presence of several black cultural group members dressed as slaves, playing their drums in celebration of a princess who, ever since the founding of the MNU, is no longer seen as a heroine in the eyes of blacks, having been replaced by Zumbi dos Palmares.[16] By participating in the official quincentennial of Portuguese discovery, these organizations adopted a stance contrary to the one taken during the lead-up to the centennial of the abolition of slavery, in 1988. At that time, much of the black population was encouraged by black organizations, including *blocos afro*, to turn their backs on the official celebrations, in rejection of the hypocrisy of a society that had freed slaves from slavery without devising strategies to include them in society as free workers.[17]

Other recent events marked the celebration of this Bahianness-founded-on-blackness and its ties to local power. The most extreme was the orchestrated public reaction to the national campaign to impeach Senator Antônio Carlos Magalhães following a corruption scandal, which culminated in his resignation in late May 2001. Demonstrations of support for Magalhães featured both the intellectual and artistic elite of Bahia, as well as popular manifestations in Pelourinho, confirming the totalitarian character of the idea of Bahia that permeates all classes of society. From the first group, the embattled senator received a show of support by Gal Costa, Zélia Gattai, Dona Canô, and other illustrious Bahians. While these supporters were immediately attacked by Brazilian intellectual critics, their stance is not surprising. Such individuals are openly committed — even if symbolically — to the Bahian oligarchy, and it is no coincidence that they also represent icons of Bahianness. As part of one of the city's newest public projects, the expansion of the Avenida Paralela was named the Dona Canô Overpass. Gal Costa, like most Bahian artists, solicits the "blessings" of Bahia's traditional politicians. This practice is common during Carnaval, when almost all of the electric floats stop, one by one, in front of the VIP box to celebrate the main representatives of the state's political oligarchy, who are often wearing a *bloco afro* costume. The friendship between former anarchist Zelia Gattai and former Communist Jorge Amado and Senator Magalhães is nothing new, either, since it was useful, among other things, in providing impetus to the Pelourinho revitalization project. In a public ceremony, Amado pronounced, "Historical downtown is the most faithful portrait of the mystical, jovial, and festive spirit that enraptures Bahia and its people. The importance of this heritage is priceless."[18]

Popular manifestations of support for the politician took place on the streets, clearly capturing the relationship between black culture, official Bahian culture, and local politics. The most important black cultural groups of Salvador, including Olodum, Ilê Aiyê, Filhos de Gandhy, Didá, and other famous capoeira masters and *baianas de acarajé*, went to Pelourinho to honor Magalhães in an event organized by his own party and intended to look like a spontaneous demonstration on the part of the "Bahian people." The stage for this enactment, which blends Bahianness, blackness, and politics, was none other than the supposed locus of black cultural production, and the city's most popular postcard image: Pelourinho.

Confirming the tendency to spread the notion that Bahia's ideological disposition is natural and spontaneous, the newspaper *Correio da Bahia* (the state's second-largest newspaper, owned by Magalhães's political group) described the event as follows:

Bahia was in the historical downtown, where every street, every alley, and every avenue was taken over by the people. From north to south, from west to east in the state, Bahians of all colors and races, of all creed and cultures, were there to salute [the senator] in caravans from over 300 cities. *Baianas*, capoeira groups, *bandas afro*, *pagode* [samba] groups, Filhos de Gandhy buglers, artists, politicians, and business owners were mingling with the common people, who were there to show Brazil the love that Bahia feels for [Magalhães]. With their *berimbaus* [single-string musical instrument] in hand, old masters of Angolan capoeira also showed their support. . . . Joyfully filling the already-festive streets of Pelourinho with black slave music, the band Didá, led by Neguinho do Samba, brought even more joy to the demonstration. . . . In addition to taxi drivers, other groups also went to the airport. . . . The percussion group Meninos do Nordeste, composed of young musicians from Nordeste de Amaralina, played its drums from the outside. . . . Inside the lobby, several improvised samba circles entertained people.[19]

By promoting the idea of Bahianness, the state government contributes to the consolidation of a totalitarian discourse in which blackness is both celebrated as central and paradoxically trapped in a secondary role. To evaluate the transformations brought by black cultural production within the ruling order of power of Bahian society, one must consider the electoral rewards and uninterrupted power of the old Bahian oligarchy. Thus, the title "Black Rome," generally used to emphasize the power of black culture in Bahia, can also indicate the dominance of the noun *Rome*. For centuries, Roman politicians strategically used culture and entertainment as demagogic vehicles of political domination.

Even though the *blocos afro* and many other black organizations combat racial inequality by developing social service projects and employing strategies of mobilization that challenge Brazil's notion of harmonious racial relations, these groups allow their image and cultural production to be used in the construction of a totalitarian notion of Bahianness. Defining itself as natural and spontaneous, this Bahianness-grounded-on-blackness accommodates conflicts and convinces those who are placed on the margins that they are at the center of "Bahia of All Saints, Enchantments, and *Axés*." While many scholars and activists have critiqued the myth of racial democracy for its ability to disguise inequalities and avoid confrontations, the myth of *baianidade*, feeding off the myth of Mama Africa, has had a very similar effect.

Scholars often fail to recognize the participation of black cultural agents in the commoditization and appropriation of black cultural production because of a romantic and often Manichean perspective that abounds in analyses of popular culture. This view is grounded on a dichotomy that juxtaposes the *elite* and the *people* and identifies the latter as the victims of the former. In this manner, the commoditization of samba schools from Rio or of the black cultural production of Bahia are seen as simply a continuation of the white appropriation of everything that "belongs to blacks," from their bodies to their symbols. Farias (1999) argues that this view ends up reinforcing two perverse ideas: that people (in this case, black people) are not viewed as subjects but mere objects, just like their cultural products; and that this is a relationship between plunderers and plundered, thus downplaying both the complexity of this kind of relationship and the agency of the cultural producers. While there is a great deal of manipulation on the part of profit-driven tourism agents and self-serving politicians, black cultural producers also objectify and manipulate black cultural expressions, albeit for different purposes.

Acknowledging the participation of black cultural organizations in strengthening the totalitarian ideology of Bahia is a polemic stance. Social scientists must recognize that oppressed minorities themselves produce identities as objects that often assume the functions of a commodity. Michael Hanchard argues that the reduction of Afro-Brazilian culture to objects of consumption is due, in great part, to the culturalist practices carried out by black activists. Such culturalist practices divorce culture from politics, Hanchard states, and "operate as ends in themselves rather than as a means to a more comprehensive, heterogeneous set of ethico-political activities. In culturalist practices, Afro-Brazilian and Afro-diasporic symbols and artifacts become reified and commodified; culture becomes a thing, not a deeply political process" (1994, 21).

In contrast, I situate myself among those who contend that culture is political, since the production of meanings takes place in hierarchical contexts and will always somehow impact the existing configuration of power (see, e.g., Alvarez et al. 1998; Wade 1999; Yúdice 2003; and Butler 1998). It is thus not possible to state that some movements are more cultural and others more political. As Alvarez et al. argue, *political culture* — the dimension of what counts as political in every society, the domain of practices and institutions — can only be transformed if the hegemonic *cultural politics* — the dimension of identity and subjectivity where disembodied struggles over meanings and representations take place—are disputed, disrupted, and altered. In order to bring about social transformation, the recognizably political activities of voting, campaigning, and lobbying must be coupled with the construction of new narratives and representations. Therefore, as much as I recognize the agency of cultural producers in the objectification of culture, I question to what extent the characteristics of the identities they are constructing contribute to challenging or reinforcing the existing order of things. I argue that the raciology and the body-centricity of the renewed black identities jeopardize their capacity to overcome racism and racial inequality.

Wade (1999) notes that scholars tend to contrast counterculture with modern capitalist consumption and juxtapose local identities with global hegemony. A way out of this binary understanding, he argues, is to see local identities as constructed within a globalized context, as material productions that have been maneuvered as objects or commodities. The understanding of culture as a set of objects that individuals and social movements can possess is the result of decentralizing and fragmenting processes that have occurred primarily since the end of the twentieth century. However, this process of the objectification of culture does not prevent identities from positioning themselves in opposition to capitalism, or even to the state. Power struggles have led oppressed groups to discuss culture as something fixed and corporal, and even as property.

Also explaining that the use of culture as a set of symbols should be situated in the context of globalization, George Yúdice (2003) argues that grassroots organizations have begun to conceive of culture as more than just a way of life—it is also seen as a resource which is ever more connected with political and economic dimensions. Culture has, in fact, become an expedient, since it has become increasingly instrumentalized to achieve such different, but interconnected, goals as economic growth, the reduction of unemployment, the elevation of self-esteem, and the fight against racism. While the instrumentalization of culture reveals the penetration of the logic of capital in every domain of life, disenfranchised groups have astutely managed this trend for their own benefit. For Yúdice, the employment of culture as an expedient does not mean that culture is necessarily becoming more materialized. One of the consequences of its expedient uses is, in effect, the non-materialization of culture, witnessed in the rise of cultural property rights, the decision of "native tribes" to patent their culture, and in the struggles over the definition of cultural heritage, especially in places like Bahia, where tourism plays such a significant role.

In his analysis of Colombia, Wade demonstrates that for the state and the market, black culture is generally conceived as a set of representations. For contemporary black social organizations, however, these representations reflect attempts by individuals and groups to exert control over their own lives. The black group he studied, for example, conceives of culture as *a way of life*, but this is in permanent tension with its practices of culture as *representation*.[20] Cultural events such as shows and performances are also proof that the material cannot be separated from the symbolic, even when the market attempts to herald the events as a "piece of culture." The event *represents* black culture, but at the same time it *is* black culture, even if within it black cultural products are commoditized, sold, and consumed.

Similarly, black cultural organizations in Bahia experience culture and its representations as both a way of life and as objects and sets of symbols. The process of commoditizing a renewed black culture requires that certain objects be selected for its identification and representation. Like other black identities of the diaspora, those constructed in Bahia use aesthetics as a political form of discourse and representation. Analyses of the production of contemporary global black identities have frequently discussed the use of objects from black aesthetics in the construction of identities, demonstrating that the manufactured aspect of these identities developed from the intersection of objects and symbols. The process is not unique to Bahia. Brazil's so-called black culture is also defined through the affirmation of certain meaningful practices — mainly those that are perceived as ludic — within the logic of producing and consuming cultural goods.

The pessimistic view of mass consumption and the need to consume in order to have access to dignity within capitalism (Adorno and Horkheimer 1997) gave way to postmodern perspectives that view cultural production and consumption as spaces of agency and construction of identities (Canclini 2001). Hence, we must understand how a spectacularized society dominated by mass consumption can be a space for subjects to realize themselves without becoming alienated. To do so, we must visualize postmodern identities as part of the world of commodities and as vehicles for individual and collective agency. The objectification of identities is not necessarily alienating. In order to spread and reproduce, cultures inevitably need to be objectified. The cultural objects that travel and transit are resignified as they promote both the culture from which they arose and the one into which they are being incorporated.

Commoditization might be accused of reducing black culture to a limited set of black cultural expressions, symbols, and objects that can be

exchanged, commercialized, and consumed, therefore affecting their political meaning. At the same time, however, people who identify as black have
taken advantage of the increasing commoditization of black objects and
symbols to appropriate and manipulate these same cultural commodities
for political ends. Black cultural producers in Brazil have continually gone
in search of black objects and symbols in the international arena, a phenomenon that has been further intensified as a result of globalization.
Private consumption of commodities has allowed individuals, especially
youth, to express themselves and construct their identities. Canclini argues
that consumption is not a locus of depoliticized actions and irrational
impulses, but rather "a site that is good for thinking, where a good part of
economic, sociopolitical, and psychological rationality is organized in all
societies" (2001, 5).

What frequently struck researchers as an essentialist attitude on behalf
of social movements and grassroots organizations may actually be a posses-
sive use of culture by groups who have felt historically dispossessed. By
recognizing the role played by dispossession, I do not mean to support the
notion that, in order to compensate for material deprivation, culture
should be understood as property. In the previous chapter, I argued against
the proposal put forward by some scholars and activists that black culture
must be recovered for black people. The logic behind that notion is that in
order to fight the myth of racial democracy, it is necessary to "extricate"
black culture from the hands of nonblacks. For my part, I do not believe it
is possible or desirable to "reclaim" samba, capoeira, Candomblé, and
other Afro-Brazilian cultural expressions as "black things" that should be
practiced only by black people, because culture is not circumscribed within
neat and clear-cut boundaries. Whether we define culture as a way of life or
as signifying practices, its irreducibility and collective nature do not allow
us to erect fences around it. We cannot "disentangle" or "purify" black
culture by prohibiting nonblacks from partaking in it. And even though
objectification is necessary for culture to circulate, ultimately culture is not
a "thing."

The emphasis on culture and identities as property to be owned instead
of experiences to be lived is a reflection of the anxieties of the current times,
addressing yet not resolving the problems that emerge from the immediate
association between "race" and body. We must explore the place occupied
by the black body in these processes of objectification and commoditization. On the one side is black agency, which uses the body and the embodiment of objects as tools of affirmation through the politics of visualization,

placing aesthetics as an interface between identity and commodity. On the other side, and in tandem, is the appropriation, by the structures of power, of not only the objects of black aesthetics but also of the commoditized black body itself, despite its resignifications. Body-centered identities, those that place excessive emphasis on the body as an arena for self-representation, emerge as both a reaction to, and historical products of, raciology.

One must therefore analyze the circumstances that favor the attribution and limitation of culture to the body. In this context, the body is proof that an individual retains a given culture, determining ethnicity, assigning group membership, and therefore dictating how to act and what stereotypes must be followed. Internal group differences, such as divisions according to age, gender, and class, are thus repressed. Notions of absolute ethnicity create a sense of culture as something organic, owned by the individual, which helps to perpetuate the very racist origins it seeks to challenge (Gilroy 2000).

Several historians have described how masters made use of their slaves' artistic gifts. Slave music and dance were exhibited during events and meetings held in masters' houses — whether it was to exploit the slaves' exotic dances and music by presenting samba and *lundu* performances for guests, or to show their slaves' refinement and capability in mastering European cultural forms such as classical orchestra music or piano. Such masters even rented out their slaves to perform at social gatherings at other families' houses. "Almost as soon as there was an African presence in Brazil, the richer Portuguese colonists started looking for musical talents among their slaves. . . . It was soon a matter of prestige to have a slave orchestra. . . . Such possessions entertained not only the plantation-owner but also his or her family. They could be put on show to entertain, and impress, their guests, and visitors" (Fryer 2000, 134).

The spectacularization of black culture is less prominent today; however, it has not disappeared, but simply undergone transformation over the centuries. It continues to be a source of entertainment for the dominant classes. The hyper-affirmation of black culture and consequently of black people during Carnaval can be seen as an example of this continuation. While some scholars believe that such hyper-affirmation brings about a positive meaning for blackness, we have to question once again the meanings of prefixes such as *hyper* or *super*, as we have done in previous chapters with the *super*-humanity of black athletes, associated with the underlying and still predominant idea that in order to deny the *under*- or *sub*-humanity of blacks, it is necessary to seek a *hyper*-, *ultra*-, or *over*-affirmation.

In her analysis of Carnaval in Rio de Janeiro, Myriam Santos, for example, argues that even though it is restricted to this annual event, the prominence enjoyed by blacks is a positive thing. "Samba is recognized for its beauty and occupies a special place among the other varieties of popular, urban music and dance in Brazil. At least once a year, black and poor people are the center of attention in Rio. On this occasion, rather than being poor, underprivileged, downtrodden victims of discrimination, they are the masters of samba, performing for foreign audiences and members of the Brazilian elite, thus inverting established relationships" (Santos 1999, 75). Unlike Santos, I do not see in this a reason for celebration, especially when this prominent position is determined hierarchically and a priori. Despite the fact that analysts preach the virtues of a supposed inversion typical of Carnaval, allowing blacks to momentarily shine, I believe such inversion simply confirms the existing order of things.

The process initiated in the 1930s, in which select symbols of black culture were shifted from the margins to the center of the narratives of the nation, represented more than just a *destigmatization* of black culture, as Sansone argues (2000a). Instead, I contend that the resignification of these symbols, and the new meanings acquired by the black bodies that allegedly produce them, has led to a *restigmatization* of black culture which, understood as a limited set of symbols, now stands for a contagious joy that is easily diluted into the totalitarian discourse of Bahianness. The replacement of pejorative ideas about blackness for new images associated with inherent beauty, sensuality, and *gingado* perpetuates the stereotyping of blackness according to aesthetic and artistic abilities. These realms, brokered mainly by the state and by the tourism and leisure industries, have portrayed blackness as a "nearby alterity" and as part of a "domestic non-routine" (Farias 1998, 70).

The automatic inversion of values does not allow for a way out of the cycle of binary oppositions, and it ultimately contributes to the spread of notions of reverse racism. Contrary to popular belief, reverse racism is not discrimination by blacks against whites, but rather the celebration of certain attributes considered part of the racial character, trapping an entire people into one or two essential characteristics. It is the perpetuation of racism by means of celebration. The ubiquity and preeminence attributed to beautiful and glamorous—albeit racialized—bodies do nothing to change quotidian forms of racial hierarchy. As a consequence, historical associations between blackness and subhumanity, brutality, crime, and hypersexuality remain untouched. As Gilroy argues, the enthusiasm demonstrated by the political elite toward the products of blackness has not been accompanied by an equivalent zeal for the human beings that routinely produce such culture. "In general, those who profit from the commoditization of black culture do not have the least interest in the black people who produce it" (Gilroy 2000, 270).

The hyper-affirmation of the black body in the realm of culture as a set of symbols creates a comfort zone (often celebrated as a boon to black self-esteem) that becomes ever more artificial as dissident cultures become increasingly more spectacle-like and aestheticized. Thus, black culture ends up taking the form of what Gilroy (2000) terms "revolutionary conservatism" since it is revolutionary in appearance but conservative in content, ultimately creating updated versions of old regimes of truth about "race" and gender. "Conservatism is signaled loud and clear in the joyless rigidity of the gender roles that are specified in an absolutist approach to both ethics and racial particularity and, above all, in a gloomy presentation of black humanity composed of limited creatures who require tradition, pedagogy, and organization" (Gilroy 2000, 206). Resistance therefore turns hollow, and antagonism is transformed into an empty challenge. By being domesticated and transformed into a pillar of an authoritarian notion of Bahianness—whether it be by the market or the state—black culture runs the risk of becoming an arena that allows little concrete resistance against the system that reproduces racial dominance and class and gender inequalities.

Producers of black culture in Bahia are continuously dealing with the power exerted by the political elite. In part, such power benefits from economic woes (politicians take advantage, for example, of the *blocos afros'* financial difficulties), but this is not the only justification for increasing political dominance over black organizations. Power also involves knowledge, ideas, and leadership. In order to expand, power seduces, solicits, induces, and gains consent. It does not flow solely from top to bottom, since it depends on the legitimization of the subordinated. Power therefore does not just constrict and prevent; it also produces new types of knowledge, new representations, and new practices that require consent in order to circulate. Black culture produced in Bahia operates within a context permeated by a pervasive totalitarian ideology of Bahianness which is the backdrop for producers of black culture. The authoritarianism of Bahian rulers is not limited to the aggressive repression of strikes, protests, and popular demonstrations against the ruling order; it is also perpetuated by the clientelistic relationships developed within a context of cordial racism.

Thus, the power exerted is not explicit coercion, and it is also carried out in the symbolic — yet no less concrete — realm of representations.

A recent event illustrates the ongoing process by which the establishment is absorbing the symbols of Africanness invented in Bahia: the choice of Salvador's Carnaval theme for 2002. Announced in August 2001 by the mayor's office, the theme "Africa and Its Presence in Bahia" led this edition of Carnaval to become popularly known as Carnaváfrica. The ceremony launching the theme, during which a decree was signed creating the contest to choose that year's logo and slogan, included the city's main *blocos afro*, the most famous capoeira masters, *baianas de acarajé*, and representatives from Candomblé *terreiros*.

Also attending the event was Mama Africa herself, literally embodied by a black woman dressed in a colorful "African outfit" and sporting an elaborate "African hairstyle." Swaying her arms in large, circular movements and gently tapping her feet on the ground like the dancers of Ilê Aiyê, Mama Africa sang a song while dancing among the guests. When the drums played by the young black men dressed in green, yellow, and red went silent, Mama Africa stood still to listen to the mayor's speech. Praising the African contribution that makes Bahia so unique, the mayor associated the Africanness of Bahia's people with their capacity to be happy even while suffering, an ability he termed "resistance": "Choosing Africa is an homage to all of us, to Salvador, to a wonderful people who know how to live with difficulties, with suffering, but who get back up on their feet, who resist. It is the call for freedom, for solidarity. Africa is therefore everything; she's our mother. I think we once again hit the nail on its head, because everyone will pay homage to her majesty, Africa."[21]

Once again, Africanness was revered in the ludic sphere of Carnaval. Not surprisingly, Africa was claimed as the mother of all Bahians, including the mayor of Salvador and the voracious elites to whom his administration catered. Akin to wet nurses during the time of slavery, whose breasts were suckled as an endless source of force and vitality by a thirsty ruling class, Mama Africa has been milked by a local elite that profits heavily from black cultural production and its representations of blackness, old and new. Undeniably, one does not have full control over the potential uses and abuses of cultural symbols, even when they are created to produce new meanings that will ideally free blackness from a stereotypical role. Yet new representations of blackness produced by black grassroots organizations, and employed by politicians and the tourism industry, have not surpassed the centrality of "race" and its inherent meanings. The new format of blackness has retained the old content of raciology, where the black body is expected to perform its contagious culture. Perhaps we could envision a radical politics of difference not as politics that celebrate the differences between human groups, but politics that propose a radical difference with regard to what is already out there, what we take for granted, or consider natural to our beings.

Epilogue

The truth is that there are no races: there is nothing in the world that can do all we ask race to do for us . . . even the biologist's notion has only limited uses. . . . Talk of "race" is particularly distressing for those of us who take culture seriously. For, where race works — in places where "gross differences of morphology" are correlated with "subtle differences" of temperament, belief, and intention — it works as an attempt at metonym for culture, and it does so only at the price of biologizing what *is* culture, ideology.
— Kwame Anthony Appiah, *In My Father's House*

In the autobiographical *Coal to Cream: A Black Man's Journey beyond Color to an Affirmation of Race*, Eugene Robinson asserts the importance of "race" and the feelings it generates in the life of black Americans. In a reversal of his initial enthusiasm for the conviviality among people of different colors that he encountered on his trip to Brazil, Robinson opts for the familiar racial separation he experienced back home. Disappointed with the striking levels of Brazilian racial inequality, which at first he had not noticed, the author extols the benefits of "racial anger" for those who are victims of racism. He equates racial anger with rocket fuel: "It can go up in flames at the wrong moment and lead to a spectacular self-destruction on the launching pad, but it can also cause the rocket to detonate a target better than anything else on earth" (1999, 180).

Bothered by the absence of racial anger among black Brazilians, Robinson contends that even though it may appear to be a privilege to live without the constant presence of "race," which he recognizes as a "weight," this makes it impossible for blacks to unite or become stronger: "Having that anger inside was oddly soothing. It was a weight to carry around, a heavy weight. But I could see that black Brazilians seemed to pay an awfully high price for the privilege of living without that weight. Without it, they had no sense of themselves as joined, embattled, mutually reinforced. Without it, they had no game face to show the world. Without it, they had no basis for demands, no scoreboard to tally gains and losses, no foreknowledge to cushion defeat and no suspicion to temper victory. Without it, they had no motor, no juice, and steam. No chance" (1999, 180).

While the author employs the logic of winners versus losers, ubiquitous in U.S. discourses and interpretations of the world, his statement reveals that "race" is, above all, the result of racism, thus confirming an argument I have defended throughout this book. Robinson makes it clear that the "engine," the "sustenance" that unites blacks — even as it separates them into another category of humans — is the fruit of the same racism that discriminates and mistreats. The racial anger that he commends, even if it has not gained wider grassroots support in Brazil, has nevertheless inspired black activism and fueled antiracist movements in that country. The United States does not hold monopoly over that. The lifelong work of the black intellectual and activist Abdias do Nascimento is possibly the greatest example of fierce reaction against Brazilian racism. The *blocos afro*, the MNU, and the NGOs defending the implementation of the recent racial laws are other examples of the raciological antiracist struggle in Brazil.

The question is whether fueling racial anger is ultimately beneficial for those who have had to live with the weight of racism in their lives — that is, all of us. Contrary to what is frequently believed, racism affects entire societies and not just racial minorities. As the growing field of critical studies of whiteness has shown, racism shapes whites as much as it shapes blacks, and — in the case of Latin American countries — the great variety of *mestiços*. This is more complicated than the mere self-endowment of whites and light-skinned individuals with feelings of superiority. The workings of racism are intimately intertwined with the operations of gender, class, and national affiliation. As we heard in the statements of the young members of the *blocos afro*, racism impinges differently on men and women, and this distinction is further nuanced by the shades of their skin. And this does not happen only in the outside world. It helps to recall that within the *blocos*, light-skinned boys and girls have their authenticity questioned. Would racial anger (against whites) help make them "blacker," and thus more accepted? It would probably help them as much as racial discrimination against blacks by lighter-skinned *mestiços* helps make the latter "whiter."

Anti-black racism influences the quality of life of *mestiços*, too, as they also encounter barriers in those arenas where aesthetics occupies a central position. The realms of dating, marriage, and access to jobs that require "good appearance" are not easily navigated by *mestiços*. No matter how much they try to distance themselves from blackness — already a horrible enough effect of racism — there are features of the *mestiço* body that "taint" their alleged whiteness. Brazilians learn from an early age to read the signs of beauty and ugliness, and the symbols of access and restriction that are inscribed onto bodily features such as skin color, hair type, and nose shape. Constituting a wider economy of signs, these elements designate those who are worthy of respect or even deference, and those who are not to be taken seriously.

The effects of racism on white middle- and upper-class Brazilians are no less hazardous for the well-being of the nation. Belief in black inferiority informs the pervasive authoritarianism of Brazilian society and the expectation that the poor and blacks should "know their place." Despite the national narratives of racial democracy and cordiality, Brazilian society is very hierarchical. Social relations are predominantly grounded on the notion that certain people are superior and entitled to give orders and others are inferior and expected to obey. Skin color, gender, age, body language, clothing, and ability to employ the rules of Portuguese grammar constitute the main traits according to which individuals are interpreted and classified within these authoritarian practices.

Notions of white superiority have both local and global consequences. While it informs authoritarianism at home, it also positions Brazil within a wider transnational racial hierarchy. Latin American whites are deemed "less white" than U.S. American whites. And this is not only because of how they have internalized myths of *mestizaje/mestiçagem*. It is not just because they view themselves as belonging to cosmic races, meta-races, or racial democracies. It is also because whiteness is a global force that, operating together with colonialism and capitalism, has positioned some nations in the core and others in the periphery. Thus, even racial minorities from core countries enjoy the privileges of whiteness when compared with those who come from the peripheries and semiperipheries of the world.

The process of being "unwhitened" is a frequent experience for many Brazilian immigrants in the United States. Those with lighter skin tone usually face racism for the first time in their lives upon moving to the United States and being inserted into a different racial order. Part of their response to racism is to heighten Brazil's myth of racial democracy and emphasize their own African cultural inheritance. The central place occupied by samba and capoeira in Brazilian events performed outside Brazil attests to that. On the other hand, these same individuals frequently "recover" their whiteness, and the authority that comes with it, upon reentering Brazilian territory, or simply by being among other, darker-skinned, immigrants. Thus, the meanings of blackness and whiteness, as well as the effects of racism, should be examined both in local and global contexts, as I have attempted to do in this book.

There is no doubt that "race" matters in Brazil. A country that experienced more than three and a half centuries of slavery, and more recent governmental policy explicitly aimed at whitening the population, not to mention everyday forms of color discrimination in domestic life, cannot be imagined to be immune to the power of "race." Although it has no racial laws, institutional barriers to blacks have abounded. Present-day racial inequalities cannot be attributed solely to a history of slavery. Racist representations and their influence on reality have been constantly renewed and disseminated. However, it is one thing to recognize the social existence of "race" and its material and immaterial consequences for the lives of flesh-and-bone human beings; it is quite another to solidify "race" by transforming it into a political tool. To propose overcoming "race" in the future does not mean to deny its present-day results. Given that Brazil is already racialized, antiracist strategies are not the source of race-based thought. Brazilians do not live on a neutral racial ground, a racial tabula rasa. But antiracist strategies and policies should be aimed at combating the causes of racism and not just its consequences. They should not work as oil that lubricates the raciology machine.

How is it possible to promote anti-racism without further endorsing the idea that there are insurmountable barriers that divide us? The solution lies in promoting cultural transformation. The struggle against racism must take place not only in the realm of law, but also in the sphere of language, representations, and everyday life. It is not feasible to change political culture without transforming cultural politics. By producing new representations and spreading their meanings, it is possible to replace old patterns of inequality and difference. Thus, we must overcome the misguided manner in which we think about equality. *Equal* should not be understood as *same* — that is, those with whom we share a nearly identical appearance. To see equality as sameness is like viewing racelessness as whiteness. It is a formulation that allows "white" to be the neutral standard from which black differs; or "man" to be the neutral standard against which women are compared. "Equality as sameness is a gendered formulation of equality, because it secures gender privilege through naming women as different and men as the neutral standard of the same. . . . The sameness of men requires the difference that is women, just as whiteness requires people of color" (Wendy Brown 1995, 153).

Nikolas Rose (1996) warns us that we should not exalt the advantages of identity projects, but rather evaluate the high price being paid for them. Whether they are racial, national, or gender based, identities are recent machinations, and they act from the outside in, and not vice versa, as we tend to believe. Identities do not reflect a person's intimate or spiritual state, but rather a reaction to the history of subjectification and its ambiguous legacies. This more skeptical way of looking at identities was already present in Frantz Fanon's call, in the 1950s, for the liberation from color:

> As I begin to recognize that the Negro is the symbol of sin, I catch myself
> hating the Negro. But then I recognize that I am a Negro. There are two
> ways out of this conflict. Either I ask others to pay no attention to my
> skin, or else I want them to be aware of it. I try then to find value for what
> is bad—since I have unthinkingly conceded that the black man is the
> color of evil. In order to terminate this neurotic situation, in which I am
> compelled to choose an unhealthy, conflictual solution, fed on fantasies,
> hostile, inhuman in short, I have only one solution: to rise above this
> absurd drama that others have staged round me, to reject the two terms
> that are equally unacceptable, and, through one human being, to reach
> out for the universal. (1991 [1952], 197)

Once we take into account how much wrongdoing and suffering the belief in the idea of "race" has caused throughout the history of humankind, what does it mean to embrace the affirmation of difference based on "race"? What is really at stake when we try to find a permanent space for black singularity? By forgetting its historic bases and its association with the horrors of slavery and racism, we commit the dangerous mistake of transforming black singularity into something static and immutable. Seen in this manner, it functions as a shield for its supposed beneficiaries, allegedly protecting them from the infinity of choices that define human experience and ultimately imposing a narrower definition of black identity. Reacting against this, I have aligned myself in this work with those who conceive of Africa and the connection among Afro-descendants in an alternative fashion, where the diaspora is understood as a dynamic force that challenges the belief in an absolute identity.

As modern counter-discourses, black identity narratives cannot claim a notion of primordial purity, because the very construction of blackness has been deeply imbued by Western forms and codes from the first moment of the dispersion of black peoples. In addition, the most important aspect of cultures of resistance is not the expression of some lost origin or a supposed essence that should remain uncontaminated, but the adoption of a critical voice that seeks, above all, to transform our conditions of existence. We know that such a transformation will not occur through a mere inversion of values, by replacing negative stereotypes with positive ones, or by adopting Afrocentrism to counter Eurocentrism. None of these dislodges the United States from its hegemonic central position of exporter of racial technologies. None of them prevents capitalism from marketing the products of ethnicity.

The construction of identities reflects a complex historical production of some subjects as marginal or inferior or subhuman, and others as central, superior, and bearers of an exclusivist human condition. The formation of such racial subjects has taken place within the orders of discipline, regulation, and domination. These orders are produced not only in mainstream society but also within the racialized groups fighting against racism. Grounded in the notion of culture as organic, ethnic absolutisms have led to oppressive formulas of identity. The narrow understanding of culture and identities as properties to be owned rather than lived reflects the anxieties produced by racism, yet it does not constitute a liberating response to them. My critique of limiting notions of blackness is intended to challenge static notions of identity and expand the reach of the agency of the oppressed. If we take into consideration the centuries of slavery and racism in the Americas, it becomes a vast understatement to claim that the self-esteem of slaves or current victims of racism was or is threatened. More than self-esteem, the very human condition is torn to pieces in contexts marked by slavery or racism. Thus, it is human dignity that needs to be restored, for all, equally.

It is probably less troubling for scholars in Brazil today to defend the use of "race." This ensures that their analyses will be viewed favorably by activists, authorizing outsiders to address a topic they are often not "automatically connected to through color." As discussed previously, it is not only the historical beneficiaries of racial hierarchies that do not want to give up raciology; many of those who have been racially oppressed and subordinated believe that consolation can be found within the very same logic that has produced their suffering. It has not been easy, therefore, to opt for the opposite path: to deconstruct essences and argue that the idea of "race" needs to be transcended, as I have done here as part of my larger battle against racism. I hope that this book can be useful above all to those who are racially oppressed, at least to inspire the thought that we *can* move beyond our structures of feeling.

While I was writing this book, I was constantly reflecting upon the role of academic knowledge. One cannot deny that academic production influences daily life and helps constitute everyday forms of thinking. Just as the premises of scientific racism shaped popular beliefs in the past, current academic analyses are also absorbed by mainstream society, albeit in diffuse and often confused forms. I understand that scholarly work has the duty to challenge common sense. It should be employed to help us understand our fears and to overcome our anxieties and build widespread hope in the construction of a planetary humanity. Although racialized thought is deeply engrained in the social, cultural, and psychological structures of our societies, blackness, whiteness, and the sordid fantasy of "race" do not need be insurmountable factors of our lives. As *beliefs*, they require our devotion and faith in order to exist. We can, nonetheless, challenge these impositions that have imprisoned us in our bodies for so long. Thus, anti-racist strategies will only succeed once representations lie at their core, and once these representations are deconstructed and reconstructed with the goal of moving beyond, instead of within, raciology.

With regard to my own identity, all I can add is that more important than being Brazilian, *nordestina*, female, Bahian, *mestiça*, or claiming any other identity that would grant me fragmented rights within the Babylonic structure of capitalism, I opt to be increasingly human. I want to strengthen my own humanity, and not in an egotistical way. The humanity inside me is what bonds me to others, to the world, to history, and to the continued need to resist and transform, in the "I and I" mode of the Rastafari message sung globally by Bob Marley and locally by Edson Gomes: an "I" that contains alterity within it, and an "I" that learns about the past of our ancestors as it yearns for a better future for our descendants, for it is an "I" tethered to the world.

NOTES

Introduction

1 With regard to unicentrism in black movements, Gilroy states, "We have seen that the authoritarian and proto-fascist formations of twentieth-century black political culture have often been animated by an intense desire to recover the lost glories of the African past. The desire to restore that departed greatness has not always been matched by an equivalent enthusiasm to remedy the plight of Africa in the present" (2000, 323).

2 The interviews sought to first identify personal information such as profession and age and then to investigate the tourists' interest in Bahia: what they were looking for, if they were able to find what they were looking for; and in which places they believed they would find what they were looking for.

3 The Portuguese term *mestiço* shares similarities with the Spanish term *mestizo* — since both indicate racial mixture. However, there are also several differences between the two. First, the ideologies of *mestizaje* in Spanish America, and *mestiçagem* in Brazil, are quite distinct from country to country. Second, while *mestizo* usually refers to a mix between a white and an indigenous partner, *mestiço* in Brazil almost always refers to a racial mixture that includes a black component, even though the role played by blackness has frequently been secondary.

4 Kamel (2006, 61) explains that the differences between blacks and whites are grounded on economic reasons: "Blacks and browns are the majority among the poor because our economic system has always promoted the concentration of income: those who were poor (slaves, by definition, had no property) have been doomed to continue poor." Similarly, Kamel contends, "The social mechanisms of exclusion have as victims the poor, be they white, black, brown, yellow or indigenous. And the main mechanism of reproduction of poverty is the low quality of our public education" (66). Kamel clearly states, "Our problem is poverty and not a supposed racial inequality" (71).

5 Kamel explains that if racism exists in Brazil, it is because of individual attitudes: "Where there are men gathered, there are also all kinds of feelings, including the worst kind" (2006, 20). Because Kamel explains all inequalities on the basis of poverty and rebuffs the role played by racism in the daily life of individuals, he

explicitly argues that poor whites undergo the same afflictions as poor blacks in Brazil: "In a country where after Abolition there never were institutional barriers to the social ascension of blacks, a country where access to public jobs and positions in institutions of public education are based solely on merit, a country where 19 million whites are poor and undergo the same suffering as poor blacks, the implementation of policies of racial preference will not guarantee good-quality education for all the poor and giving them the opportunity to overcome poverty according to their merits but rather will risk putting Brazil in the path of a nightmare: the emergence of racial hatred, something that we have not experienced until now" (39–40). Either Kamel is confusing legal with institutional barriers or he is ignoring the concrete barriers imposed on black ascension in institutions as varied as the Catholic church, the army, recreational clubs, and private companies that have purposefully excluded black candidates from their hiring processes. There is irrefutable evidence of these barriers in the literature on institutional racism in Brazil, including George Reid Andrews's *Blacks and Whites in São Paulo, Brazil, 1888–1998*, and Jeffrey Dávila's *Diploma of Whiteness: Race and Social Policy in Brazil, 1917–1945*.

6 Comparing the U.S. and Brazilian "models" of race relations, Antônio Sérgio Guimarães states that, in contrast with the violent and segregationist pattern of the former, the Brazilian model seemed to be "gentler" because it was a "very complex and ambiguous system of racial differentiation, based mainly on phenotypical differences, and solidified in a chromatic vocabulary" (1999, 39). Because of their differences, these two systems were taken as opposite poles, and their similarities were ignored. This view only began to change after the civil rights movement in the United States secured its first victories. From that moment on, social scientists and black militants in Brazil began to notice more similarities than differences when comparing race relations in Brazil and the United States (Guimarães 1999).

7 One of the most important strategies instituted by the federal government to support the construction of a distinct black identity is the "Diretrizes Curriculares Nacionais para a Educação das Relações Étnico-Raciais e para o Ensino de História e Cultura Afro-Brasileira e Africana" (National Curriculum Guidelines for Ethnic-Racial Relations Education and for Teaching Afro-Brazilian and African History and Culture), approved in 2004. Its main objective is to "recognize and value the identity, history, and culture of Afro-Brazilians, as well as ensure the recognition and equality of the valorization of Brazil's African roots, alongside its indigenous, European, and Asian roots" (Ministério da Educação 2004, 9).

8 The other color categories are *branco* (white), *preto* (black), *amarelo* (yellow, used for individuals of Asian descent), and *indígena* (indigenous).

9 Quantitative research carried out since the late 1970s by Hasenbalg and Valle Silva (1988; 1993) demonstrated that *mulatos/pardos* enjoy the same life standards as blacks.

10 The "comb test" was used in South Africa when there was doubt surrounding

someone's racial origin. A fine-toothed comb would be run through an individual's hair, and if it ran through it easily, the verdict was "white." If it did not, the result was "black." In 2004, the Brazilian Association of Anthropology (ABA) made a public statement in which it defined UnB's practice as authoritarian. See Maio and Ventura (2005) for a thorough analysis of UnB's quota system and selection practices.

11 In spite of the vast spectrum of skin-color categories in Brazil and the resulting impression of the dilution of whiteness and blackness, in moments of conflict the extreme opposite poles "black" and "white" emerge and are recognized. Sheriff explains that three distinct discourses of race and color terms exist in Brazil: a descriptive discourse of one's appearance, a pragmatic register based on euphemisms, and a bipolar race discourse that classifies blacks versus whites. Sheriff defines the latter as the "bedrock reality of racialized polarization and opposition" that "truly articulates a system of racial classification" (2001, 57). Although I do not agree with the hierarchy and rigidity of Sheriff's scheme, I find her explanation useful in understanding how, depending on the context of the interaction, whiteness and blackness can become very marked categories.

12 I emphasize that the book is a reminder that racism invented races because this is, evidently, not a new idea. Many of the arguments raised in *Divisões perigosas* had already been discussed by Célia Marinho de Azevedo in her important book *Anti-Racismo e seus Paradoxos: Reflexões sobre cota racial, raça e racismo* (2004). Despite its in-depth analyses of the contradictions of the antiracist movement, Azevedo's book did not receive the attention it deserved, especially if compared to the splash that accompanied the publication of *Divisões perigosas*.

13 Yvonne Maggie, one of the book's organizers, declared in an interview with Adam Stepan that, by implementing racial quotas and the EIR, "We are creating a monster, and a monster that will transform our society into a racist and very dangerous society" (see Stepan's documentary *Wide Angle: Brazil in Black and White* [2007]).

Chapter 1: Bahia in the Black Atlantic

1 One of the study packets produced by Ilê Aiyê states that Africa is divided into four geographical regions (west, east, central, and southern), but that a single identity nevertheless traverses it: "These regions represent two large cultural areas . . . without losing the strength of one cultural identity, regardless of obstacles, regardless of limits imposed by European colonizers" (Ilê Aiyê 2000, 2).

2 The *Dicionário Aurélio da língua portuguesa* defines *banzo* as a "mortal nostalgia that attacked blacks brought enslaved from Africa."

3 With regards to Brazil's so-called returning blacks, the Agudás, who settled in the Bight of Benin, see Cunha (1985) and Guran (1999).

4 Osvalrísio, Ilê Aiyê director, interview with TV Cultura.

5 Elsewhere I argue that Freyre established a dichotomy between the "young

mulata"—whose hypersexuality is so irresistible that it is described as leading unavoidably to miscegenation—and the "elderly black woman"—the quintessential cook whose body no longer offers the pleasures of sex but still pleases the desires of the stomach. Jorge Amado explored this duality and further disseminated these stereotypes in his novels (Pinho 2006a).

6 Matory (1997; 1999) demonstrates that since the end of the nineteenth century, Candomblé leaders began establishing contacts with Africa, initiating their championing of the Yoruba religion and people and the deliberate celebration of their greatness. The idea of Yoruba sophistication reverberated throughout the Afro-Latino world and became a hallmark for those calling for African purity in the black cultures of the New World.

7 Sansome (2000a) defines the "black community" as a politicized group comprised of black militants and intellectuals who are constantly searching for diacritical signs of blackness, thus attending Candomblé rituals, wearing "African" clothing, and so on.

8 According to Antônio Risério (1995), the name Ilê Aiyê was suggested to the *bloco* by a Yugoslavian anthropologist, which is an example of the invention of tradition.

9 The middle passage refers to the longest and most arduous crossing of the Atlantic by the slave ships. It also refers to the transformation—metaphorically represented by the experience endured on a slave ship—of the identities of individuals from several specific ethnic groups into a new type of identity as generic Africans or blacks.

10 "Faraó divindade do Egito," by Lazinho, an Olodum composer, and "Civilização do Congo," by Ademário, an Ilê Aiyê composer.

11 For more on the Rastafari movement, see Pinho (1995).

12 Like Ilê Aiyê, Muzenza is located in the neighborhood of Liberdade, but while Ilê only accepts individuals of dark skin complexion, Muzenza also has *mestiços* and whites among its members.

13 The volume *Brazilian Popular Music and Globalization*, edited by Charles A. Perrone and Christopher Dunn, contains several important articles on the music of the *blocos afro*.

14 "Civilização do Congo," by Ademário, of Ilê Aiyê.

15 "Canto para o Senegal," by Banda Reflexus; "Madagascar Olodum," by Rey Zulu, Olodum; "Negrice Cristal," by César Maravilha, Ilê Aiyê; and "Denúncia," by Tita Lopes, Olodum.

16 "Baianidade Nagô," by Evany Ed Stalo, Banda Mel. *Nagô* is a generic designation given in Brazil to the Yoruba-speaking African groups that came from the former Kingdom of Dahomey and southern Nigeria (Dantas 1988, 34). In Brazil, the term *Nagô* has been used interchangeably with Yoruba, both by scholars and activists.

17 "Faraó divindade do Egito," by Luciano Gomes dos Santos, Olodum.

18 "Deusa do ébano," by Geraldo Lima; "Negrume da noite," by Paulinho do Reco; and "Canto da cor," by Moisés and Simão, all from Ilê Aiyê.

19 "Faraó divindade do Egito," by Luciano Gomes dos Santos; and "Salvador não inerte," by Bobôco and Beto Jamaica, Olodum.

20 *Trios elétricos* are big trucks with sound systems that parade in Bahia's Carnaval. They comprise the so-called *blocos de trio*, Carnaval groups whose members are mainly upper- and middle-class white youth. Ilê Aiyê was founded as a response to discrimination against blacks by these *blocos de trio*.

21 As mentioned before, Liberdade is a black neighborhood where the *blocos afro*, Ilê Aiyê and Muzenza are located. It also means freedom in Portuguese.

22 "Eu sou negão," by Gerônimo.

23 "Um povo comum pensar," by Suka, Olodum.

24 "Denúncia," by Tita Lopes, Olodum.

25 "The integrity of the nation becomes the integrity of its masculinity. In fact, it can be a nation only if the correct version of gender hierarchy has been established and reproduced" (Gilroy 2000, 127).

26 Hermano Vianna explains that the adoption of transnational symbols also occurred in the funk dances in Rio de Janeiro, at which "the dancers that moved to Soul Grand Prix . . . created a style of dress that fused the various visual cues they were receiving, including record covers. This was the time of Afros, of multicolored platform shoes, bell-bottom pants, James Brown-inspired dancing — everything connected to the expression 'Black is Beautiful' " (1988, 27).

27 Because of its moist and fertile soil, the region of the Recôncavo was one of the major sites of the sugarcane plantation economy in Brazil. It is therefore marked by a long history of slavery and its aftermath.

28 Members of ACBANTU (Associação Cultural de Preservação do Patrimônio Bantu — Cultural Association for the Preservation of Bantu Heritage), a Bahian NGO whose main objective is to contribute to the recovery of original Bantu traditions and carry on exchanges with similar entities nationally and internationally, mentioned that Angolans have traveled to Bahia in search of Bantu traditions that had been "lost" in Africa yet preserved in Brazil.

29 *Correio da Bahia*, 10 March 2004 (Andréia Santana).

30 The construction of a black image of Bahia was also fueled by researchers and writers, as we shall see in more detail in chapter 5.

31 http://olodum.uol.com.br/, accessed 2001.

32 Olodum has spread Afro-Bahian music throughout the world, performing in New York's Central Park and in many European countries. Internationally known singers such as Paul Simon and Michael Jackson have gone to Brazil to record with the group.

33 The idea that blacks in Bahia or Brazil have more awareness about their African origins is quite present in the imaginary of black militants in the United States, as can be noted in the comments of rapper M-1, from the group Dead Prez: "When I think about Brazil, I think about black people talking Portuguese, you see? I think of Africans, of Africa. . . . I feel they are closer or more connected to Africa. I see [them as] a step forward in the struggle of black people. In the spirituality

of the people from there I see a great step forward in the resistance against colonial domination; in the understanding of Africa's importance, I see a strategy of less brain-washing than has been applied here." *Rap Internacional*, 1, no. 3, 2001.

34 This article by Rachel Jackson Christmas, which originally appeared in the *New York Times*, was reprinted in an anthology organized by David Hellwig (1992) that contains several other articles that refer to the importance of the exchange of experiences between Brazilian and African-American blacks. Among these, I would highlight the articles by R. L. Jackson, Niani D. Brown, and Gloria Calomee.

35 Even though there are older Candomblé *terreiros* than Opô Afonjá in Bahia— e.g., the temple of Casa Branca—African American tourists predominantly seek out Mãe Stella de Oxóssi's *terreiro*. I believe this is because of the compatibility of the discourses employed by African Americans and by Mãe Stella, who departs from syncretism and projects Africa as the source of fundamental knowledge.

36 In Sansone's definition (2000b), Bahia sells traditional products such as Candomblé, *orixá* figurines, capoeira, traditional African food, percussion instruments, and so on; quasi-traditional products such as world music, popular painting, capoeira schools, new Candomblé *terreiros*, and the popular dance companies that travel throughout the West; and new traditional products, related mainly to Bahian carnaval, such as costumes, musical instruments, souvenirs, and so on. The most prized products are sold in the shops of Olodum, Ilê Aiyê, and Ara Ketu, located in Pelourinho.

37 Interviews with African American tourists in Cachoeira, Bahia, in August 2000.

38 The notion that the black experience in the United States was more "modern" than the Brazilian one is also endorsed by some theorists in the United States. Sheila Walker (2002) argues that African Americans exchange their blackness— represented by a politicized and modern racial identity—for the Africanness of black Brazilians; in other words, their capacity for cultural retention.

39 Recently, Representative Charles Rangel (Democrat, New York) introduced House Concurrent Resolution 47, which aims at reinforcing the connections between African descendants on the American continent. His opening statement emphasizes this notion of diaspora brotherhood: "These people are our brothers and sisters through slave trafficking, and like us, are suffering similar problems. The ships that brought us to the U.S. could very well have brought us to the Dominican Republic, Colombia, or Brazil. I have introduced this bill as a way for us to remember our common history and the need to work together to resolve our common problems." Press release of the Global Afro Latino and Caribbean Initiative, Latin American and Caribbean Studies, Hunter College.

40 The Sisterhood of the Good Death (Irmandade da Boa Morte) has existed since 1823, and is comprised entirely of black women over the age of 50 who worship Our Lady of Glory. The sisters are adepts of both Catholicism and Candomblé.

The festival always takes place during the second half of August and includes a procession, masses, an Afro-Brazilian supper offered to the community by the sisters, and a samba circle at the end.

Chapter 2: Afro Identity Made in Bahia

1 Some scholars, however, argue that the origin of the modern theory of identity is not to be found in Barth's work. Leo Despres has stated that before Barth, in the 1950s, A. L. Epstein and J. Clyde Mitchell had already undertaken an analysis of ethnicity in Africa and should therefore be considered the true pioneers of the anthropological theory of identity (Ruben 1992).

2 "Ethnic identity, then, if used in an uncritical fashion, could well be nothing more than a naive folk concept, feeding the illusion that an entity which has duration and specificity is produced by auto- and hetero-ascription of ethnic markers, or, what boils down to the same thing, by boundary production" (Roosens 1994, 84).

3 Candomblé is divided into "nations" such as Jeje (Ewe-Fon), Angola (Bantu), and Nagô and Ketu (both Yoruba). The term *nation* lost its initial meaning as "ethnic origin," having acquired more of a political than a theological meaning. It is currently employed in Candomblé not as a claim to a specific African ancestry but to refer to a social identity constructed within the temples.

4 On the subject of integrationism and nationalism present in the Brazilian black movement of the 1930s, Sueli Carneiro states, "Blacks are the ones with the most nationalistic feelings and also the most rejected people of this nation, and they developed a profoundly nationalist perspective because they do not have anywhere to which they can return; we do not know where to return to, we do not have any records of our origins on the African continent. . . . Thus, we had to adopt the nationalist vision heavily expressed by black movement struggles, by the Frente Negra Brasileira" (2000, 25).

5 *A Voz da Raça*, 3, no. 62 (February 1937), cited in Maués (1991, 121).

6 The poetry of these expressions is lost in translation: Ilê praises itself in its songs as "*o mais belo dos belos*," to which I am adding "*o mais velho dos velhos*," highlighting the importance of antiquity for the myth of Mama Africa.

7 See Burdick's (1998) discussion of the meanings of Candomblé for Afro-Brazilian activists and how this informs their opposition to Protestantism.

8 *Jornal A Tarde*, 12 February 1975.

9 In order to protect the identity of the young interviewees — whom I define as the *blocos'* discourse interlocutors — I have not used their names, referring to them only by their positions within Ilê Aiyê and Olodum. When I refer to those I define as the *discourse producers* (such as directors, composers, or teachers), I use their names and positions within the *bloco*. These individuals are public figures who are accustomed to giving interviews not only to academic researchers but also to reporters.

10 *Quilombolas* were the dwellers of the *quilombos*, communities formed by runaway slaves in Brazil.

11 "África, entrada do mundo / Negra desposando a luz, luminária natural que nos conduz / Mama, mama Africana / Entregou ao Ilê Aiyê a gênese da negritude baiana / Copa, tronco, raiz / A liberdade quis, árvore da afro-descendência / Ilê Aiyê projeto da diferença / A horta da nossa história irrigada por novos quilombolas / Comendo raiz africana, a matriz, Ilê Aiyê continua nobre e feliz / Segue, avance a trajetória, estação primeira Curuzu, morada do guarda memória / Corpo de ébano, farda africana, apito preto, Ilê Aiyê guarda a memória do seu jeito / Apita ré, fazendo a história, Ilê Aiyê guarda atento, guarda a memória."12. Statement to *A Tarde*, December 1991, cited in Guerreiro (2000, 30).

12 Interview with author, July 1999, Salvador.

13 For Pierucci, "the axis of 'equivalence' that allows for this 'black' identification on a planetwide level is located in the experience of the same *negrophobia*. In other words, the possibility of a common identification is based on the fact that black communities, as different as they might be in cultural resources and in their historical pasts, have been nevertheless looked at and treated by the dominant culture of the west as 'the same thing' " (1999, 158).

14 "In this world of overdetermined racial signs, an outstandingly good but temperamental natural athlete is exactly what we would expect a savage African to become. The notion of black beauty is a more complex issue, but even that need not be a doorway into liberation from the idea of race and its non-negotiable natural hierarchies. It, too, can cement the most destructive bonds between blackness and the body to the obvious detriment of any possible connections between blackness and the mind" (Gilroy 2000, 173).

Chapter 3: Africa on the Body

1 According to Thomas (1997), four million slaves were brought to Brazil.

2 Mariza Corrêa (1982) analyzed the passage from the condition of slave to the condition of black in Brazil. She states that *slaves* became *blacks*, racially and biologically defined, soon after abolition.

3 Job-market practices of requiring a "good appearance" or which specify age, sex, color, height, marital status, family situation, pregnancy status, etc., are prohibited under Brazilian law (art. 7, paragraph 30 of the federal constitution; article 373, a, of the Consolidated Labor Law, and Law 9,029/95, art. 1).

4 Describing the "black types" that appear most frequently in movies made in the United States, Stuart Hall (1997b) discusses the figure of the Bad Buck, represented in the cinema as a tall, muscular, violent, angry black man who is a potential rapist.

5 Brazil was the only Latin American country to participate in the First International Conference on Race, held in 1911. Anthropologist João Batista Lacerda presented his thesis "Sur les métis," in which he argued that Brazil's miscegena-

tion process would lead the country to a "whiter future." He said that it would take three generations to complete the entire lightening process (both moral and physical) of the Brazilian population (Schwarcz 2001).

6 For more information on whiteness in Brazil, see Pinho (2009).

7 In the beginning of the 1990s, there were approximately 30 Afro-Brazilian cultural groups registered in Salvador, with an average of 20,000 members. In addition, there were over 2,000 Afro-Brazilian houses of worship, dozens of capoeira, theater, and Afro-Brazilian dance schools, and at least a dozen strictly political groups (Agier 1992).

8 In Salvador there is another school built in a Candomblé *terreiro*: Escola Ana Eugênia dos Santos, located in the Ilê Axé Opô Afonjá terreiro, in São Gonçalo do Retiro, in the neighborhood of Cabula.

9 Project plan sent to potential supporters requesting financing. This plan was shared with me by one of Ilê Aiyê's directors.

10 Ibid. The Odebrecht Foundation is one of the project's main financial supporters.

11 http://olodum.uol.com.br/, accessed 2001.

12 http://olodum.uol.com.br/, accessed 2001.

13 In Brazil, most full-time schools operate on two shifts, with students attending classes either in the morning or in the afternoon.

14 Statistics show that in times of high inflation and poverty, Brazilians decrease their consumption of essential products such as food and clothing, but surprisingly, they do not alter their consumption of hair products.

15 "Ilê Aiyê," by Paulinho Camafeu.

16 Melo made his comments during a debate between the editors of *Revista Raça* and several academics discussing the impact of the then recently launched magazine (Kofes 1996).

17 http://www.goyalopes.com.br, accessed 7 June 2008.

18 "Todo mundo é afro," *Revista Veja*, 20 February 2003.

19 A very extreme example of the merchandising of supposedly black objects in the tourism sector are crocheted "Rasta caps," typically green, yellow, and red, fashioned with crudely made plastic braids or dreadlocks — intended, I believe, to look "comical." In general, these wiglike hats are purchased only during Carnaval to be used as a gag, something which in and of itself deserves a more detailed analysis.

20 In their social projects, black organizations in Bahia generally use alternatives based on educational, pedagogical, cultural, moral, legal, and political strategies. Often, embedded within these approaches is the goal to later transform these into public, government-instituted policies to combat racism.

21 Several black "cultural" organizations carry out work that, intentionally or not, leads to increased black self-esteem. For Myriam Santos, samba schools in Rio de Janeiro "develop a cultural and artistic production that strengthens its members' self-esteem, and these activities . . . go against the grain of the growing rationalization of society at-large, opening up important spaces for freedom" (1999, 59).

22 This feeling of self-worth is also closely associated with the fact that they belong

to a famous group, as was expressed to me in an interview with a member of Ilê Aiyê: "I am proud to wear Ilê's outfits. As soon as I put these clothes on, as soon as I put on Ilê Aiyê's clothes, . . . it's a whole new thing, it changes, it completely changes. I feel an actual sense of joy. As soon as you put on the clothes from an entity you belong to, you are no longer . . . you are no longer in the middle of a crowd, you become unique, you know?"

23 "Auto-estima: Um sonho de libertação," by Juracy Tavares da Silva and Nelson Borderô.

24 The interviewee refers to the Brazilian soccer player now known as Ronaldo, who shaves his head, and not to the younger soccer player, Ronaldinho Gaúcho.

25 I have personally heard this type of discourse several times at Ilê Aiyê rehearsals, during many Black Beauty Evenings, and in interviews with the group's leaders on local television stations.

26 "Cenário negro da simpatia do Ilê," by Amilton Nêga Fulô and Genivaldo.

27 Gilroy (2000) employs the concept of "camp mentality" to refer to the excluding logic of national, ethnic, and racial absolutisms. Beyond expressing the concrete reality of institutions such as concentration camps and refugee camps, the term is a metaphor for the rigidity of "race" and nation. For Gilroy, the most effective reaction against camp mentalities come from those who are "between camps," such as diasporic thinkers who have traveled between continents and different ways of thinking.

28 "Lowered self-esteem and a negative self-image inhibit any type of movement toward demands, whether these be in the intellectual or affective realms. Prince Charmings living as toads, they believe they are only capable of croaking until the spell is broken and it is possible to reclaim their royalty. For example, the strength resulting from the (re)appropriation of origin values certainly facilitates the transition from fear and shame at not being white to pride in being black, and stimulates the impulse to demand human rights, among them those related to citizenship" (Ribeiro 1999, 242).

29 There has been a noticeable increase in the use of the expression "self-esteem" in Brazilian television advertisements. One advertisement for a loan company delivers the message, "Request a personal loan now and increase your self-esteem."

30 The appropriation of the term *self-esteem* often occurs in conjunction with the appropriation of the expression *empowerment*. The discourse of Comunidade Solidária during Fernando Henrique Cardoso's government can be considered emblematic in this sense.

Chapter 4: Africa in the Soul

1 Just to remind the reader: I consider the discourse producers of *blocos afro* to be the directors, teachers, songwriters, and any other person directly responsible for formulating the discourse, while the *discourse interlocutors* are primarily the younger members, who receive and reformulate the produced narratives.

2 Luíza Brunet, to a television reporter during a samba school rehearsal, January 1998.

3 *Correio Popular* 1, no. 47 (15 February 1988). Another example of the stereotyping of *mulatas* was confirmed in the Datafolha poll, "Cordial Racism," carried out in 1995. In response to the question (posed only to men) "As far as you know or imagine, who is better in bed, white women, *mulatas*, or black women?" thirty-two percent of the men interviewed said that *mulatas* were better, whereas twenty-three percent said there is no difference/they're all the same (Datafolha 1995).

4 Stuart Hall (1996c, 10) calls attention to Foucault's discussion of the double-sided character of subjection–subjectification.

5 For more information about the construction of samba as a national symbol, see Vianna (1995).

6 Several scholars have defended the idea that the black movement should take back the ethnic cultural manifestations that have undergone the process of being labeled as Brazilian, such as Ortiz (1985), Munanga (1990; 1996; 1999), and Carneiro (2000), among others.

7 It is necessary to underscore, however, that musical genres such as jazz, blues, rock, and more recently rap are simultaneously black and modern, in addition to being obviously hybrid. This illustrates the difficulty of segregating a "black culture" from a "white culture."

8 Writing on the meaning of *soul*, Ulf Hannerz explains that the term is used to confer identity and common values upon disadvantaged American blacks: "By talking about people who have soul, about soul music, and about soul food, . . . by talking to others of his group in these terms, he identifies with them and confers the same role on them. Using soul rhetoric is a way of convincing others of one's own worth and of their worth" (1968, 27).

9 The word *negão* (*negona* in the feminine) is derived from *negrão* (the augmented form of *negro*) literally "big black man." This term has several meanings depending on the context and tone of voice used. It can be used to express the notion of the black male as large, threatening, and violent; it can have a sexual connotation; or it can also be a term of endearment, as in *meu negão* or *minha negona*. I opted to not translate it as "nigger" because, unlike in the United States, *negão* and *negona* are not used only by "insiders." Furthermore, I believe that even when resignified and reappropriated by the racially oppressed, the term *nigger* is very controversial and always carries a negative ring to it. The word *negão*, in contrast, does not have negative connotations unless explicitly indicated by tone of voice. In fact, interviewees frequently mentioned the importance of tone of voice in discussing the meaning of utterances such as *negão, negona, neguinha, neguinho*, and so on.

10 This is a rather summary explanation of Foucault's concept of biopolitics (1978). For him, biopolitics is also linked to racism, since it creates a notion of "pure community" that, in order to continue existing, must eliminate the biological types that threaten it.

11 The Parliamentary Inquiry on Racism was conceived and implemented by Rep-

resentative Juca Ferreira, from the Green Party, in March 1999. Over the course of 70 days, four public hearings and one seminar were held, and 17 statements were gathered from representatives of the *blocos de trio* under investigation: Eva, Beijo, Pinel, Cheiro de Amor, and Nu outro-Eva. This data was taken from the Inquiry's final report, kindly shared with me by Representative Ferreira.

12 As expressed in one of Ilê Aiyê's songs, composed in honor of the group's 21st anniversary, "I'm 21, I'm an adult, my skin is black, I have reached adulthood."

13 "The varying importance of color throughout Brazil's several regions, as well as its perception and categorization in the labor market, at home, and at work, demonstrate precisely that color is nothing more than the bodily mark of race, or to put it differently, its codification. The importance of color seems to vary specifically in function of the demographic percentage of blacks in each region and in each different kind of situation where they compete with whites" (Guimarães 1995, 57).

14 F. James Davis provides an extensive panorama of the changing definitions of blackness in the United States in his book *Who Is Black? One Nation's Definition*. Besides demonstrating that the one-drop rule was not always hegemonic in the history of the United States as a whole or in all of its states, Davis also describes the difficulties faced by light-skinned individuals of mixed race in terms of racial classification, indicating the imprecision of the one-drop rule.

15 I thank my colleagues Robert Stam and Darién Davis for pointing this out in our conversations about U.S.-centrism in the African diaspora.

16 Interview provided to the local TV Itapoan newscast, 1997, emphasis added.

17 Guimarães argues that "races are social constructs, forms of identity based on an erroneous biological idea, but socially functional for constructing, maintaining, and reproducing differences and privileges" (1999, 67).

18 For Guimarães, all ethnic formations require a "forcibly essentialist definition" (1999, 59).

19 Guimarães not only defends the use of the term *race* but also argues that it should be used without quotation marks. "In the social sciences, the non-use of racial categories by means of the abusive use of quotation marks in order to denote race as a native or socially constructed category lost meaning as soon as it became clear, through deconstructive criticism, that after all, more immediate notions such as 'skin color' or 'hair type' were not any more natural than the notion of 'race'" (1999, 178).

Chapter 5: Milking Mama Africa

1 The idea that Brazilians constituted a "sad people" (*povo triste*) was developed by Paulo Prado in his 1928 essay "Retrato do Brasil: Ensaio sobre a tristeza brasileira." Prado explained that the melancholy of Brazilian people stemmed from their sexual excesses and vices, which had existed ever since the earliest years of

colonization. The nudity of indigenous women and the sensuality of black women led Brazilians to became a tired and lethargic people.

2 Holanda also states that "the Brazilian contribution to civilization is cordiality — we shall give the world the 'cordial man'" (1990 [1936], 106).

3 "And not only Bahian urbanity, politeness, gentleness, civility, good taste, religiosity, tenderness, civics, and intelligence, but also a little of the malice, the humor, the jocularity that compensates for the excess in dignity, solemnity, and elegance itself" (Freyre 1990, 10).

4 In *Tenda dos milagres* (1969), there are several sections in which Amado boldly describes police repression toward Candomblé *terreiros*, relating such authoritarian practice to the racist ideas of Nina Rodrigues, which could still be heard in academic and official speeches.

5 The *obá-mangbá*, or *obá de Xangô*, is a hierarchical position in the *terreiro* Ilê Axé Opô Afonjá and represents the 12 ministers of Xangô. This position is offered to nonpractitioners of Candomblé, chosen for their prestige to represent the old court of Oyó, the ancient political capital of the Yoruba (Matory 2001, 186).

6 According to Dantas, the title of the book points to the divided world inhabited by the Candomblé temples in the state of Sergipe: a world divided between dominant whites and dominated blacks. Vovó Nagô (Nagô Grandmother) refers to the African grandparents of one of the *mães de santo* interviewed by Dantas. Papai Branco (White Daddy) refers to the slave master of this *mãe de santo*'s mother, who was described by her mother as a patron and protector, thus indicating that the relationship between dominant whites and dominated blacks were quite complex, involving negotiation and patronage.

7 Born in Cilicia, now known as Arabia, sometime in the third century, Cosmas and Damian were twin brothers who practiced medicine without charging fees. Their cult was introduced by the Portuguese in Brazil as early as the 1530s.

8 This idea of Bahia as a nursery is found in the works of Bahians influenced by Freyre, such as Nelson Sampaio, who in 1943 called Bahia a "Brazilian matriarch" (quoted in Freyre 1944, 121).

9 Ilhéus is a good example of the relationship between Jorge Amado's work and the formation of a public image for the state of Bahia. The state's third-largest tourist attraction is cited in many Amado novels, and the author allowed the mayor's office to use images he created in publicity campaigns promoting tourism in the city (*Folha de São Paulo*, 8 July 2001). In Ilhéus, tourists can purchase chocolates shaped like female and male genitals, respectively called "Gabriela's flower" and "Nacib's cacao."

10 *Abará* is an Afro-Bahian delicacy made of mashed black-eyed peas and cooked in banana leaves. *Cocadas* are Afro-Bahian delicacies made of coconut and sugar. Both items are available for sale in the trays of the *baianas de acarajé*.

11 *Guias* are the beaded necklaces used by Candomblé practitioners. The color of the beads corresponds to a specific *orixá*. *Balangandans* are the good luck charms

used by the *baianas de acarajé*, usually made of metal, in the form of medals, keys, *figas*, etc.

12 The "implicit spaces" are those where being black does not, in principle, represent a problem or obstacle for individuals (e.g., the streets, neighborhoods, soccer teams, Catholic churches). In these spaces, racism and themes connected to blackness are topics to be avoided; they are the places where the important thing is to be cordial and relate well to everyone else (Sansone 1995b).

13 "Mystical Bahia," http://www.senado.gov.br/web/senador/acm/index.htm (Antônio Carlos Magalhães's Web site), accessed 2001. Not surprisingly, the background audio playing on this Web site is capoeira music.

14 http://www.senado.gov.br/web/senador/acm/index.htm, accessed 2001.

15 Sansone (2000b) considers the presidents of *blocos afros*, among other exponents of black cultural production in Bahia, to be representatives and spokespersons of the black community since they constitute a select group that decisively affects the discourses and representations of Afro-Bahian culture.

16 In 1978, the Movimento Negro Unificado contra a Discriminação Racial (MNUCDR—Black Movement United Against Racial Discrimination) proclaimed November 20 to be the National Day of Black Awareness. One of the objectives was to replace the importance attributed to May 13 (Abolition Day), which until that moment had been imposed as the main date dedicated to blacks, and to remove Princess Isabel from her throne as the heroine of blacks.

17 One of the slogans used by the black movement's campaign of nonparticipation in the official celebrations of the Abolition Centennial was, "They gave me freedom papers, but no work papers."

18 From the special issue on Jorge Amado, published in *Folha de São Paulo* on 8 July 2001.

19 Excerpts from news stories, entitled "[Magalhães] returns to Bahia to win the 2002 elections," "[Pelourinho] wears the colors of Bahia to greet [Magalhães]," and "Bahian people greet their greatest leader," *Correio da Bahia*, 6 January 2001.

20 The Colombian rap group Wade studied calls itself the "Ashanty Cultural and Ethno-Educational Association" and was founded in the mid-1980s as a dance and music group, using rudimentary instruments such as boxes and buckets. In 1992, Ashanty emerged as a rap and reggae group with a strong political and social agenda. Like Bahia's *blocos afro*, the group is influenced by international black cultural production, such as the black movement in the United States, Spike Lee's movies, Nelson Mandela's speeches, and a high esteem for Africanisms.

21 From the local television news program *TVE Notícias*, broadcast on TVE Bahia on 8 September 2001.

REFERENCES

Adorno, T., and Horkheimer, M. 1978. "A indústria cultural: O Ilusionismo como mistificação de massa." *Teoria da cultura de massa*, edited by Luís Lima. Rio de Janeiro: Paz e Terra.

Agier, Michel. 1991. "Classe ou raça? Socialização, trabalho e identidade opcionais." *Bahia: Análise e dados*, vol. 1. Salvador: Centro de Estatística e Informações.

———. 1992. "Etnopolítica: A dinâmica do espaço afro-baiano." *Estudos Afro-Asiáticos* 22, 99–115.

Alencastro, Luiz Felipe de. 2000. *O trato dos viventes: Formação do Brasil no Atlântico Sul*. São Paulo: Companhia das Letras.

Alvarez, Sonia, Evelina Dagnino, and Arturo Escobar, eds. 1998. *Cultures of Politics, Politics of Cultures: Re-visioning Latin American Social Movements*. Boulder, Colo.: Westview Press.

Amado, Jorge. 1958. *Gabriela, cravo e canela*. São Paulo: Martins.

———. 1963. *Jubiabá*. São Paulo: Martins.

———. 1966. *Dona Flor e seus dois maridos, história moral e de amor*. São Paulo: Martins.

———. 1973. *Tereza Batista cansada de guerra*. São Paulo: Martins.

———. 1977. *Tieta do agreste*. Rio de Janeiro: Record.

———. 1978. *Tenda dos milagres*. Rio de Janeiro: Record.

Amma-Psique e Negritude Quilombhoje. 1999. *Gostando mais de nós mesmos: Perguntas e respostas sobre auto-estima e questão racial*. São Paulo: Editora Gente.

Anderson, Benedict. 1991. *Imagined Communities: Reflections on the Origins and Spread of Nationalism*. 2nd edition. New York: Verso.

Andrews, George Reid. 1991a. *Blacks and Whites in São Paulo, Brazil, 1888–1988*. Madison: University of Wisconsin Press.

———. 1991b. "O protesto político negro em São Paulo, 1888–1988." *Estudos Afro-Asiáticos* 21, 27–48.

———. 2004. *Afro-Latin America, 1800–2000*. New York: Oxford University Press.

Anta Diop, Ckeik. 1980. "Origem dos antigos egípcios." *História geral da África*, vol. 3, edited by G. Mokhtar, 39–70. São Paulo: Ática/UNESCO.

Appiah, Kwame Anthony. 1992. *In My Father's House: Africa in the Philosophy of Culture*. New York: Oxford University Press.

Araújo Pinho, Osmundo S. 1998. "A Bahia no fundamental: Notas para uma interpretação do discurso ideológico da baianidade." *Revista Brasileira de Ciências Sociais* 13, no. 36 (February), 109–20.

———. 1999. "'Só se vê na Bahia': A imagem típica e a imagem crítica do Pelourinho afro-baiano." *Brasil: Um país de negros?* edited by Jeferson Bacelar and Carlos Caroso, 87–110. Rio de Janeiro: Pallas, Salvador, Centro de Estudos Afro-Asiáticos.

———. 2000. "Perspectivas sobre a produção da 'cultura baiana': Miscigenação, misticismo e mercado." Paper presented at the 22nd annual meeting of the Associação Brasileira de Antropologia, Brasília, 16–19 July.

———. 2001. "*Fogo na Babilonia*: Reggae, Black Counterculture, and Globalization in Brazil." *Brazilian Popular Music and Globalization*, edited by Charles A. Perrone and Christopher Dunn. Gainesville: University Press of Florida.

Asante, Molefi. 1987. "The Search for an Afrocentric Method." *The Afrocentric Idea*. Philadelphia: Temple University Press.

———. 1990. *Kemet, Afrocentricity and Knowledge*. Trenton, N.J.: Africa World Press.

Azevedo, Célia Maria Marinho de. 1995. "O abolicionismo transatlântico e a memória do paraíso racial brasileiro." *Estudos Afro-Asiáticos* 30, 151–62.

———. 2003. *Abolicionismo: Estados Unidos e Brasil. Uma história comparada*. São Paulo: Editora Annablume.

———. 2004. *Anti-racismo e seus paradoxos: Reflexões sobre cota racial, raça e racismo*. São Paulo: Editora Annablume.

Bacelar, Jeferson, and Carlos Caroso, eds. 1999. *Brasil: Um país de negros?* Rio de Janeiro: Pallas, Salvador, Centro de Estudos Afro-Asiáticos.

Balibar, Étienne, and Immanuel Wallerstein. 1991. *Race, Nation and Class: Ambiguous Identities*. London: Verso.

Bandeira, Claudio. 1999. "Agreement against Discrimination," *A Tarde* (Salvador da Bahia), 14 May.

Banks, Marcus. 1996. *Ethnicity: Anthropological Constructions*. London: Routledge.

Banton, Michael. 1987. *Racial Theories*. Cambridge: Cambridge University Press.

Barbosa, Márcio, ed. 1998. *Frente Negra Brasileira: Depoimentos*. São Paulo: Quilombhoje Literatura.

Barkty, Sandra Lee. 1982. "Narcissism, Femininity and Alienation." *Social Theory and Practice* 8 (Summer), 127–43.

Barret, Leonard. 1988. *The Rastafarians*. Boston: Beacon Press.

Barth, Fredrik. 1969. *Ethnic Groups and Boundaries*. Boston: Brown and Company.

Bastide, Roger. 1953. *Estudos afro-brasileiros*. São Paulo: USP, Perspectiva.

———. 1971. *As religiões africanas no Brasil*. São Paulo: USP, Pioneira.

———. 1974. *As Américas negras*. São Paulo: Difel.

Beauvoir, Simone de. 1993 [1953]. *The Second Sex*. New York: Alfred A. Knopf.

Benhabib, Seyla. 2002. *The Claims of Culture: Equality and Diversity in the Global Era*. Princeton, N.J.: Princeton University Press.

Bhabha, Homi. 1990. *Nation and Narration*. London: Routledge.

———. 1992. "A questão do 'outro': Diferença, discriminação e o discurso do colonialismo." *Pós-modernismo e política*, edited by Heloísa Buarque de Holanda, 177–203. Rio de Janeiro: Rocco.

Birman, Patrícia. 1990. "Beleza negra." *Estudos Afro-Asiáticos* 18, 5–12.

Brandão, Carlos Rodrigues. 1986. *Identidade e etnia: construção da pessoa e resistência cultural*. São Paulo: Brasiliense.

———. 1989. "O negro de hoje visto pelo branco de agora." *Estudos Afro-Asiáticos* 17, 5–28.

Briggs, Charles L. 1996. "The Politics of Discursive Authority in Research on the 'Invention of Tradition.'" *Cultural Anthropology* 11, no. 4, 435–69.

Brown, Niani Dee. 1992. "Black Consciousness vs. Racism in Brazil." *African-American Reflections on Brazil's Racial Paradise*, edited by David J. Hellwig, 225–48. Philadelphia: Temple University Press.

Brown, Wendy. 1995. *States of Injury*. Princeton, N.J.: Princeton University Press.

Browning, Barbara. *Infectious Rhythm: Metaphors of Contagion and the Spread of African Culture*. New York: Routledge.

Bruner, Edward M. 1996. "Tourism in Ghana: The Representation of Slavery and the Return of the Black Diaspora." *American Anthropologist* 98, no. 2 (June), 290–304.

Buarque de Holanda Ferreira, Aurélio. 2004. *Novo Dicionário Aurélio da Língua Portuguesa*. 3rd edition. Curitiba: Editora Positivo.

Burdick, John. 1998. *Blessed Anastácia: Women, Race and Popular Christianity in Brazil*. New York: Routledge.

Butler, Judith. 1998. "Merely Cultural." *New Left Review* no. 227 (January–February), 33–44.

Butler, Kim. 1998. *Freedoms Given, Freedoms Won: Afro-Brazilians in Post-Abolition São Paulo and Salvador*. New Brunswick, N.J.: Rutgers University Press.

Caldeira, Teresa Pires do Rio. 1984. *A política dos outros*. São Paulo: Brasiliense.

Calomee, Gloria. 1992. "Brazil and the Blacks of South America." *African-American Reflections on Brazil's Racial Paradise*, edited by David J. Hellwig, 249–52. Philadelphia: Temple University Press.

Campos, Djalma, and Cristina Núbia. 1999. "Famosos e generosos." *Revista Raça* 4, no. 29 (January), 34–41.

Canclini, Nestor. 2001. *Consumers and Citizens: Globalization and Multicultural Conflicts*. Minneapolis, University of Minnesota Press.

Carby, Hazel. 1982. "White Woman Listen! Black Feminism and the Boundaries of Sisterhood." *The Empire Strikes Back: Race and Racism in 70s Britain*, edited by the Centre for Contemporary Cultural Studies, 212–35. London: Hutchinson / Centre for Contemporary Cultural Studies, University of Birmingham.

Cardoso de Oliveira, Roberto. 1975. *Identidade, etnia e estrutura social*. São Paulo: Livraria Pioneira Editora.

Carneiro, Sueli. 1999. "Black Women's Identity in Brazil." *Race in Contemporary Brazil*, edited by Rebecca Reichmann, 217–28. University Park: Pennsylvania State University Press.

———. 2000. "Sueli Carneiro: Uma guerreira contra o racismo." Interview in *Caros Amigos* 3, no. 35, 24–29.

Carneiro da Cunha, Manuela. 1985. *Negros, estrangeiros: Os escravos libertos e sua volta à África*. São Paulo: Brasiliense.

Castro, Nádia de Araújo, and Vanda Sá Barreto, eds. 1998. *Trabalho e desigualdades raciais: Negros e brancos no mercado de trabalho em Salvador*. São Paulo: Annablume Editora.

Chauí, Marilena. 2000. *Brasil: Mito fundador e sociedade autoritária*. São Paulo: Ed. Fundação Perseu Abramo.

Christmas, Rachel Jackson. 1992. "In Harmony with Brazil's African Pulse." *African-American Reflections on Brazil's Racial Paradise*, edited by David J. Hellwig, 253–58. Philadelphia: Temple University Press.

Clifford, James. 1994. "Diasporas." *Cultural Anthropology* 9, no. 3 (August), 302–38.

Cohen, Abner. 1974. *Urban Ethnicity*. London: Routledge and Kegan Paul.

Connerton, Paul. 1989. *How Societies Remember*. Cambridge: Cambridge University Press.

Corrêa, Mariza. 1982. *As ilusões da liberdade: A escola Nina Rodrigues e a antropologia no Brasil*, PhD dissertation, Instituto de Filosofia e Ciências Humanas, Universidade de Campinas.

———. 1996. "Sobre a invenção da mulata." *Cadernos Pagu* 6–7, 35–50.

Crowley, Daniel. 1984. *African Myth and Black Reality in Bahian Carnaval*. UCLA Monograph Series, no. 25. Los Angeles: Museum of Cultural History.

Cunha, Olivia. M. Gomes da. 1991. *Corações rastafaris: Lazer, política e religião em Salvador*. Master's thesis, Museu Nacional (Rio de Janeiro).

———. 1998. "Black Movements and the Politics of Identity in Brazil." *Cultures of Politics, Politics of Cultures: Re-visioning Latin American Social Movements*, edited by Sonia Alvarez, Evelina Dagnino, and Arturo Escobar, 220–51. Boulder, Colo.: Westview Press.

Cunha Jr., Henrique. 1996. "As estratégias de combate ao racismo, movimentos negros na escola, na universidade e no pensamento brasileiro." *Estratégias e políticas de combate à discriminação racial*, edited by Kabengele Munanga, 147–56. São Paulo: Edusp.

CUT, CGT, Força Sindical. 1995. "Racismo à brasileira." "300 Anos de Zumbi," special issue, *Cadernos do CEAS*, 39–56.

Dagnino, Evelina. 1994. "Os movimentos sociais e a emergência de uma nova noção de cidadania." *Os anos 90: Política e sociedade no Brasil*, 103–15. São Paulo: Editora Brasiliense.

Da Matta, Roberto. 1981. *Carnavais, malandros e heróis*. Rio de Janeiro: Zahar.

Dantas, Beatriz Góis. 1982. "Repensando a pureza Nagô." *Religião e Sociedade* 8, 15–20.

———. 1988. *Vovó nagô e papai branco: Usos e abusos da África no Brasil*. Rio de Janeiro: Graal.

Datafolha. 1995. *Racismo cordial*. São Paulo: Editora Ática.

Davies, Carole Boyce. 1999. "Beyond Unicentricity: Transcultural Black Presences." *Research in African Literature* 30, no. 2, 96–109.

Dávila, Jeffrey. 2003. *Diploma of Whiteness: Race and Social Policy in Brazil, 1917–1945*. Durham, N.C.: Duke University Press.

Davis, Darién. 1999. *Avoiding the Dark: Race and the Forging of National Culture in Modern Brazil*. Aldershot, UK: Ashgate.

Davis, F. James. 2001. *Who Is Black? One Nation's Definitions*. 10th Anniversary Edition. University Park: Pennsylvania State University Press.

Deleuze, Gilles, and Félix Guattari. 1987. *A Thousand Plateaus: Capitalism and Schizophrenia*. Minneapolis: University of Minnesota Press.

Dias Filho, Antônio Jonas. 1996. "As mulatas que não estão no mapa." *Cadernos Pagu*, 6–7, 51–66.

Diawara, Mantia. 1998. *In Search of Africa*. Cambridge, Mass.: Harvard University Press.

Du Bois, W. E. B. 1990 [1903]. *The Souls of Black Folk*. New York: Vintage Books / Library of America.

Dunn, Christopher. 1992. "Afro-Bahian Carnival: A Stage for Protest." *Afro-Hispanic Review* 11, no. 1–3, 11–20.

———. 2001. *Brutality Garden: Tropicália and the Emergence of a Brazilian Counterculture*. Chapel Hill: University of North Carolina Press.

Erasmus, Zimitri. 2000. "Hair Politics." *Senses of Culture*, edited by Sarah Nuttall and Cheryl-Ann Michael, 380–92. Cape Town: Oxford University Press.

Eriksen, Thomas. 2002. *Ethnicity and Nationalism: Anthropological Perspectives*. London: Pluto Press.

Fanon, Frantz. 1991 [1952]. *Black Skin, White Masks*. New York: Grove Press.

Farias, Edson. 1999. "Orfeus em tempo de modernidade no carnaval carioca." *Estudos Afro-Asiáticos* 34, 49–79.

Featherstone, Mike, ed. 1990. *Global Culture: Nationalism, Globalization and Modernity*. London: Sage Publications.

Ferme, Mariane Ferme. 2001. *The Underneath of Things: Violence, History, and the Everyday in Sierra Leone*. Berkeley: University of California Press.

Fernandes, Florestan. 1972. *O negro no mundo dos brancos*. São Paulo: Difel.

Ferreira, Ivone. 1998. "Apartheid baiano." *Revista Raça* 3, no. 22 (June), 72–77.

Finley, Cheryl. 2001. "The Door of (No) Return." *Common-Place* 1, no. 4 (July), www.common-place.org.

Foucault, Michel. 1978. *The History of Sexuality*. Vol 1. Translated by Robert Hurley. New York: Pantheon.

———. 1980. "The Eye of Power." *Power/Knowledge: Selected Interviews and Other Writings, 1972–1977*, edited by Colin Gordon, 146–65. New York: Pantheon.

———. 1988. *Technologies of the Self: A Seminar with Michel Foucault*, edited by Luther H. Martin, Huck Gutman, and Patrick H. Hutton. Cambridge, Mass.: University of Massachusetts Press.

———. 1995. *Discipline and Punish: The Birth of the Prison*. Translated by Alan Sheridan. New York, Vintage Books.

———. 1996. *Microfísica do poder*. Rio de Janeiro: Graal.

Fraser, Nancy. 1998. "Heterosexism, Misrecognition and Capitalism: A Response to Judith Butler." *New Left Review*, no. 228, 140–49.

Frazier, Edward Franklin. 1942. "The negro family in Bahia, Brazil." *American Sociological Review* 4, no. 7, 465–78.

———. 1968 [1944]. "A comparison of negro-white relations in Brazil and the United States." *On Race Relations*, 82–102. Chicago: University of Chicago Press.

———. 1969. *The Negro Family in the United States*. Chicago: University of Chicago.

Freyre, Gilberto. 1926. "Bahia à tarde," *Diário de Pernambuco*, 19 March 1926.

———. 1937. *Novos estudos afro-brasileiros*. Rio de Janeiro: Civilização Brasileira.

———. 1952 [1926]. *Manifesto regionalista*. Recife: Região.

———. 1989. *Casa Grande & Senzala*. Rio de Janeiro: Record.

———. 1990. *Bahia e baianos*, edited by Edson Nery da Fonseca. Salvador: Empresa Gráfica da Bahia.

Friedman, Jonathan. 1990. "Being in the World: Globalization and Localization." *Global Culture: Nationalism, Globalization and Modernity*, edited by Mike Featherstone, 311–28. London: Sage Publications.

Fry, Peter. 1977. "Feijoada e Soul Food: notas sobre a manipulação de símbolos étnicos e nacionais." *Cadernos de Opinião* 4, 13–23.

———. 1982. *Para inglês ver*. Rio de Janeiro: Zahar.

———. 1991. "Politicamente correto num lugar, incorreto noutro? Relações raciais no Brasil, nos E. Unidos, em Moçambique e no Zimbábue." *Estudos Afro-Asiáticos* 21, 167–77.

———. 1995–96. "O que a Cinderela negra tem a dizer sobre a 'política racial' no Brasil." *Revista USP* 28, 122–35.

———. 2000. "Politics, Nationality and the Meanings of 'Race.'" "Brazil. Burden of the Past, Promise of the Future," special issue of *Daedalus: Journal of the American Academy of Arts and Sciences* 129, no. 2 (Spring), 83–118.

———. 2005. *A persistência da raça: Ensaios antropológicos sobre o Brasil e a África austral*. Rio de Janeiro: Civilização Brasileira.

Fry, Peter, Sérgio Carrara, and Ana Luiza Martins-Costa. 1988. "Negros e brancos no Carnaval da Velha República." *Escravidão e invenção da liberdade*, edited by J. J. Reis, 232–63. São Paulo: Brasiliense.

Fry, Peter, Yvonne Maggie, Marcos Chor Maio, Simone Monteiro, and Ricardo Ventura Santos, eds. 2007. *Divisões perigosas: Políticas raciais no Brasil contemporâneo*. Rio de Janeiro: Civilização Brasileira.

Fryer, Peter. 2000. *Rhythms of Resistance: African Musical Heritage in Brazil*. Hanover, N.H.: University Press of New England.

Gilroy, Paul. 1987. *There Ain't No Black in the Union Jack*. London: Hutchinson.

———. 1993a. *The Black Atlantic, Modernity and Double Consciousness*. London: Verso.

———. 1993b. *Small Acts: Thoughts on the Politics of Black Cultures*. London: Serpent's Tail.

———. 1994. "Urban Social Movements, 'Race' and Community." *Colonial Discourse and Post-Colonial Theory, A Reader*, edited by Patrik Williams and Laura Chrisman, 404–20. New York: Columbia University Press.

——. 2000. *Against Race: Imagining Political Culture Beyond the Color Line*. Cambridge, Mass.: Harvard University Press.

——. 2001. "Driving While Black." *Car Cultures*, edited by Daniel Miller, 81–104. Oxford: Berg Publishers.

——. 2002. "Neither Jews nor Germans: Where Is Liberalism Taking Us?" Interview with Paul Gilroy. *Open Democracy*. http://www.opendemocracy.org, accessed 6 December 2002.

Gobineau, Arthur Comte de. 1983 [1853–55]. *Essai sur l'inegalité des races humaines*. Paris: Editions Gallimard.

Godi, Antonio J. V. dos Santos. 1991. "De índio a negro, ou o reverso." *Cantos e toques: Etnografias do espaço negro na Bahia*. Caderno CRH. Salvador: Editora Fator, Universidade Federal da Bahia.

Goffman, Erving. 1963. *Stigma: Note on the Management of Spoiled Identity*. Englewood Cliffs, N.J.: Prentice-Hall.

Goldstein, Donna. 2003. *Laughter out of Place: Race, Class, Violence, and Sexuality in a Rio Shantytown*. Berkeley: University of California Press.

Gomes, Marco Aurélio A. de Filgueiras, ed. 1995. *Pelo Pelô: História, cultura e cidade*. Salvador: Editora da Universidade Federal da Bahia.

Gomes, Olívia Maria dos Santos. 1988. "Impressões da festa: Blocos afro sob o olhar da imprensa baiana." *Estudos Afro-Asiáticos* 16, no. 1, 171–87.

Gonzales, Lelia. 1985. "The Unified Black Movement: A New Stage in Black Political Mobilization." *Race, Class and Power in Brazil*, edited by Pierre-Michel Fontaine, 120–34. Los Angeles: Center for Afro-American Studies, University of California.

Gonzales, Lélia, and Carlos Hasenbalg. 1982. *Lugar de negro*. Rio de Janeiro: Editora Marco Zero.

Gordon, Edmund T., and Mark Anderson. 1999. "The African Diaspora: Toward an Ethnography of Diasporic Identification." *Journal of American Folklore* 112, no. 445, 282–96.

Gramsci, Antonio. 1992. *Prison Notebooks*. Edited by Joseph A. Buttigieg. Translated by Joseph A. Buttigieg and Antonio Callari. New York: Columbia University Press.

Grande enciclopédia portuguesa e brasileira. 1946. Lisbon and Rio de Janeiro: Editorial Enciclopédia Limitada.

Grosz, Elizabeth. 1988. "Conclusion: A Note on Essentialism and Difference." *Feminist Knowledge: Critics and Construct*, edited by S. Gunew, 332–44. London: Routledge.

Guerreiro, Goli. 2000. *A trama dos tambores: A música afro-pop de Salvador*. São Paulo: Editora 34, 2000.

Guimarães, Antônio Sérgio. 1994. "Brasil-Estados Unidos: Um diálogo que forja nossa identidade racial." *Estudos Afro-Asiáticos* 26, 141–47.

REFERENCES

———. 1995–96. "O recente anti-racismo brasileiro: o que dizem os jornais diários." *Revista USP* 28, 84–95.

———. 1997. "Raça, racismo e grupos de cor no Brasil." *Estudos Afro-Asiáticos* 27, 45–63.

———. 1999. *Racismo e anti-racismo no Brasil*. São Paulo: Editora 34.

———. 2006. "Depois da democracia racial." *Tempo Social: Revista de Sociologia da USP* 18, no. 2 (November), 269–90.

Guanaes, Nizan. 2006. Interview. *Revista Raça* 94 (January).

Guran, Milton. 1999. *Agudás : Os "brasileiros" do Benim*. Rio de Janeiro: Editora Nova Fonteira / Editora Gama Filho.

Haley, Alex. 1976. *Roots*. Garden City, N.Y.: Doubleday.

Hall, Stuart. 1992. "The Question of Cultural Identity." *Modernity and Its Futures*, edited by Stuart Hall, David Held, and Tony McGrew, 273–326. Cambridge: Polity Press / Open University.

———. 1993. "Cultural Identity and Diaspora." *Colonial Discourse and Post-Colonial Theory*, edited by Patrick Williams and Laura Chrisman, 392–403. New York: Harvester Wheatsheaf.

———. 1995. "New Cultures for Old." *A Place in the World? Places, Cultures, and Globalization*, edited by Doreen Massey and Pat Jess, 175–213. Oxford: Oxford University Press.

———. 1996a. "New Ethnicities." *Stuart Hall: Critical Dialogues in Cultural Studies*, edited by David Morley and Kuan-Hsing Chen, 441–49. London: Routledge.

———. 1996b. "What Is This 'Black' in Black Popular Culture?" *Stuart Hall: Critical Dialogues in Cultural Studies*, edited by David Morley and Kuan-Hsing Chen, 441–49. London: Routledge.

———. 1996c. "Who Needs 'Identity'?" *Questions of Cultural Identity*, edited by Stuart Hall and Paul du Gay, 1–17. London: Sage.

———. 1997a. *Representation: Cultural Representations and Signifying Practices*. London: Sage / Open University.

———. 1997b. *Identidade cultural*. Coleção Memo. São Paulo: Fundação Memorial da América Latina.

Hanchard, Michael. 1988. "Raça, hegemonia e subordinação na cultura popular." *Estudos Afro-Asiáticos* 21, 5–25.

———. 1994. *Orpheus and Power: The Movimento Negro of Rio de Janeiro and Sao Paulo, Brazil, 1945–1988*. Princeton, N.J.: Princeton University Press.

———. 1995. "Fazendo a exceção: Narrativas de igualdade racial no Brasil, no México e em Cuba." *Estudos Afro-Asiáticos* 28, 203–17.

———. 1996a. "Cinderela negra? Raça e esfera pública no Brasil." *Estudos Afro-Asiáticos* 30, 41–59.

———. 1996b. "Resposta a Luiza Bairros." *Afro-Ásia* 18, 227–33.

Hannerz, Ulf. 1968. "The Significance of Soul." *Trans-Action Magazine* July / August, 15–30.

Haraway, Donna. 1996. "Race: Universal Donors in a Vampire Culture." *Modest_*

Witness@Second_Millennium.FemaleMan©_Meets_OncoMouse™: Feminism and Technoscience. London: Routledge.

Hasenbalg, Carlos. 1985. "Race and Socioeconomic Inequalities in Brazil." *Race, Class and Power in Brazil*, edited by Pierre-Michel Fontaine, 25–41. Los Angeles: Center for Afro-American Studies, University of California.

———. 1992. *Relações raciais no Brasil contemporâneo.* Rio de Janeiro: Rio Fundo Editora.

———. 1996. "Entre o mito e os fatos: racismo e relações raciais no Brasil." *Raça, ciência e sociedade*, edited by Marcos Chor Maio and Ricardo Ventura Santos, 235–49. Rio de Janeiro: Fiocruz/CCBB.

Hasenbalg, Carlos, and Nelson do Valle Silva. 1988. *Estrutura social, mobilidade e raça.* Rio de Janeiro: Vértice.

———. 1993. "Notas sobre desigualdade racial e política no Brasil." *Estudos Afro-Asiáticos* 25, 141–59.

Hellwig, David J., ed. 1992. *African-American Reflections on Brazil's Racial Paradise.* Philadelphia: Temple University Press.

Hernandez-Reguant, Ariana. 1999. "Kwanzaa and the US Ethnic Mosaic." *Representations of Blackness and the Performance of Identities*, edited by Jean Muteba Rahier, 101–22. Westport, Conn.: Bergin and Garvey.

Herskovits, Melville. 1941. *The Myth of the Negro Past.* New York: Harper and Bros.

———. 1943 "The Negro in Bahia, Brazil: A Problem in Method." *American Sociological Review* 8, no. 7, 394–404.

———. 1966a [1948]. "The Contribution of Afroamerican Studies to Africanist Research." *The New World Negro*, 12–23. Bloomington: Indiana University Press.

———. 1966b [1948]. *The New World Negro.* Bloomington: Indiana University Press.

Hill, Robert A., ed. 1983. *The Marcus Garvey and Universal Negro Improvement Association Papers,* vol. 2. Berkeley: University of California Press.

Hobsbawm, Eric, and Terence Ranger. 1983. *The Invention of Tradition.* Cambridge: Cambridge University Press.

Holanda, Sérgio Buarque de. 1990 [1936]. *Raízes do Brasil.* Rio de Janeiro: José Olympio.

hooks, bell. 1992. *Black Looks: Race and Representation.* Cambridge, Mass.: South End Press.

———. 1994. "Postmodern Blackness." *Colonial Discourse and Post-Colonial Theory: A Reader*, edited by Patrick Williams and Laura Chrisman, 421–27. New York: Columbia University Press.

———. 1997. *Wounds of Passion.* New York: Henry Holt and Company.

———. 2000. *Where We Stand: Class Matters.* New York: Routledge.

Howe, Stephen. 1998. *Afrocentrism: Mythical Pasts and Imagined Homes.* London: Verso.

Ianni, Otávio. 1991. "A questão racial no Brasil." *Desigualdade racial no Brasil contemporâneo*, edited by Peggy A. Lovell, 15–32. Belo Horizonte: UFMG/Cedeplar.

Ilê Aiyê. 1982. "O conceito de política nos blocos negros e afoxés." Paper presented

REFERENCES

at the Sociedade de Estudos da Cultura Negra no Brasil meeting, Salvador, Bahia.

——. 2000. *África: Ventre Fértil do Mundo*. Caderno de Educaçâo Ilê Aiyê.

Jackson, Richard L. 1992. "Mestizage vs. Black Identity: The Color Crisis in Latin America." *African-American Reflections on Brazil's Racial Paradise*, edited by David J. Hellwig, 216–24. Philadelphia: Temple University Press.

Johnson, Paul C. 2002. *Secrets, Gossip, and Gods: The Transformation of Brazilian Candomblé*. Oxford: Oxford University Press, 2002.

Kamel, Ali. 2006. *Não somos racistas: Uma reação aos que querem nos transformar numa nação bicolor*. Rio de Janeiro: Editora Nova Fronteira.

Kofes, Suely. 1996. "Gênero e raça em revista: Debate com os editores da *Revista Raça Brasil*." *Cadernos Pagu* 6–7, 241–96.

Kraay, Hendrik, ed. 1998. *Afro-Brazilian Culture and Politics: Bahia, 1790s to 1990s*. Armonk, N.Y.: M. E. Sharpe.

Landes, Ruth. 1994 [1947]. *City of Women*. Albuquerque: University of New Mexico Press.

Lima, Ari. 1995. "Espaço, lazer, música e diferença cultural na Bahia." *Estudos Afro-Asiáticos* 31, 151–67.

——. 2001. "Black or Brau. Music and Black Subjectivity in a Global Context." *Brazilian Popular Music and Globalization*, edited by Charles A. Perrone and Christopher Dunn, 220–32. Gainesville: University Press of Florida.

Lopes, Jose Sergio Leite. 2000. "Class, Ethnicity, and Color in the Making of Brazilian Football." *Daedalus: Journal of the American Academy of Arts and Sciences* 129, no. 2 (Spring), 239–70.

Lovell, Peggy A., ed. 1991. *Desigualdade racial no Brasil contemporâneo*. Belo Horizonte: UFMG /Cedeplar.

Luz, Marco Aurélio. 1993. *Cultura negra e ideologia do recalque*. Rio de Janeiro: Achiamé.

M-1 [Mutulu Olugabala]. 2001. Interview. *Rap Internacional* 1, no. 3.

Machado, Vanda. 1999. *Ilê Axé: Vivência e invenção pedagógica. As crianças do Opô Afonjá*. Salvador: Edufba.

Maciel, Cléber da Silva. 1987. *Discriminações raciais*. Campinas: Editora da Unicamp.

Maggie, Yvone. 1994. "Cor, hierarquia e sistema de classificação." *Estudos Históricos* 7, no. 14, 149–60.

——. 1996. "'Aqueles a quem foi negada a cor do dia': As categorias cor e raça na cultura brasileira," *Raça, ciência e sociedade*, edited by Maio Marcos Chor and Ricardo Ventura Santos, 225–34. Rio de Janeiro: Fiocruz/CCBB.

Maio, Marcos Chor, and Ricardo Ventura Santos, eds. 1996. *Raça, ciência e sociedade*. Rio de Janeiro: Fiocruz/CCBB.

——. 2005. "Política de cotas raciais, os 'olhos da sociedade' e os usos da antropologia: O caso do vestibular da Universidade de Brasília (UNB)." *Horizontes Antropológicos* 11, no. 23 (January–June), 181–214.

——. 2007. "Cotas e racismo." *Divisões perigosas: Políticas raciais no Brasil contempo-*

râneo, edited by Peter Fry, Yvonne Maggie, Marcos Chor Maio, Simone Monteiro, and Ricardo Ventura Santos, 161–65. Rio de Janeiro: Civilização Brasileira.

Martínez-Hechazábal, Lourdes. 1999. "Hibridismo e diasporização em Black Atlantic: O caso de Chombo." *Estudos Afro-Asiáticos* 35, 81–96.

Matory, Lorand. 1997. "The English Professors of Brazil: On the Diasporic Roots of the Yorúbá Nation." *Bulletin of the Society for Comparative Studies in Society and History*, 1997, 72–103.

———. 1999. "Man in the 'City of Women.'" Paper presented at "From Local to Global: Rethinking Yoruba Religious Traditions for the Next Millenium," Florida International University, December 9–12.

———. 2001. The 'Cult of Nations' and the ritualization of their purity. *The South Atlantic Quaterly* 100, no. 1 (Winter), 171–214.

Maués, Maria Angélica Motta. 1991. "Da 'branca senhora' ao 'herói negro': A trajetória de um discurso racial." *Estudos Afro-Asiáticos* 21, 119–29.

Mbembe, Achille. 2000. "African Modes of Self Writing." *African Journals Online*, CODESRIA Bulletin/Bulletin du CODESRIA 1, no. 1, 4–18.

McClintock, Anne. 1997. "Soap and Commodity Spectacle." *Representation: Cultural Representations and Signifying Practices*, edited by Stuart Hall, 280–82. London: Sage Publications.

Meade, Teresa, and Gregory Alonso Pirio. 1988. "In Search of the Afro-American 'Eldorado': Attempts by North American Blacks to Enter Brazil in the 1920s." *Luso-Brazilian Review* 25, no. 1, 85–110.

Memmi, Albert. 1993. *O racismo: Descrição, definição, tratamento*. Lisbon: Editorial Caminho.

Militão, José Roberto. 2007. "A reflexão que vale a pena ser feita: contra as cotas raciais." *Divisões perigosas: Políticas raciais no Brasil contemporâneo*, edited by Peter Fry, Yvonne Maggie, Marcos Chor Maio, Simone Monteiro, and Ricardo Ventura Santos, 325–32. Rio de Janeiro: Civilização Brasileira.

Ministério da Educação, Conselho Nacional de Educação. 2004. *Diretrizes curriculares nacionais para a educação das relações étnico-raciais e para o ensino de história e cultura Afro-Brasileira e Africana*. Parecer N.°: CNE/CP 003/2004. Brasília, DF, October.

Mintz, Sidney, and Richard Price. 1992. *The Birth of African-American Culture: An Anthropological Perspective*. Boston: Beacon Press.

Mohanty, C. T. 1988. "Under Western Eyes." *Feminist Review* 30 (Autumn), 61–88.

Montes, Maria Lúcia. 1996. "Raça e identidade: entre o espelho, a invenção e a ideologia." *Raça e diversidade*, edited by L. Schwarcz and R. S. Queiroz, 47–75. São Paulo: Edusp.

Moreira Leite, Dante. 1983. *O caráter nacional brasileiro: História de uma ideologia*. São Paulo: Livraria Pioneira Editora.

Morrison, Toni. 1988. *Beloved*. New York: Penguin Books.

———. 1994. *The Bluest Eye*. New York: Penguin Books.

Movimento Negro Unificado. 1988. *MNU: 1978–1988, Dez anos de luta contra o racismo*. São Paulo: Confraria do Livro.

Munanga, Kabengele. 1990. "Negritude afro-brasileira: Perspectivas e dificuldades." *Revista de Antropologia* (São Paulo) 33, 109–17.

———. 1996a. "As facetas de um racismo silenciado." *Raça e diversidade*, edited by Lilia M. Schwarcz and Renato da Silva Queiroz, 213–29. São Paulo: Edusp.

———, ed. 1996b. *Estratégias e políticas de combate à discriminação racial*. São Paulo: Edusp.

———. 1996c, "O anti-racismo no Brasil." *Estratégias e políticas de combate à discriminação racial*, Kabengele Munanga, 79–94. São Paulo: Edusp.

———. 1996d. "Mestiçagem e experiências interculturais no Brasil." *Negras imagens*, edited by Lilia M. Schwarcz and Letícia V. S. Reis. São Paulo: Edusp.

———. 1998. *Rediscutindo a mestiçagem no Brasil: Identidade nacional versus identidade negra*. Petrópolis: Vozes.

Nascimento, Abdias do. 1961. *Dramas para negros e prólogos para brancos*. Rio de Janeiro: Teatro Experimental do Negro.

———. 1968. *O negro revoltado*. Rio de Janeiro: GRD.

———. 1979. *Mixture or Massacre? Genocide of a Black People*. Buffalo, N.Y.: Afrodiaspora.

Nascimento, Elisa N. 1981. *Pan-africanismo na América do Sul*. Petrópolis: Vozes.

N'ganga, João Paulo. 1995. *Preto no branco: A regra e a exceção*. Porto: Edições Afrontamento.

Nogueira, Oracy. 1985. *Tanto preto quanto branco: Estudo de relações raciais*. São Paulo: T. A. Queiroz.

Novo Dicionário Eletrônico Aurélio, version 5.0. CD-ROM. 2004.

Nuttall, Sarah, ed. 2006. *Beautiful Ugly: African and Diaspora Aesthetics*. Durham, N.C.: Duke University Press, 2006.

Ojo-Ade, Femi. 1995. "Cultura africana: Do velho e do novo; os anos 90." *Afro-Ásia* 16, 36–53.

Ortiz, Renato. 1985. *Cultura brasileira e identidade nacional*. Rio de Janeiro: Brasiliense.

Penha-Lopes, Vânia. 1997. "An Unsavory Union: Poverty, Racism, and the Murders of Street Youth in Brazil." *Globalization and Survival in the Black Diaspora: The New Urban Challenge*, edited by Charles Green, 149–68. Albany: State University of New York Press.

Perrone, Charles A., and Christopher Dunn, eds. 2001. *Brazilian Popular Music and Globalization*. Gainsville: University Press of Florida, 2001.

Pessanha, Ricardo, and Chris McGowan. 1991. *The Brazilian Sound: Samba, Bossa Nova and the Popular Music of Brazil*. New York: Billboard Books.

Pierucci, Flávio. 1999. *Ciladas da diferença*. São Paulo: Editora 34.

Pinho, Patricia de Santana. 1995. "Rastafarianismo e mundialização." *Revista de Cultura Vozes* 89, no. 5 (September–October), 53–76.

———. 2001. Review of *Rhythms of Resistance: African Musical Heritage in Brazil*, by Peter Fryer, *Hispanic American Historical Review* 81, no. 2, 423–24.

———. 2002. "Comment trouver l'Afrique a Bahia en suivant les ethno-touristes Afro-Americains." *Cahiers du Brésil Contemporain* 49–50, 97–107.

———. 2002. "Rotas e raízes da cultura negra." Review of *O atlântico negro*, by Paul Gilroy. *Novos Estudos CEBRAP* 62 (March), 183–87.

———. 2003. "Viajando a la tierra de *Ashé*: Turismo etnico afro-americano en Bahia, Brasil." *Revista del Caribe* 41 (June), 76–82.

———. 2004. *Reinvenções da África na Bahia*. São Paulo: Editora Annablume, 2004.

———. 2005. "Descentrando os Estados Unidos nos estudos sobre negritude no Brasil." *Revista Brasileira de Ciências Sociais* 59, 37–50.

———. 2006. "Afro-Aesthetics in Brazil." *Beautiful Ugly: African and Diaspora Aesthetics*, edited by Sarah Nuttall, 266–89. Durham, N.C.: Duke University Press, 2006.

———. 2006. "Gilberto Freyre e a baianidade." *Gilberto Freyre e os estudos latinoamericanos*, edited by Malcolm McNee and Joshua Lund, 227–54. Pittsburgh: Instituto Internacional de Literatura Iberoamericana, 2006.

———. 2008. "African-American Roots Tourism in Brazil." *Latin American Perspectives* 35, no. 3 (May), 70–86.

———. 2009. "White but Not Quite: Tones and Overtones of Whiteness in Brazil." *Small Axe: A Caribbean Journal of Criticism* 29, 39–56.

Pinto, Regina Pahim. 1990. "Movimento Negro e etnicidade." *Estudos Afro-Asiáticos* 19, 109–24.

Piscitelli, Adriana. 1996. "Sexo tropical: Comentários sobre gênero e raça em alguns textos da mídia brasileira." *Cadernos Pagu* 6–7, 9–35.

Prandi, Reginaldo. 1991. *Os candomblés de São Paulo*. São Paulo: Hucitec/Edusp.

———. 1996. *Herdeiras do Axé*. São Paulo: Hucitec.

Queiroz, Delcele Mascarenhas. 1999. " ' . . . um dia eu vou abrir a porta da frente': Mulheres negras, educação e mercado de trabalho." *Educação e os afro-brasileiros: Trajetórias, identidades e alternativas*, edited by Jocélio Teles dos Santos, 135–52. Salvador: Universidade Federal da Bahia/Programa A Cor da Bahia/Coleção Novos Toques.

Quijano, Anibal. 2000. "Coloniality of Power, Eurocentrism, and Latin America." *Nepantla: Views from South* 1, no. 3, 533–80.

Raeders, Georges. 1988. *O Conde Gobineau no Brasil*. Rio de Janeiro: Paz e Terra.

Rahier, Jean Muteba. 1997. "Blackness and the Racial/Spacial Order, Migrations, and Miss Ecuador 1995–1996." *American-Anthropologist* 100, no. 2 (June), 421–30.

———. 1999a. "Introduction." *Representations of Blackness and the Performance of Identities*, edited by Jean Muteba Rahier, xiii–xxvi. Westport, Conn.: Bergin and Garvey.

———, ed. 1999b. *Representations of Blackness and the Performance of Identities*. Westport, Conn.: Bergin and Garvey.

Ramos, Arthur. 1956. *O negro na civilização brasileira*. Rio de Janeiro: Casa do Estudante.

Reis, João José, ed. 1987. *Escravidão e invenção da liberdade*. São Paulo: Brasiliense.

Ribeiro, Fernando Rosa. 1993. "Apartheid e democracia racial: raça e nação no Brasil e na África do Sul." *Estudos Afro-Asiáticos* 24, 95–120.

———. 1995. "O que é ser negro ou africano, afinal de contas?" *Estudos Afro-Asiáticos* 27, 203–11.

———. 1997. "Ideologia nacional, antropologia e a questão racial." *Estudos Afro-Asiáticos* 31, 79–119.

Ribeiro, João Ubaldo. 2000. "O complexo." *A Tarde* (Salvador), 26 March.

Ribeiro, Ronilda. 1996. *Alma africana no Brasil: Os iorubás*. São Paulo: Editora Oduduwa.

———. 1999a. "Identidade do afro-descendente e sentimento de pertença a networks organizados em torno da temática racial." *Brasil: Um país de negros?* edited by Jeferson Bacelar and Carlos Caroso, 235–52. Rio de Janeiro: Pallas, Salvador, Centro de Estudos Afro-Asiáticos.

———. 1999b. "Políticas de ação afirmativa e a temática racial no Projeto de Educação para a Paz." *Educação e os afro-brasileiros: Trajetórias, identidades e alternativas*. Salvador: Universidade Federal da Bahia/Programa A Cor da Bahia/Coleção Novos Toques.

Risério, Antônio. 1981. *Carnaval Ijexá*. Salvador: Corrupio.

———. 1995. "Carnaval, as cores da mudança." *Afro-Ásia* 16, 90–106.

———. 2007. *A utopia brasileira e os movimentos negros*. São Paulo: Editora 34.

Robinson, Eugene. 1999. *Coal to Cream: A Black Man's Journey beyond Color to an Affirmation of Race*. New York: Free Press.

Rodrigues, Nina. 1935. *Os africanos no Brasil*. São Paulo: Companhia Editora Nacional.

Rolnik, Raquel. 1989. "Territórios negros nas cidades brasileiras etnicidade e cidade em São Paulo e no Rio de Janeiro." *Estudos Afro-Asiáticos* 17, 29–41.

Romero, Sílvio. 1943. *História da literatura brasileira*. Rio de Janeiro: José Olympio.

Roosens, Eugeen. 1994. *The Anthropology of Ethnicity: Beyond 'Ethnic Groups and Boundaries.'* Amsterdam: Hel Spinhuis.

Rose, Nikolas. 1996. *Inventing Our Selves: Psychology, Power, and Personhood*. London: Cambridge University Press.

Ruben, Guilermo Raul. 1986. "Teoria da identidade: Uma Crítica." *Anuário Antropológico*, 77–92.

———. 1992. "A teoria da identidade na antropologia: Um exercício de etnografia do pensamento moderno." *Roberto Cardoso de Oliveira: Homenagem*, edited by Mariza Corrêa and Roque Laraia. Campinas: IFCH/Unicamp.

Rutherford, Jonathan, ed. 1990. *Identity: Community, Culture, Difference*. London: Lawrence and Wishart.

Safran, William. 1991. "Diasporas in Modern Society: Myths of Homeland and Return," *Diaspora* 1, no. 1, 83–99.

Said, Edward. 2003. *Orientalism*. New York: Vintage.

Salah, Jacques. 2000. "A cidade como personagem." *Bahia, a Cidade de Jorge Amado. Atas do ciclo de palestras "A Bahia de Jorge Amado."* Salvador: Casa de Palavras.

Salzman, Jack, David Lionel Smith, and Cornel West, eds. 1996. *Encyclopedia of African-American Culture and History*. New York: Macmillan.

Sansone, Lívio. 1995. "Nem somente preto ou negro: O sistema de classificação racial no Brasil que muda." *Afro-Ásia* 18, 165–87.

———. 1995. "O local e o global na Afro-Bahia contemporânea." *Revista Brasileira de Ciências Sociais* 29, vol. 10 (October), 65–84.

———. 2000a. *De África a afro: Usos e abusos da África na cultura de elite e na cultura popular no Brasil.* Rio de Janeiro: Editora da UCAM.

———. 2000b. "Os objetos da cultura negra: Consumo, mercantilização, globalização e a criação de culturas negras no Brasil." *Mana–Estudos de Antropologia Social* 6, no. 1, 87–119.

Santos, Jocélio Teles dos. 1991. "As políticas públicas e a população afro-brasileira." *Bahia: Análise e dados,* vol. 1. Salvador: Centro de Estatística e Informações.

———. 2005. *O poder da cultura e a cultura no poder: A disputa simbólica da herança cultural negra no Brasil.* Salvador: Editora da Universidade Federal da Bahia.

Santos, Joel Rufino dos. 1996. "O negro como lugar." *Raça, ciência e sociedade,* edited by Marcos Chor Maio and Ricardo Ventura Santos, 219–23. Rio de Janeiro: Fiocruz/CCBB.

Santos, Myriam Sepúlveda dos. 1998. "O batuque negro das escolas de samba." *Estudos Afro-Asiáticos* 35 (July), 43–66.

———. 1999. "Samba Schools: The Logic of Orgy and Blackness in Rio de Janeiro." *Representations of Blackness and the Performance of Identities,* edited by Jean Muteba Rahier, 69–89. Westport, Conn.: Bergin and Garvey.

Santos Rodrigues, João Jorge dos. 1983. "A música do Ilê Aiyê e a educação consciente." *Estudos Afro-Asiáticos* 8–9, 247–51.

Sartre, Jean-Paul. 1948. *Orphée Noir,* preface to *Anthologie de la nouvell poésie nègre et malgache.* Paris: Presses Universitaires de France.

Sassen, Saskia. 1991. *The Global City: New York. London. Tokyo.* Princeton, N.J.: Princeton University Press.

Scarry, Elaine. 1999. *On Beauty and Being Just.* Princeton, N.J.: Princeton University Press.

Schwarcz, Lilia. 1995. *O espetáculo das raças: cientistas, instituições e questão racial no Brasil, 1870–1930.* São Paulo: Companhia das Letras.

———. 1996a. "As teorias raciais, uma construção histórica de finais do século XIX. O contexto brasileiro." *Raça e diversidade,* edited by Lilia Schwarcz, and Renato da Silva Queiroz, 147–85. São Paulo: Edusp.

———. 1996b. "Usos e abusos da mestiçagem e da raça no Brasil: Uma história das teorias raciais em finais do século XIX." *Afro-Ásia* 18, 77–101.

———. 1996c "Questão racial no Brasil." *Negras imagens,* edited by Lilia M. Schwarcz, and Letícia V. S. Reis, 153–77. São Paulo: Edusp.

———. 2001. *Racismo no Brasil.* 1st edition. São Paulo: Publifolha.

Schwarcz, Lilia, and Renato da Silva Queiroz, eds. 1996. *Raça e diversidade.* São Paulo: Edusp.

Schwarcz, Lilia M., and Letícia V. S. Reis, eds. 1996. *Negras imagens.* São Paulo: Edusp.

Segato, Rita. 1998. "The Color-Blind Subject of Myth; Or, Where to Find Africa in the Nation." *Annual Review of Anthropology* 27, 129–51.

Senghor, Leopold. 1982. "Sobre a negritude." *Diógene* 2, 73–82.

Seyferth, Giralda. 1989. "Identidade étnica, assimilação e cidadania: A imigração alemã e o Estado brasileiro." *Revista Brasileira de Ciências Sociais* 9, no. 26, 103–22.

Sheriff, Robin. 2001. *Dreaming Equality: Color, Race, and Racism in Urban Brazil.* New Brunswick, N.J.: Rutgers University Press, 2001.

Silva, Ana Célia da. 1996. "Ideologia do embranquecimento na educação brasileira e proposta de reversão." *Estratégias e políticas de combate à discriminação racial*, edited by Kabengele Munanga, 141–45. São Paulo: Edusp.

Silva, Carlos Benedito Rodrigues da. 2001. "Ritmos da identidade: Mestiçagens e sincretismos na cultura do Maranhão." PhD dissertation, Pontifícia Universidade Católica de São Paulo, 2001.

Silva, Denise Ferreira da. 1998. "Facts of Blackness: Brazil is Not (Quite) the United States . . . and racial politics in Brazil?" *Social Identities* 4, no. 2 (June), 201–34.

Silva, Edilson Marques da. 1998. *Negritude e fé: O resgate da auto-estima.* Santa Cruz do Rio Pardo: Faculdade de Filosofia, Ciências e Letras Carlos Queiroz.

Silva, Jônatas Conceição da. 1988a. "História de lutas negras: Memórias do surgimento do movimento negro na Bahia." *MNU: 1978–1988. Dez anos de luta contra o racismo*, 15–16. São Paulo: Confraria do Livro.

———. 1988b. "O querer é o eterno poder: História e resistência no Bloco Afro." Mimeograph.

Silva, Paula Cristina da. 1999. "Educação pluricultural e anti-racista em Salvador: Algumas experiências nos anos 80 e 90." *Educação e os afro-brasileiros: Trajetórias, identidades e alternativas*, edited by Jocélio Teles dos Santos, 133–52. Salvador: Universidade Federal da Bahia / Programa A Cor da Bahia / Coleção Novos Toques.

Silva, Vagner G., and Rita C. Amaral. 1996. "Símbolos da herança africana. Por que candomblé?" *Negras imagens*, edited by Lilia M. Schwarcz, and Letícia V. S. Reis, 195–209. São Paulo: Edusp.

Simpson, Amelia. 1993. *Xuxa: The Mega-Marketing of Gender, Race, and Modernity.* Philadelphia: Temple University Press.

Siqueira, Maria de Lourdes. 1996. "Ilê Aiyê: Uma dinâmica de educação na perspectiva cultural afro-brasileira." *Estratégias e políticas de combate à discriminação racial*, edited by Kabengele Munanga, 157–65. São Paulo: Edusp.

Skidmore, Thomas. 1991. "Raça e classe no Brasil: Perspectiva histórica." *Desigualdade racial no Brasil contemporâneo*, edited by Peggy A. Lovell, Peggy, 35–50. Belo Horizonte: UFMG / Cedeplar.

Slenes, Robert. 1995. *"Malungu, Ngoma vem!" África encoberta e descoberta no Brasil.* Cadernos do Museu da Escravatura, no. 1. Luanda: Ministério da Cultura.

Somers, Margaret. 1994. "The Narrative Constitution of Identity: A Relational and Network Approach." *Theory and Society* 23, no.5, 605–49.

Souza, Neusa Santos. 1983. *Tornar-se negro.* Rio de Janeiro: Graal.

Stam, Robert. 1997. *Tropical Multiculturalism: A Comparative History of Race in Brazilian Cinema and Culture*. Durham, N.C.: Duke University Press.

Stephens, Michelle. 2005. *Black Empire: The Masculine Global Imaginary of Caribbean Intellectuals in the United States, 1914–1962*. Durham, N.C.: Duke University Press.

Stokes, Martin. 1994. Introduction to *Ethnicity, Identity and Music: The Musical Construction of Place*. Oxford: Berg.

Stolcke, Verena. 1993. "Is Sex to Gender as Race is to Ethnicity?" *Gendered Anthropology*, edited by Teresa Del Valle, 17–37. London: Routledge.

Sundiata, Ibrahim. 1996. "Repensando o africanismo da diáspora." *Estratégias e políticas de combate à discriminação racial*, edited by Kabengele Munanga, 45–57. São Paulo: Eduspb.

Sutherland, Peter. 1999. "In Memory of the Slaves." *Representations of Blackness and the Performance of Identities*, edited by Jean Muteba Rahier, 195–211. Westport, Conn.: Bergin and Garvey.

Taylor, Charles. 1992. *The Ethics of Authenticity*. Cambridge, Mass.: Harvard University Press.

Telles, Edward. 1996. "Identidade racial, contexto urbano e mobilização política." *Afro-Ásia* 17, 121–38.

——. 1997. "A promoção da diversidade racial no Brasil: Uma visão dos Estados Unidos." *Estudos Afro-Asiáticos* 31, 91–102.

——. 2004. *Race in Another America: The Significance of Skin Color in Brazil*. Princeton, N.J.: Princeton University Press.

Thornham, Sue. 2000. *Feminist Theory and Cultural Studies: Stories of Unsettled Relations*. New York: Oxford University Press.

Thornton, John. 1998. *Africa and the Africans in the Making of the Atlantic World, 1400–1800*. Cambridge: Cambridge University Press.

Trouillot, Michel-Rolph. 1995. *Silencing the Past: Power and the Production of History*. Boston: Mass.: Beacon Press.

Twine, France Winddance. 1998. *Racism in a Racial Democracy: The Maintenance of White Supremacy in Brazil*. New Brunswick, N.J.: Rutgers University Press.

Verger, Pierre. 1991. *Orixás, deuses iorubás na África e no Novo Mundo*. São Paulo: Corrupio.

——. 1999a. *Notícias da Bahia: 1850*. Salvador: Editora Corrupio.

——. 1999b. *Notas sobre o culto aos orixás e voduns*. São Paulo: Edusp.

Vianna, Hermano. 1988. *O mundo funk carioca*. Rio de Janeiro: Jorge Zahar.

——. 1995. *O mistério do samba*. Rio de Janeiro: J. Zahar Editor Editora UFRJ.

Wade, Peter. 1997. *Race and Ethnicity in Latin America*. London: Pluto Press.

——. 1999a. "Working Culture: Making Cultural Identities in Cali, Colombia." *Current Anthropology* 40, no. 4, 449–72.

——. 1999. "Representations of Blackness in Colombian Popular Music." *Representations of Blackness and the Performance of Identities*, edited by Jean Muteba Rahier, 173–91. Westport, Conn.: Bergin and Garvey.

——. 2000. *Music, Race, and Nation*. Chicago: University of Chicago Press.

REFERENCES

———. 2005. "Rethinking Mestizaje: Ideology and Lived Experience." *Journal of Latin American Studies* 37, 239–57.

Walker, Sheila. 2002. "Africanity vs. Blackness: Race, Class and Culture in Brazil." *NACLA Report on the Americas* 35, no. 6 (May–June), 16–20.

Wallerstein, I. 1990. "Culture as the Ideological Battleground of the Modern World System." *Global Culture: Nationalism, Globalization and Modernity*, edited by Mike Featherstone, 31–56. London: Sage Publications.

Ware, Vron. 2001. "What Makes You/Him/Her/Them/Us/It White? The Making and Unmaking of Whiteness: A Global Project." Paper presented at "The Burden Of Race: 'Whiteness' and 'Blackness' in Modern South Africa." University Of Witwatersrand, Johannesburg, 5–8 July.

Weeks, Jeffrey. 1990. "The Value of Difference." *Identity: Community, Culture, Difference*, edited by Jonathan Rutherford, 88–100. London: Lawrence and Wishart.

West, Cornel. 1994. *Questão de raça*. São Paulo: Companhia das Letras.

Willens, Emílio. 1961. *Dicionário de sociologia*. Porto Alegre: Editora Globo.

Williams, Brackette. 1989. "A Class Act: Anthropology and the Race to Nation across Ethnic Terrain." *Annual Review of Anthropology* 18, 401–44.

Williams, Raymond. 1961. *The Long Revolution*. London: Chatto and Windus.

Winant, Howard. 1994. *Racial Conditions: Politics, Theory, Comparisions*. Minneapolis: University of Minnesota Press.

Wright, Michelle. 2004. *Becoming Black: Creating Identity in the African Diaspora*. Durham, N.C.: Duke University Press, 2004.

Wright, Richard. 1954. *Black Power: A Record of Reactions in a Land of Pathos*. Westport, Conn.: Greenwood Press.

Young, I. M. 1989. "Polity and Group Difference: A Critique of the Idea of Universal Citizenship." *Ethics* 99, no. 1, 250–74.

Yúdice, George. 2003. *The Expediency of Culture: Uses of Culture in the Global Era*. Durham, N.C.: Duke University Press, 2003.

Zarur, George. 2007. "Aprendizes de Feiticeiro." *Divisões perigosas: Políticas raciais no Brasil contemporâneo*, edited by Peter Fry, Yvonne Maggie, Marcos Chor Maio, Simone Monteiro, and Ricardo Ventura Santos, 127–31. Rio de Janeiro: Civilização Brasileira.

INDEX

Affirmative action, 17

Afoxés, 45, 118, 127

Africa, 1; African diaspora and, 1–2, 23–33; anticolonial struggles in, 34; Bahia and, 8, 30, 33–34, 47–48; black culture and, 24–25, 32–33; black motherhood and, 29–31, 35; *blocos afro* and, 32–40, 43–44, 91–92; Egypt and, 25; essentialism and, 31; as imagined community, 1–2, 24–25, 27, 32, 34, 36–38; invented traditions and, 28–29, 31–32, 38, 44, 72; land in, 44; motherland vs. fatherland, 29–30; music and, 33–34, 40–41, 43, 45, 91–92; pan-Africanism, 75–76; paradisiacal vs. impoverished, 36–37; production of, 29–32, 36; religious-based organizations and, 33, 72–73; savagery of, 32; as source of all knowledge, 35, 42; tribal Africa, 36–38, 42; United States and, 26, 43; as Western construction, 31

África: Ventre Fértil do Mundo (Africa: The World's Fertile Womb, textbook), 29

African Americans, 14, 28–29, 86–87, 230 n. 38

African American tourists and tourism, 7–8, 24, 34, 50–58, 90, 230 n. 35, 230 n. 37; afro objects and, 124

African diaspora, 8, 79, 101, 230 n. 39; Africa and, 1–2, 23–33; as African na-

tion, 44; Caribbean and, 30, 43; Civil Rights movement and, 45; as expatriate minority communities, 27–28; international black culture in, 26, 35, 45–46, 80–81; motherland vs. fatherland and, 29–30, 40; pan-Africanism and, 25, 31; transnational alliances of, 25–26, 28; Jewish diaspora vs., 27

Africanisms, 4, 23, 33, 37, 45; elder's blessings as, 38–39. *See also* Traditions

Africanness, 1, 31, 45, 229 n. 28, 229 n. 33; African American's disconnect from, 86–87; afro-aesthetics and, 121–26; *blocos afros* and, 49, 51–52, 78, 81, 83–87, 92–95, 116–17; in Carnaval, 214–15; colorful fabrics and, 88; commodified, 72, 87–88, 184; ethnic symbols and, 83–88; Ilê Aiyê and, 29, 34–35, 85, 91–95; music and, 86–87, 90, 92–94; pan-Africanism and, 25

Afro-aesthetics, 26, 33, 102, 128–30, 139–45; in Bahia, 125–26; blackness and, 142–43; dreadlocks as, 130; normativity of, 142–45; protesting racism and, 126; self-esteem and, 127–28, 131–34, 132, 139; tourism and, 124–26

Afro-Brazilian cuisine, 84, 185, 187–89, 237 n. 10

Afro-labeling, 122

Afro objects, 26, 46, 84–85, 128, 195–

64, 96–99, 148, 158, 162; black particularities and, 69–70; *blocos afro* and, 8, 64, 78–81, 88, 117; Brazilian black organizations and, 72–80; Candomblé and, 80, 83–84; colorful fabrics and, 88; essentialist vs. antiessentialist views of, 69–70, 98, 176; ethnic symbols and, 83–86; globalization and, 70–71; internal divisions and, 68, 70; metaphor of origin and, 67–68; new representations of blackness and, 90, 98; oppositional, 83, 85, 167; race and, 68, 170, 174, 178; social and political advancement and, 72; transnational, 33, 46; U.S. forms of, 83. *See also* Identity

Black Atlantic theory, 4, 45–46, 58–60, 124, 126; Bahia and, 47–48

Black body, 4–5, 8, 31, 58–59, 89; afro-aesthetics and, 121–26; Afro-Brazilians and, 101–2; appearance of, 3, 9, 24, 67, 75–76, 78–79, 91, 178; Bahianness and, 84, 189–94; Black Beauty Evening and, 135–38; "black is beautiful" ideal, 76, 125; *boa aparência* and, 106, 232 n. 3; in Brazilian media, 111–13; Carnaval and, 114–15; commodification of, 193, 210; dishonesty and delinquency associations, 109–10; essence of, 3, 9, 24, 67–68, 75, 78–80, 91, 148–52, 158–59, 170, 178; Eurocentric notions of, 101–2, 111; exoticization of, 112–13; filth and stench of, 101, 105–8; identity and, 64, 96–99, 148, 158, 162; Ilê Aiyê and, 5, 108–9; low self-esteem and, 101; manipulation of, 67, 109–10, 156; negative perceptions of, 102–15, 126–27; slavery and, 102–5, 107, 162, 192; technology of power and, 107; tendencies of, 3, 9, 24, 67–68, 75, 78–80, 91, 123, 142–43, 148–56, 158–59, 178, 192–93; tourism

and, 191; vigilant personal hygiene and, 106–8; whitening and, 111; of women, 30, 69, 134–39, 156–57. *See also* Afro-aesthetics; Beauty; Hairstyles

Black cultural production, 6, 51–52, 89, 183; Africa and, 24–25, 33–34; afro-aesthetics and, 126; of black beauty, 113–14, 123–24, 131, 138–39; *blocos afro* and, 64, 80–81, 134, 238 n. 15; Carnaval and, 81–82, 211–13; local power elites in Bahia and, 199–206, 213; social action projects of, 116–21

Black culture, 4, 7–8, 21–23, 64, 69, 77, 91, 183; Africa and, 24–25, 32–33; Bahianness and, 83, 183–87, 191–206, 213; becoming black and, 170; blood as transmitter of, 153–55; Brazilian national identity and, 102, 160–61, 186–87, 212; commodification and appropriation of, 70, 72, 199, 203, 207–11; contagiousness of, 184, 193–96, 212; exchange across diaspora, 26, 35, 45–46, 80–81; fetishization and, 161; modernity and, 80–81, 84; myth of Mama Africa and, 2–3, 24, 35, 51–52; paradisiacal vs. impoverished Africa, 36–37; producers of identity discourse and, 7; racism and, 117; reclaiming, 151, 159–62, 173, 210; as representations, 209; representations of blackness and, 80–81, 127–28, 130–34, 156–57; self-esteem and, 117, 130–34; slavery and, 38–39, 102–3, 211; stereotypes and, 212; symbols of, 161, 196, 212; tourism and, 212; tribal Africa, 37–38. *See also* Candomblé; Music; Samba

Black militants, 128, 229 n. 33

Blackness, 1, 3, 5, 31, 68; Bahianness and, 7, 9, 83–84, 185–87, 203–6; biology and, 162–64; black identity and, 27, 45, 90; *blocos afros* and, 2, 49,

Carneiro, Sueli, 178, 231 n. 4

Casa Grande & Senzala (Freyre), 18

Castro, Fidel, 43

Catinga (body odor), 105–6

Cesta do Povo (supermarket), 203–4

Che Guevara, 43

Chico César, 1

Christmas, Rachel Jackson, 51, 230 n. 34

Civil Rights movement, 26, 33, 45

Clifford, James, 28

Clothing. *See* Afro-style clothing

Cohen, Abner, 66

Cohen, Ronald, 66–67

Comb test, 226–27 n. 10

Connerton, Paul, 155, 157

Cuba, 43; as branch of Mama Africa, 39–40

Cultural politics, 2–3, 8, 13–14, 72, 81, 127, 161–62, 207–8; in Bahia, 199–206, 213; black organizations and, 78; black particularity and, 179; black symbols and, 196

Culture, 3–4, 21, 66, 78, 91; beauty and, 114; black culture for the black race, 158–70; bounded, 159–60; nature and, 156, 158, 180; as objects, 181, 209–10; politics and, 3, 8, 13–14, 72, 78, 81, 127, 157, 162, 179, 196, 199–208, 213; race and, 12–13, 68, 148, 222; as representations, 9–10, 127, 131, 195, 209; as a way of life, 181, 209; women's bodies and, 156

DaMatta, Roberto, 128

Dance and dancing: *batuques,* 117–18; dance parties, 45; as natural ability of blacks, 151–56, 193. *See also* Samba

Dantas, Beatriz Góis, 186–87

Davis, Darién, 74

de Beauvoir, Simone, 35, 148

Delany, Martin, 29–30

Deracialization, 167–68

Diaspora. *See* Africa and African diaspora; Jewish diaspora

Didara (women's clothing line), 123–24

Divisões perigosas: Políticas raciais no Brasil contemporâneo, 16–17

Dreadlocks, 87, 128–30, 143–44

Du Bois, W.E.B., 28

Dunn, Christopher, 40, 128

Education, 75, 114, 121, 233 n. 8, 233 n. 13; educational outreach programs, 119–20

Egypt, 41–42; myth of Mama Africa and, 38–39

Elder's blessings, 37–38

Entrudos (pre-lent festivals), 82

Erasmus, Zimitri, 130

Essentialism, 5, 148, 170, 180; appearance and, 9, 89; identity and, 95–96, 98, 174, 179; invented traditions and, 29; myth of Mama Africa and, 31, 69; natural characteristics of blacks and, 139, 142–43, 151–56, 158, 192–93; Pan-African scholars and, 31; racism and, 212

Estatuto da Igualdade Racial (Racial Equality Statute), 10–12, 14, 17–18, 21

Ethiopia, 40–43; myth of Mama Africa and, 38–39

Ethnic Groups and Boundaries (Barth), 66

Ethnic identity. *See* Black and ethnic identity; Identity

Fanon, Frantz, 28, 176, 178

Fatherland, 29–30

Feijoada, 160, 183, 198

Ferme, Mariane, 123

Festival of the Bonfim Church, 195

Foreman, George, 34

Foucault, Michel, 107–8, 135, 139, 157–58, 164, 235 n. 10; on subjection-subjectification, 235 n. 4

39; social action projects of, 119–21; song lyrics of, 39–40, 43, 122–23, 133–34, 231 n. 6, 228 n. 13–15, 18; surveillance strategies in, 69, 134–35; tribal Africa and, 37–38

Jamaica, 43; as branch of Mama Africa, 39–40; dreadlocks in, 129–30
Jewish diaspora, 27

Kamel, Ali, 12–14, 225 nn. 4–5
King Jr., Martin Luther, 26

Lallement, Avé, 191
Landes, Ruth, 49
Landless movement, 21
Latinamente, 43
Liberdade, 229 n. 21
Light skinned: in *blocos afro*, 218–19; immigrants in U.S., 220
Lopes, Goya, 123–24
Lourdes, Maria de Siqueira, 119

Macarini, Romilda, 15
Magalhães, Antônio Carlos (Bahian Senator), 195–96
Maids: policing of personal hygiene of, 106
Malcolm X, 26
Malê de Balê (*bloco afro*), 43
Mama Africa, myth of, 2–3, 231 n. 6; African anti-colonialism and, 34; African character and, 26; Afro-referenced identities and, 64, 66–67; Bahia and, 9, 30, 35; becoming black and, 67; black bodies and, 9, 30–31, 66, 69; black motherhood and, 31, 35; *blocos afro* and, 2–3, 24, 34–35, 51–52; colorful fabrics and, 88; Egypt and Ethiopia and, 38–39; essentialism and, 9, 31, 58–59, 69, 98, 148; ethnic symbols and, 85; imagined community and, 44; Jamaica

and, 39–40; liberating aspects of, 58–59; Marcus Garvey and, 25; *mestiçagem* and, 30; motherland vs. fatherland and, 29–30; slave experience and, 38; song lyrics and, 1, 39–40. *See also* Myth
Mandela, Nelson, 26
Marley, Bob, 40
Masters and the Slaves, The (Freyre), 76
Maués, Maria Angélica, 128
Mbembe, Achille, 27–28, 32, 57, 177
Melo, Roberto, 123
Mendes, Nelson, 95
Mestiçagem (Brazil's cultural and racial mixture), 13–14, 16, 18–19, 21, 30, 76, 161, 219; Bahianness and, 184; binary racial classification and, 167; break with, 159
Mestiços, 68, 115, 167–68
Militão, José Roberto, 17
Modernity and tradition, 80–81, 84, 87–88, 90
Mohanty, Chandra, 16
Morrison, Toni, 89, 110
Motherhood, 31
Motherland, 29–30
Movimento Negro Unificado contra a Discriminação Racial, 76–77
Movimento Pro-Mestiçagem, 17–18
Muhammad Ali, 34
Mulatas, 105, 190, 235 n. 3
Munanga, Kabengele, 159, 162, 169–70, 198–99
Music, 49, 58–60, 198; African diaspora and, 32–33, 40–41; African rhythms, 90, 92, 94; black struggles and, 45; *blocos afro* and, 38–47, 51–52, 80–81, 86–88, 91–94, 228 n. 13; exchange across Black Atlantic, 45–46; funk music, 45, 50, 229 n. 26; hip hop, 45, 98; modernity and transnationalism in, 40; musical promiscuity, 92–93; as natural ability of blacks, 151–56; pro-

representations of blacks and, 73, 127; police repression and, 104, 237 n. 4; quality of life and, 104; racial anger, 217–19; racial profiling in U.S., 109; reverse, 212; scientific racism, 103; slavery and, 103–5; U.S. model and, 167–69

Racismo cordial, 20, 213

Raffia fiber, 84–85

Rastafarianism, 40, 43, 223; dreadlocks and, 129–30

Rede Globo, 154

Reggae music, 40, 50, 81, 86–88

Reinvenções da África na Bahia, 5–6

Religious-based organizations, 72–73. *See also* Candomblé

Restaurants, 188–89

Revista Raça (magazine), 123, 233 n. 16

Rhythms. *See under* Music

Ribeiro, Ronilda, 127

Rio de Janeiro, 53, 186

Risério, Antônio, 13, 21, 41; on funk dance parties, 45; on re-Africanization of Carnaval, 81

Robinson, Eugene, 217–18

Rodrigues, Nina, 81–82, 237 n. 4

"Roma Negra," 48–49

Roosens, Eugeen, 68, 167

Roots (Haley), 26

Roots tourism. *See* African-American tourists and tourism

Rose, Nikolas, 157–58, 221

Safran, William, 27

Salvador, 24; Africanness of, 24. *See also* Bahia

Samba, 22, 33; mythical Africa and, 32; as national symbol, 159–60, 199, 212, 220, 235 n. 5; as natural ability, 154; reclaiming of, 161

Sansone, Lívio, 58, 84, 120, 228 n. 7, 230 n. 36, 238 n. 15

Santos, Jocélio Teles dos, 187

Santos, Myriam, 201, 212

Sartre, Jean-Paul, 175

Scarry, Elaine, 110, 113–14

Schwarcz, Lilia, 174

Scientific racism, 103, 171–72

Segato, Rita, 161

Selassie, Haile, 40, 43

Self-esteem, 101–2, 110, 121, 162, 233 nn. 21–22, 234 nn. 28–30; beauty pageants and, 137–38; blackening and, 121; *blocos afro* and, 117, 120; new representations of blackness and, 127–28, 130–34; political power and, 140–41; raising of in 1970s, 33–34; stereotypes and, 139, 141; women's magazines and, 123

Senegal, 41

Silva, Denise Ferreira da, 16

Silva, Juracy, 91, 94, 133

Siqueira, Maria de Lourdes, 119

Slavery, 38, 47–48, 229 n. 27, 232 nn. 1–2; African American tourists and, 53–55; *Black Atlantic* and, 46; black bodies and, 162; blackness in Brazil and, 102–7, 142, 144, 154–55; entertainment and, 211; filth and stench and, 106–8; racism and, 103–5; soap operas and, 111–12; U.S. vs. Brazil, 13

Soap operas, 111–12

Soul food, 160

Soul music, 26, 45, 235 n. 8

Souls of Black Folk, The (Du Bois), 28

Souza, Neusa Santos, 150

Staring, 110

Stephens, Michelle, 30

Stereotypes, 109, 141, 156; of black motherhood, 31; of *mulatas*, 105, 190, 235 n. 3; politics of representation and, 139

Stigmas, 130–31

Structures of feeling, 4, 64, 70, 170

Sutherland, Peter, 55–57

Patricia de Santana Pinho is assistant professor in
the Department of Latin American, Caribbean,
and U.S. Latino Studies at the State
University of New York at Albany.

Library of Congress Cataloging-in-Publication Data
Pinho, Patricia de Santana.
[Reinvenções da Africa na Bahia. English]
Mama Africa : reinventing blackness in Bahia /
Patricia de Santana Pinho ; original edition
translated by Elena Langdon.
p. cm.
Includes bibliographical references and index.
ISBN 978-0-8223-4654-8 (cloth : alk. paper)
ISBN 978-0-8223-4646-3 (pbk. : alk. paper)
1. Blacks — Race identity — Brazil — Bahia (State)
2. Bahia (Brazil : State) — Race relations.
3. Bahia (Brazil : State) — Civilization — African
influences. I. Title.
F2551.P5613   2010
305.896'08142 — dc22   2009041156